Genius and Monologue

Genius and Monologue

KEN FRIEDEN

CORNELL UNIVERSITY PRESS

Ithaca and London

Cornell University Press gratefully acknowledges
a grant from the Andrew W. Mellon foundation
that aided in bringing this book to publication.

First published 1985 by Cornell University Press.

International Standard Book Number 0-8014-1804-6
Library of Congress Catalog Card Number 85-47700
Printed in the United States of America
Librarians: Library of Congress cataloging information
appears on the last page of the book.

The paper in this book is acid-free and meets
the guidelines for permanence and durability
of the Committee on Production Guidelines for
Book Longevity of the Council on Library Resources.

Contents

Preface   7

Abbreviations of Classical Works   11

Introduction   15

PART ONE   *Philosophy of Genius*

   1.   Greek Gods, *daimōn*, and Socrates' *daimonion*   27

   2.   Hebrew Angels, *satan*, and Philo's *logoi*   48

   3.   The Eighteenth-Century Introjection of Genius   66

   4.   The Transcendence of Monologue   84

PART TWO   *Literature of Monologue*

   5.   Pre-Shakespearean and Shakespearean Soliloquies   111

   6.   Coleridge's Conversational Pretense   134

   7.   Poe's Narrative Monologues   154

   8.   The Genius of Internal Monologue   169

Conclusions   189

Selected Bibliography   195

Index   207

How one must first distinguish between artworks.—All that is thought, written, painted, composed, even built and sculpted, belongs either to monological art or to art before witnesses. Among the latter is also to be reckoned even that illusory monologue art which includes belief in God, the entire lyric of prayer: because for a pious person there is no solitude—we were the first to make this discovery, we the godless. I know no deeper distinction in the entire optics of the artist than this: whether he looks toward the emerging artwork (toward "himself"—) from the standpoint of the witness or "has forgotten the world": as is the essence of every monological artwork—it rests *on forgetting*, it is the music of forgetting.

—FRIEDRICH NIETZSCHE, *Die fröhliche Wissenschaft*

Preface

Genius is the intellectual obsession of our time, and monologue is one symptom of the disorder. Monologues of solitude and madness have reached epidemic proportions. This book confronts modernity by reviewing Western traditions of genius and monologue, inspiration and individuality, from a rhetorical standpoint. A person no longer *has a genius*, a guardian spirit; twentieth-century myth suggests that an especially creative person *is a genius*. Ancient mythology has not disappeared but has been turned inward.

From biblical narratives to modern literature, as the prophet becomes the man of genius, invention displaces divine inspiration. Yet transcendent ideas continue to guide the modern genius, whose creative exertions never secure autonomy. Although the contemporary persona of the genius rings hollow, no original figure can be severed from the masks it has successively worn: the guise of the prophet, the poetry of imagination, the rhetoric of consciousness. These are not movements in a continuous historical narrative, but turning points that disrupt an elusive continuity.

Despite my disclaimers, some readers will misunderstand *Genius and Monologue* as a history of ideas. The opening chapters on Greek and Hebrew traditions are not gestures toward comprehensiveness; I have merely focused on certain recurrent configurations in the Western rhetoric of inspiration and individuality. I employ the methods of rhetorical, not historical, criticism. Without intending to narrate an

intellectual history, I interpret emblematic linguistic and literary forms
that are linked to the philosophy of genius and the literature of monologue. Intertextual relationships make this a drama in which words
are the central characters.

Part One, Philosophy of Genius, begins with Socrates' "divine sign,"
a precursor of the Latin guardian *genius*. Biblical and midrashic traditions supplement the Greco-Roman context through their representations of angels and *satan* as divine emissaries. Eighteenth-century
aestheticians such as Shaftesbury, Addison, Young, and Kant revive
and transform these ancient origins. The classical conception of a
supernatural guardian spirit is gradually supplanted by modern ideas
of an individual extraordinary mind. Following Husserl's phenomenology, which may represent the last possible struggle to maintain a
monadic consciousness, monological subjectivity is deconstructed by
Heidegger and Derrida.

Part Two, Literature of Monologue, examines paradigmatic literary
monologues in drama, lyric, and narrative. For pre-Shakespearean
soliloquists, solitary speech is linked to prayer and guilt. Shakespeare's soliloquists, after they lose the communicative relation to
God, encounter radical psychological anomalies at the threshold of
reason. Coleridge's conversation poems transform the contemplative
voice into an independent, lyrical form, but his visionary poems disrupt this apparent continuity. Poe's mad narrators extend the range
of first-person fiction—toward the abyss. Diverse conventions of internal monologue culminate with Joyce's Mollylogue, in which stream
of consciousness cedes to stream of text: "Language speaks."

Quotations are central to this intertextual study. In a rhetorical
analysis, however, the distinction between "use" and "mention" of
words is sometimes difficult to maintain. Literary motifs combine
themes and the words that embody them. Textual analysis has the
appearance of a mosaic in which every tile is a word, a tessera from
previous contexts. The mortar of quotation marks is everywhere essential, yet not always perceptible.

All translations in this book are my own except where otherwise
indicated: I have chosen to perform this first interpretive act myself.
In responding to the uniqueness of each original text, my translations
and commentaries are intended to return the reader to the sources,
cited in the footnotes. I also mention existing translations when they

are especially useful, and offer page references to those translations even when the English version quoted here is my own.

Work on *Genius and Monologue* began with the help of a Special Humanities Fellowship at the University of Chicago (1977–79), continued through the support of a German Academic Exchange Grant at the Universities of Freiburg and Berlin (1979–81), and was completed during a Yale University Fellowship (1981–84). I am grateful for this generous assistance.

Of the many teachers and friends who have made this book possible, I especially thank: James Adler, Harold Bloom, Jane Bottner, Leslie Brisman, Thomas Cole, Paul de Man, Jacques Derrida, Howard Felperin, Steven Fraade, Janina Frankel, Thomas Gould, Karsten Harries, Geoffrey Hartman, Lewis Klausner, Paul Miklowitz, J. Hillis Miller, Maurice Natanson, Fred Oscanyan, Elana Ponet, James Ponet, Paul Ricoeur, Michael Theunissen, Ernst Tugendhat, Heinrich Weidmann, and Dolora Wojciehowski. Thanks also go to the students in my Yale College seminar "Literary Monologue from Shakespeare to Joyce," who continued the dialogue while this book was in the final stages of revision.

To my family I owe the profoundest debt.

K.F.

New Haven, Connecticut

Abbreviations of Classical Works

Apol.	Plato, *Apology*
De Cher.	Philo, *De cherubim*
De Civ. Dei	St. Augustine, *De civitate dei*
De Conf. Ling.	Philo, *De confusione linguarum*
De Dec.	Philo, *De decalogo*
De Fug.	Philo, *De fuga et inventione*
De Gig.	Philo, *De gigantibus*
De Migr. Abr.	Philo, *De migratione Abrahami*
De Opif.	Philo, *De opificio mundi*
De Somn.	Philo, *De somniis*
Diss.	Maximus of Tyre, *Dissertations*
Il.	Homer, *Iliad*
Od.	Homer, *Odyssey*
Quis. Rer. Div.	Philo, *Quis rerum divinarum Heres*
Quod Det.	Philo, *Quod Deterius potiori insidiari solet*

Genius and Monologue

Introduction

I

English "genius" retains traces of an intertextual history that transforms and introjects the archaic, mythological *daimōn*. Following Greek sources, Roman religion posits that every man has a genius, a familiar spirit; eighteenth-century aesthetics maintains that a great poet has genius; and today an extraordinarily creative person is a genius. The mythological past has been covered over by an exaggerated faith in subjectivity, individual speech, "monologue." While no pure genius can be quarried from buried strata, research may discern residues of opposing rhetorical systems that have generated particular surface formations. Analysis of literary and philosophic texts suggests, for example, that subjective monologue is a transformation of theological genius.

Ancient religions characteristically refer to frequent communications between divine and human realms. In the Greek context, Hesiodic *daimones* are essentially spirits, mediators between gods and men. Homer employs the singular *daimōn* more abstractly, implying an indefinite notion of divinity or fate. Distinct versions of the *daimōn* conflict within Plato's dialogues, and Socrates' *daimonion* is a nodal point at which Plato revises the prevailing traditions of Hellenic spirituality. The *daimonion*, Socrates' customary divine sign or voice, hovers between divinity and subjectivity, inspiration and internal speech. Ever since Plato's philosophical biography, literary texts have confronted the tensions between monologue as prayer (dialogue with God) and as solitary contemplation (dialogue with oneself).

Ancient Hebrew texts refer to *malachim*, angels or divine messengers, mediators between God and men. In a monotheistic framework, angels take the place of pagan minor deities, and Philo explicitly identifies Greek *daimones* and *logoi* with Hebrew *malachim*. Whereas Plato's texts displace plural *daimones* by singular *daimōn* or *daimonion*, Hellenized Judaism drifts in the opposite direction: postbiblical commentaries and legends expand the role of angels and demons, as in the stories of Abraham, Isaac, and *satan*.

Angels and demons permeate the Judaic and Christian traditions, until the Enlightenment contests all figures of manifest divinity. Enlightened philosophers propose an ideal of the rational, self-contained subject that dispenses with transcendent assumptions, while English aesthetics specifically displaces the theological dimension of genius. Joseph Addison appropriates the ancient word at the same time that he modifies its use, while Lord Shaftesbury equates the experience of a *daimōn*, or *genius*, with soliloquy. To the extent that eighteenth-century aestheticians retain religious concerns, they characteristically introject the divine: Edward Young, for example, writes of genius as "that god within." In the associationist tradition that revises and radicalizes Young's conjectures, William Duff and Alexander Gerard understand genius as a psychological faculty. Mythical ideas of genius as mediator between gods and men cede to the popular call for original artistic creation through genius.

Seminal works of twentieth-century philosophy implicitly approach the new genius—subjectivity in language—through a dialectic of "transcendence" and "immanence." Edmund Husserl explicates the monadic or immanent sphere of consciousness by excluding the transcendent, such that only the transcendental ego remains. Based on Husserl's phenomenological method that grounds consciousness by limiting transcendent perception, existentialism briefly recasts genius in the guise of the authentic self before language merges with this last divinity. While Heidegger's early work interprets the transcendence of Dasein, his later writings move toward a nostalgic rediscovery of the divine *Logos*.

Transformations of genius have replaced divine selection by individual speech, but monologue has also eroded as a basis of subjectivity. Following the brief ascendancy of internal monologue, contemporary fiction and literary theory question the traditions that rely on this phenomenon. Modern thought thus attains its current impasse, defiant of transcendent genius and skeptical of the immanent monologue that remains. The monological subject has been unsettled or decentered by a world purged of all possible foundations. Martin Heidegger and Jacques Derrida respond to this aporia through modified notions of transcendence in language.

II

Mono-logos means "solitary speech."

Monologue is not primarily a fact of human solitude but rather a mode of linguistic individuality. Ordinary, externalized discourse is the background for deviant, internalized discourse that may perform a semantically isolated idiolect.[1] On the level of discourse, monologue is a turn away from dialogue. The language of an individual is monological to the extent that it deviates from dialogical conventions of speech. Such swerves are essential to formal innovation, but our task is to understand, not to evaluate, literary monologues.

The monadic subject has developed together with a monological conception of thought. No longer divine, *logos* grounds the speaking subject as an originator of propositions and narratives, meanings and illusions. The isolated self does not exist first in order to create its individuality afterward, however, because the "I" comes into conscious existence through languages of inwardness. The modern self strives for autonomy, although the speaking subject never exists in isolation: however insular a monologue may appear to be, it depends on interaction with communicative dialogue.

Extraordinary language philosophy comes into being when, unable to secure its authenticity, the singular subject allies itself with phenomena of linguistic deviance. Radical *mono-logos* arises as a divergence from norms of ordinary dialogical language; internal speech is only the most familiar form of solitary language, distinct from and yet associated with semantically isolated modes. While internal speech

---

[1]In this book, "deviant" and related terms are used descriptively, without pejorative connotations. The norms themselves are in flux and are not entirely insulated from what is perceived as abnormal.

is not necessarily deviant, literary monologues are typically bound up with difference, as if the monologist had an inherent tendency to deviate.[2] At the same time that monological swerves produce illusions of individuality, the achieved individual expressions threaten communal norms and tend toward meaninglessness.

European literary traditions of monologue, linked to the representation of thought, recapitulate philosophical and theological explanations of genius. In the beginning only God is capable of monologue, but sin and *satan* generate new possibilities for monological speech at a distance from God. The monologist steers a course between divinity and madness through English literary works from pre-Shakespearean drama to modernist fiction. While medieval and Renaissance plays retain the link between solitary speech and prayer, Shakespeare's schemers and meditators introduce diverse modes of deviant monologue. Marlowe and Shakespeare imply both the metaphysical and the psychological forms of soliloquy, but dialogue with God drifts toward an internal dialogue. S. T. Coleridge's conversational poetry responds to Hamlet's soliloquies and exemplifies the Romantic discourse of a speaking subject. Hints of the transcendent remain, however, and the sober conversational pretense begins to dissolve when supernatural and unconscious worlds threaten to take control. E. A. Poe's tales represent extremes of the determined villain and mad monologist, yet the subjective certainty of his speakers is disarmed by a perverse reflex.

The development of narrative internal monologue also moves between the poles of genius and monologue, the transcendent and the immanent, external forces and the independence of the subject. Arthur Schnitzler in particular shows that internal speech cannot escape implicit dialogues. Stream of consciousness in works by James Joyce flows into the stream of language as a transcendent muse. Even the postmodernist scene of writing, in which a text appears as its own monologue, derives from this line of development: discourse cannot secure a realm of isolated subjectivity. These readings are in no way comprehensive but represent a limited number of intertextual rela-

---

[2]Compare Victor Erlich, "Notes on the Uses of Monologue in Artistic Prose," *International Journal of Slavic Linguistics and Poetics*, ed. Paul Böckmann, 1/2 (1959), 223–31; and "Some Uses of Monologue in Prose-Fiction: Narrative Manner and World-View," in *Stil- und Formprobleme in der Literatur* (Heidelberg: Carl Winter, 1959), 371–78.

tionships in which literary monologue reveals a monological history of creative deviations.

In the critical tradition starting with Hédelin d'Aubignac, dramatic soliloquy is considered problematic from the standpoint of realism. Denis Diderot questions whether unrealistic soliloquies are acceptable in drama, while others defend and redefine dramatic soliloquy.[3] The aside is a further form of staged self-address, often linked with audience address. Dramatic soliloquies frequently approach a relationship to divinity, if not to deviance and madness. The conversation poem transforms the conventions of dramatic soliloquy, and first-person narrative may assume similar monological forms.

To varying degrees, literature of monologue purports to represent internal speech, but modernism tends to undermine mimetic illusions in favor of a writing that recognizes itself as such. While most monologues imply a first-person speaker, first-person narrators in particular tend to merge self-reflectively with their texts. On one level, internal monologue fictionally represents internal speech, the linguistic aspect of consciousness.[4] Stream-of-consciousness technique reproduces a fictional stream of consciousness, including internal speech and pre-

[3]Hédelin d'Aubignac, *La pratique du théâtre* (Amsterdam: Jean Frederic Bernard, 1715), 230. Denis Diderot, *Discours de la poésie dramatique*, ed. Jean-Pol Caput (Paris: Librairie Larousse, 1970), 91. See also Friedrich Düsel, *Der dramatische Monolog in der Poetik des 17. und 18. Jahrhunderts und in den Dramen Lessings* (Hamburg: Leopold Voss, 1897), 2–4; and H. M. Paull, "Dramatic Convention with Special Reference to the Soliloquy," in *Fortnightly Review*, 71 (1899), 863–70. J. J. Engel, "Über Handlung, Gespräch, und Erzählung," in *Schriften* (Berlin: Mylius, 1802), vol. 4, pp. 190–94; and Hans Sittenberger, "Der Monolog," in *Das litterarische Echo*, 15 (May 1, 1900), 1033–41. The seminal work of Friedrich Leo, *Der Monolog im Drama: Ein Beitrag zur griechisch-römischen Poetik* (Berlin: Weidmann, 1908), differs from most in that it distinguishes between soliloquy, self-address, and monologue. Modern English does not preserve this distinction, but we may wish to differentiate between soliloquy as physically isolated speech, retaining self-address and monologue for more radical forms of semantic solitude. Leo notes that, in Greek drama, self-address develops later than soliloquy. In *The Soliloquy in German Drama* (New York: Columbia University Press, 1915), 3, Erwin W. Roessler understands dramatic soliloquy as "a passage in a drama in which a character is alone upon the stage and speaks to himself, believing himself to be alone." He emphasizes the difference between dramatic forms that represent "solitude as a condition" and those that depict "aloneness as a fact." See also Wolfgang Schadewaldt, *Monolog und Selbstgespräch: Untersuchungen zur Formgeschichte der griechischen Tragödie* (Berlin: Weidmann, 1926), 29.

[4]See Lawrence Edward Bowling, "What Is the Stream of Consciousness Technique?" in *PMLA*, 65 (June 1950), 345; Francis Scarfe, *The Art of Paul Valéry* (Melbourne: William Heinemann, 1954), 111; and Robert Scholes and Robert Kellogg, *The Nature of Narrative* (London: Oxford University Press, 1966), 177. But compare Melvin Freedman, *Stream of Consciousness: A Study in Literary Method* (London: Oxford University Press, 1955).

linguistic elements. Both internal monologue and stream of consciousness tend to merge with the stream of textuality, however, to the point of renouncing mimetic pretenses.

Definitions begin to erode as we approach particular literary works. "Monologue" remains a general term denoting physically or semantically solitary speech acts that deviate from dialogical norms.

III

Genius and monologue initially appear to constitute a simple antithesis on the order of inspiration and individuality, divinity and subjectivity, God and man, or spirit and language. But both genius and monologue contain internal tensions, and the two do not signify on the same level of discourse. Genius is both transcendent and immanent spirit by virtue of the introjection that transforms a Roman mythological figure into a category of modern psychology. Monologue may be understood either as a static opposition to communicative dialogue or as a dynamic swerve away from prior conventions of discourse. In the first case, monologue is the factual solitude of isolated speech that is not addressed to another. More significantly, monologue signals the active break from norms of ordinary language and is thus allied with innovation, deviant discourse, and creativity. Monologues often strive to evade norms, although pure monologue, in the sense of a linguistic mode that has entirely freed itself from otherness, is an impossibility.

Monologue is, then, a set of literary and rhetorical forms that represent and accomplish individuality. As individuality is both a linguistic and a subjective phenomenon, individual language is not merely "the language of an individual." Before assuming anything about speaking individuals, we must understand how speech itself can be individualized, and how texts produce the appearance of individuality.

Ferdinand de Saussure's *Cours de linguistique générale*, based on the terminological categories of "language" (*langue*) and "speech" (*parole*), facilitates an understanding of individual language, deviance, and originality. Saussure never wrote a linguistics of speech, which would have been relevant to the problematics of monologue, but the boundaries of his research provide direction for further exploration. He characterizes speech most broadly as an act of discourse and further explains the physical utterance by reference to individual thoughts that occasionally permit verbal freedom. For Saussure, then, speech is primarily a physical and psychological act of expression. If Saussure's general description of speech links the speech act to individual acts of will, then individual language appears to occur in conjunction with a personal or individual thought.[5] Post-Saussurian linguists for the most part begin from this psychological premise, yet the exclusive association of speech with individual thought leads away from analysis of linguistic individuality.

In recognition of the subsystems of language, post-Saussurian linguists often refer to "individual language," formed by specialized conventions and systems that govern an individual's speech. This individual language is an intermediary term in the discussion of collective language and specific speech acts. In one sense, the individual language may be only a selection from existing forms of discourse. From the standpoint of psychological theory, Sigmund Freud writes of clichés that repeat themselves throughout our lives, and not only "a lover's discourse" follows predictable patterns.[6] To view individual language as either an unchanging norm or as a discrete psychological capacity is analogous to conceiving language as a single essence. An individual's speech follows predictable patterns, but this network of linguistic strategies does not constitute a closed system. In contrast to the traditional and fully formed locutions, original combinations of speech deviate from systems or conventions of usage. An individual language may be understood as a repertoire of common or uncommon discourse types; individual speech depends on a break from established repertoires. A deviant speech act may become a fashionable communal norm or dialect variation, when an innovative swerve from previous standards is repeated and stabilized.

Dramatic, poetic, and narrative forms of monologue are closely associated with the use of deviant literary techniques, at the boundary

[5]Ferdinand de Saussure, *Cours de linguistique générale*, ed. Charles Bally and Albert Sechehaye in 1916, newly edited by Tullio de Mauro (Paris: Payot, 1972), 31. In English, see Ferdinand de Saussure, *Course in General Linguistics*, trans. Wade Baskin (New York: McGraw-Hill, 1966). See also Robert Godel, *Les sources manuscrites du "Cours de linguistique générale"* (Geneva: E. Droz, 1957), 66. The students' notes show Saussure's inconclusive effort to understand the freedom or individuality of speech without reference to the psychology of speakers.

[6]Sigmund Freud, "Zur Dynamik der Übertragung," in the *Studienausgabe*, supp. vol. (Frankfurt am Main: S. Fischer, 1975), 159; Roland Barthes, *Fragments d'un discours amoureux* (Paris: Editions du Seuil, 1977).

between socially accepted and socially censored discourse. The potential for constituting an original discourse type structured around an unfamiliar code is evident in the development of internal monologue and stream of consciousness in twentieth-century literature.

IV

Writers on genius have always feared that personal limitations may make their subject inaccessible. Can only an ingenious subject know genius as an object of analysis? Does genius only express itself indirectly, without revealing its essence?

"Genius" is first of all a word, and these pages approach an intertextual history of inspiration and individuality by working from linguistic clues. Modern genius is a nebulous construction over unstable foundations. How must we understand the linguistic mechanisms that have generated modern philosophy of genius and literature of monologue? No attempt has been made here to provide a linear intellectual history or even to trace direct lines of influence in the transformations of genius and monologue, for contrasts are often more significant than continuities.

"Unit idea," "key word," and "master trope" seek to name what they themselves are, in diverse intellectual traditions. Much depends on the different ways of conceiving thought that they imply. In contrast to the methods of conventional history of ideas, *Genius and Monologue* examines Western inspiration and individuality by uncovering key words and rhetorical mechanisms that give rise to dominant ideology. If the unit idea presupposes an essentialist conception, the key word is connected with a functionalist approach to meaning in relation to linguistic usage, and the master trope forms part of a rhetoricist method.

Traditional intellectual history, typified by the writings of Arthur Lovejoy, relies on the assumption that essential ideas can be distinguished and defined. Despite changing forms of expression, the Chain of Being, the Good, and the Just are taken to provide solid ground for the inquiry into unit ideas. Central human experiences, we like to believe, have not changed substantially during the course of cultural development. Conventional history of ideas, then, presumes access to immutable signified conceptions beyond the configuration of signifying expressions. Based on essentialist notions of stable meaning, intellectual history sometimes quests for unifying ideas.

A more pragmatic type of research, suggested by the work of Raymond Williams, focuses on key words that predictably recur in connection with ideology. According to the modified assumptions, signified conceptions must be understood in terms of shifting means of signification. Like keys, words function to open up ways of encountering the world. Ideas cannot remain stable, as our worldview is created and revised by a kaleidoscope of changing word configurations. This functionalist conception of meaning emphasizes the manifestations of thought. *Genius and Monologue* examines key terms— "genius," "monologue," *daimōn, daimones, daimonion, malachim, logoi, satan,* "transcendence," and "immanence"—that reveal much about diverse theological and philosophical systems. Because these key words are discussed from a linguistic standpoint, they stand in implicit quotation marks throughout the present book.

The new rhetorical criticism, practiced by critics as different as Kenneth Burke and Paul de Man, dispenses with essentialist presuppositions by emphasizing the efficacy of master tropes, figures of speech that engender and dominate meaning. Beyond the control of subjective ideas or intentions, tropes determine signification. In view of this rhetorical power, essential ideas and functional keys fade into positions of subsidiary importance: tropes give rise to tropes, generating the appearance of structures and systems of thought. From a rhetoricist standpoint, *Genius and Monologue* deals with the introjection of genius and the prosopopoeia that creates illusions of monologue. An inward turn represents God within man, while the trope of masks gives a voice and a face to internal speech.

This book does not present a conventional history of ideas, but considers key words and literary forms associated with inspiration and individuality. Rather than seek to conquer some paradise of stable meanings, I offer a guided tour through pathways of the Western tradition, with only one certain end: a review of rhetorical landscapes or textual topoi with interested fellow travelers. Because these revisionary routes demand an agile guide, specialists may resent the wanderer who declines to linger in their chosen domain, while other people wish the pace were faster. The reader need not start at the beginning and may prefer to skip from chapter to chapter in accordance with personal preference. The relationships between texts are essential.

Part One

PHILOSOPHY OF GENIUS

The scraps of paper which have been worn away and
dirtied by a thousand fingers, and which we must
accept as bad money, are repugnant to every tidy
person. And the used-up, washed-out everyday words
are no less repulsive to friends of mental tidiness,
because they take on a different sense in each mouth,
and thus, as currency of a higher kind, only simulate
an illusory credit. So much more unpleasant does this
devaluation of words become when one feels that they
formerly numbered among the aristocrats of language.
   Such a degraded aristocrat, still betraying its noble
lineage through its external appearance, is the word
"genius."

—GEORG WITKOWSKI, *Miniaturen*

1 Greek Gods, *daimōn,* and Socrates' *daimonion*

There is some truth in the popular notion that Plato leads Greek thought away from polytheism, yet the exact character of his turn remains mysterious. Neither Plato's philosophy of ideas nor Socrates' skepticism fully accounts for the theological impetus of the Platonic dialogues, because their explicit statements about the gods reach no univocal conclusion. A theological development shows itself indirectly: Plato performs one answer to established religion by representing the life and death of Socrates, who continues to affirm his unique encounters with divinity even when accused and tried for impiety. This biography had no need to be historically accurate in order to influence Western theology profoundly. At the end of a long line of revisions, modern European philosophers reconceive Socrates as a determined rationalist whose individual certainty does not preclude religious experience.[1]

In the Platonic drama that transforms Greek religion, one key term is the Socratic *daimonion,* which is variously described as something divine, a customary divine voice or sign. Socrates' *daimonion* has, however, always eluded definitive interpretation. The "something divine" (or daemonic) is already enigmatic when it first appears in

---

[1] On Socrates as a prototype of modern man, see Benno Böhm, *Sokrates im achtzehnten Jahrhundert: Studien zum Werdegange des modernen Persönlichkeitsbewusstseins* (Neumünster: Karl Wachholtz, 1966), 11–19. Böhm also briefly discusses the functions of the *daimonion* (p. 16).

texts by Plato and Xenophon, and in subsequent tradition the ascribed meanings and functions only proliferate. With reason, the configuration of Greek *daimōn*, Latin *genius*, and French *génie* has been called "a wonderful confusion" (*eine wünderliche wirrnis*).[2]

The present discussion neither surveys the vast literature on Socrates' *daimonion* nor strives to recover the original form of this divine mystery. *Daimonia* will continue to lurk amid a multiplicity of textual topoi despite all efforts to curtail their operations and to deny their efficacy. If the attempt to entrap this trope is abandoned, how can one approach the active power of the *daimonion*? What are the dynamics of the *daimonion* in Plato's dialogues? Although Plato's *Apology* vividly depicts the trial and condemnation of Socrates, the significance of the Athenian decision remains controversial. Modern scholarship tends to view the accusations against Socrates as the consequence of long-standing prejudices rather than as a reaction to his alleged impiety. But the hostile response to Socrates' theological leanings is the surest indication of their importance.

Hegel provides an incisive point of departure from which to understand Socrates' "genius" as a religious innovation. Because his *Vorlesungen über die Geschichte der Philosophie* construe Socrates allegorically, as a turning point in the development of spirit, Hegel reveals the strategic significance of Socrates' references to divinity in opposition to established Greek religion. According to Hegel, the *daimonion* turns Socrates inward, away from Athenian norms, and makes Socrates a forerunner of modern subjectivity.

Following Xenophon, Hegel associates Socrates' *daimonion* with the charge that he recognizes or imports novel divinities (*kaina daimonia*), although in fact Socrates introduces a novel form of divinity. The dispute over the grounds for Socrates' conviction rests on shades of meaning, however, and the significance of Socrates' theology emerges only in light of its context. If Socrates was charged with impiety as a consequence of his *daimonion*, then this figure must have been incompatible with the established religious language. In order to understand how this may have been the case, it is necessary to examine the traditional theological terminology.

Daimonion is a key word that cannot be firmly grasped apart from

[2]S. v. "Genie," by R. Hildebrandt, in *Deutsches Wörterbuch*, ed. Jakob Grimm and Wilhelm Grimm (Leipzig, 1854). This translation is my own, as are all translations hereafter, except where otherwise indicated.

the ancient vault it unlocks: *daimōn* and *theos* are basic terms in Greek piety. The complexity of Socrates' *daimonion* derives in part from ambiguous links to the evolving tradition of *daimones*, guardian spirits. Homer and Hesiod are necessarily the ground of Platonic theology, and yet no map of this ground can master the turn that Plato gives to his precursors.

A first analytic gesture returns to the *daimonion* of Socrates by way of Hegel's allegorical reading. Subsequently, an approach to the classical *daimōn* prepares for a strategic reading of Socrates' defense against his Athenian accusers, as presented in Plato's *Apology*. Against the background of *daimones* and *daimōn*, the Socratic *daimonion* revises the polytheistic tradition and moves toward a form of abstract monotheism.

Hegel's "Socrates"

For Hegel, spirit is essentially related to language,[3] and thus Socrates, a turning point in spirit, appears as a decisive moment in the historical text of philosophy. According to the *Vorlesungen über die Geschichte der Philosophie*, Socrates is "not only a most important figure in the history of philosophy—the most interesting in the philosophy of antiquity—but also a world-historical person."[4] Emblem of a philosophic *Aufhebung*, Socrates does not merely oppose Greek custom but retains both sides of the dialectic in himself. Hegel's Socrates allegorizes the development of spirit toward self-certain, self-determinative subjectivity: his destiny is a double movement of "turning back into himself" (*Rückkehr in sich*) and "decision out of himself" (*Entscheidung aus sich*). To the extent that Socrates represents the decision of subjectivity against Greek law, Hegel believes that he was necessarily an enemy of the state and rightly convicted.

The *daimonion* appears to confirm Socrates' position as an outsider

[3]See, for example, Hegel's *Phänomenologie des Geistes*, ed. Johannes Hoffmeister (Hamburg: Felix Meiner, 1952): "We again see *language* as the existence of spirit. It is the self-consciousness existing for others, which is immediately *present as such*, and as *this* is universal" (p. 458).

[4]Georg Wilhelm Friedrich Hegel, *Vorlesungen über die Geschichte der Philosophie*, in *Werke in zwanzig Bänden* (Frankfurt am Main: Suhrkamp, 1974), vol. 18, p. 441 (henceforth cited as *VGP*). A translation by E. S. Haldane and Frances H. Simson, first published in 1894, has been reprinted under the title *Hegel's Lectures on the History of Philosophy*, 3 vols. (New York: Humanities Press, 1974).

in relation to Athenian norms. Hegel asserts that the first accusation, "that Socrates did not hold to be gods, those which the Athenian people held to be, did not have the old gods, but rather imported new ones," is connected with the *daimonion* (*VGP* 498).[5] In short, the *daimōn* of Socrates was "a different mode [*eine andere Weise*] from that which was valid in the Greek religion." Religious innovation makes Socrates an enemy of the Athenians at the same time that he is "the hero who, in place of the Delphic god, established the principle: man knows in himself what the true is; he must look into himself" (*VGP* 502–3). Socrates is thus both a hero in the development of spirit and an enemy of his contemporaries.

Skeptical of the prophetic powers that some readers attribute to Socrates' *daimonion*, Hegel finds a similarity between Socrates' trances and abnormal states of consciousness. He writes that the *daimonion*, or "genius" of Socrates, "is not Socrates himself, not his opinion, conviction, rather something unconscious [*ein Bewusstloses*]; Socrates is driven" (*VGP* 491). The "something divine" at once becomes something unconscious, external (*das Äusserliche*) and yet subjective (*ein Subjektives*).[6] Socrates' oracle takes on "the form of a knowing, that at the same time is bound up with an unconsciousness,—a knowing, that can also occur in other circumstances as a magnetic condition [of mesmerism]" (*VGP* 491). While Hegel never explicitly rejects the

[5]As evidence of this connection, Hegel repeats the account given by Xenophon at the start of his *Memorabilia*. He approves Xenophon's version, but where Xenophon reports that Socrates believed that "the *daimonion* gave a sign to him [*eautōi sēmainein*]" (*Mem.* I.1.2), Hegel mistranslates *daimonion* as "the voice of God" (*die Stimme Gottes*) (p. 499). In Xenophon's *Memorabilia*, Socrates defends himself by noting that his *daimonion* is not so different from innocent forms of prophecy. But Hegel repeats Xenophon's account only to show that Socrates was in fact guilty. A. E. Taylor, in his *Varia Socratica* (Oxford: James Parker, 1911), questions the association of the *daimonion* with Socrates' indictment: "If Socrates believed that 'heaven' gave him revelations by means of the *sēmeion*, he believed neither more nor less than any of his neighbors who put their faith in omens, or consulted a soothsayer about their dreams. And it follows at once that if Socrates could be charged with impiety for believing in the prophetic significance of his 'sign,' Anytus and Meletus could equally have brought a successful *graphē asebeias* against any Athenian who believed in dreams and omens, that is, against the great majority of the *dēmos*" (pp. 10–11). But Taylor attributes greater rationality and consistency to Athenian jurors than they need have possessed. And since Hegel treats the life of Socrates as an allegory of spirit, rather than as a literal history, Taylor's reasoning does not disqualify Hegel's reading of Xenophon.

[6]Neither the ordinary language nor the psychology of Hegel's time distinguished between *bewusstlos* and *vorbewusst*, "consciousless" (or "unconscious") and "preconscious." Hegel's coinage plays on a second meaning of *bewusstlos* as "senseless" and leads to an extended discussion of abnormal psychological states.

prophetic image of Socrates, he makes the supposedly pathological manifestation of the *daimonion* appear far more compelling than its divinity.

Hegel bases his theory that the Socratic *daimonion* is "something unconscious" on the *Symposium* 220cd.[7] Plato's Alcibiades associates Socrates' motionlessness with the depth of his meditations, and Hegel takes this anecdote as evidence of the profundity of his spirit. But Hegel is not satisfied with the trance as a sign of Socrates' reflective depths and calls it a cataleptic state in which Socrates is "completely dead as a sentient consciousness"; this is "a physical tearing away of the inner abstraction from the concrete bodily being, a tearing away, in which the individual separates himself from his inner self" (*VGP* 449). While Socrates' thought represents a particular level of world-historical consciousness, his trances are pathological (*krankhaft*), and Hegel later argues with increasing urgency that Socrates' *daimonion* is linked to cataleptic trances (*VGP* 495). Neither Plato nor Xenophon associates the *daimonion* with Socrates' trancelike states. Hegel makes this connection in order that the pathological Socrates may function as an allegory of his relationship to the Athenian people: Socrates is like a sleepwalker, and Athens is like a waking person. Hegel's allegory directly contrasts Socrates' self-interpretation as a gadfly that rouses the sleeping horse, Athens (*Apol.* 30e–31a).[8] Despite Socrates' own references to the Delphic exhortation "Know thyself," Hegel suggests that Socrates himself was incapable of self-knowledge in relation to his experience of the *daimonion*.

From the start of his exposition on Socrates' *daimonion*, Hegel main-

[7]According to Alcibiades, "On one occasion some idea came to him [*synnoēsas*] early in the morning, and he stood there contemplating [*skopōn*] it. When he made no progress, he wouldn't give up, but went on inquiring [*zētōn*]. At noon he was still there; men were noticing him and saying to each other in marvel that Socrates had been standing there considering [*phrontizōn*] since sunrise. Finally, in the evening some of the Ionians took their meal, brought out their mats and lay down in the cooling air—this was in the summer, of course—to see whether he would also stand through the night. He stood there until morning, and then at sunrise he said his prayers to the sun and went away." The words used to describe Socrates' thought process are incompatible with a dysfunctional, pathological condition. I have consulted and modified the translations from Plato that appear in the *Collected Dialogues*, ed. Edith Hamilton and Huntington Cairns, Bollingen Series (Princeton: Princeton University Press, 1963).

[8]Compare Heraklitus' use of the sleeping/waking opposition, in Hermann Diels and Walther Kranz, *Die Fragmente der Vorsokratiker* (which I shall henceforth cite as Diels and Kranz), 3 vols. (Berlin: Weidmann, 1954) B1, B21, B26, B73, B88, B89; and see also the discussion of divination in the *Timaeus* 71de.

tains a cautious distance: "In connection with this famous *Genius* of Socrates, as a so much talked-about bizarrerie of his imagining, neither the idea of guardian spirit or angel, nor that of conscience, should occur to us" (*VGP* 490–91). The *daimonion*, or "genius," is a "bizarrerie" of his imagination, and *we* must guard against conceiving it as a guardian spirit or angel. Although Socrates is characterized as "one who is certain in himself," his *daimonion* does not represent anything universal, such as conscience (*Gewissen*). The *daimonion* stands opposite the universality of Socratic reason: the revelations of the *daimonion* concern mere particulars and are thus "less significant than those of his spirit, of his thinking" (*VGP* 501). But even if the *daimonion* proves inferior to intellectual self-determination or conscience, what convinces Hegel that it is not to be imagined as a guardian spirit (*Schutzgeist*) or angel (*Engel*)?

Hegel relies in part, no doubt, on the opinion Schleiermacher expresses in his contemporary edition of Plato's dialogues. Schleiermacher's note to the *Apology* 27c argues that neither Socrates nor Meletus understood the *daimonion* as "a particular being [*Wesen*] of a higher kind." Rather the *daimonion* is "only a special effect [*Wirkung*] or revelation of the, or of an indefinite, higher being."[9] Hegel's tone is significant, however, when he denies all argument its place and asserts that "the idea of a guardian spirit, angel," should not even occur to us. Hegel claims that Socrates believed himself to possess what *we* should not seriously consider.

Hegel ultimately evades any direct confrontation with questions of the divinity of the *daimonion*. Although he opts for an allegorical reading of Socrates as a moment in the development of spirit, Hegel reduces the occurrence of the *daimonion* to a psychological aberration.[10] Furthermore, Hegel preserves for the *daimonion* a middle ground

---

[9]Plato, *Werke*, 2d ed., trans. F. Schleiermacher (Berlin: Realschulbuchhandlung, 1818/ 1804), pt. 1, vol. 2, pp. 432–33.

[10]Hegel's psychological reading of Socrates is exaggerated and literalized by L. F. Lélut's *Du démon de Socrate*, 2d ed. (Paris: J.J.B. Ballière, 1856): "Socrates was a *Theosophist*, a *visionary*, and, to say the word, a *madman*; this opinion is the only true one" (p. 93). Søren Kierkegaard responds with hostility to the 1836 edition of Lélut's book in *The Concept of Irony*, trans. Lee M. Capel (Bloomington: Indiana University Press, 1968): "There has also been considerable difficulty with this daimon quite recently, and I see from a publication by Heinsius that a psychiatrist in Paris, F. Lélut, has been so self-wise as to claim: 'Socrates was afflicted with that madness which in technical language is called hallucination'" (p. 186n). Yet Kierkegaard does not take issue with Hegel as regards the *daimonion*.

"between the exteriority of the oracle and the pure interiority of spirit" (*VGP* 495). Socrates appears to Hegel as prophet of internal certainty (*innere Gewissheit*), but to Socrates' contemporaries, this certainty appears as a new god. From the standpoint of the Athenians, then, Hegel considers the accusation against Socrates as completely correct, and Hegel ratifies their condemnation of him.

Like many other post-Enlightenment thinkers, Hegel recognizes Socrates' significance as a self-determinative consciousness and yet cannot accept his theological innovation. The meaning of the *daimonion* remains a problem for modern thought, because this mysterious agency can neither be identified with a guardian spirit nor reduced to the voice of conscience. Hegel chooses to understand the activity of the *daimonion* as an expression of a pathological condition in which Socrates loses rational awareness and submits himself to "something unconscious." Although modern interpreters acknowledge the significance of Socrates as an individual, they deny the divine influence of the *daimonion*.

Hesiodic *daimones* and Homeric *daimōn*

Daimones and *daimōn* are precursors of the Socratic *daimonion*. *Daimones* appear influentially in Hesiod as minor deities, guardians over men; *daimōn* occurs often in Homer and reveals a plenitude of meanings close to the omnipresent *theos*. The moment of Socratic subjectivity depends on its opposition to the shadowy terminology it displaces.

Hesiod narrates the history and activity of *daimones* in two central passages of the *Works and Days*. In a double narrative of decline, Pandora first exposes men to all the ills of life; afterward the golden race is followed by silver, bronze, semidivine, and iron generations. The first two generations transmigrate and become spirits, *epichthonioi* and *hypochthonioi*:

> But after earth covered over this generation,
> They are called the earth-dwelling spirits,
> Noble warders-off of evil, protectors of mortal men,
> Who keep watch over judgments and wicked deeds,
> Clad in mist wandering everywhere over the earth. . . .
> But after earth covered over this generation,

They are called by men the blessed dwellers under the earth,
Second in order, but nevertheless honor attends upon these also.[11]

Echoes of the Hesiodic daemonology in expressions attributed to
Thales, Theognis, Heraklitus, and Empedocles attest to its prevalence.[12] In most instances, the guardian spirits are souls of the dead.
Passages in Aeschylus, Sophocles, Euripides, and Plato,[13] Xenocrates,
Plutarch, Maximus of Tyre, and Apuleius,[14] further repeat and revise
the image of *daimones*. The tension between *daimones* and *daimōn* recurs
in Socrates' life: just as the traditional *daimones* precondition the charge
that Socrates recognizes novel divinities (*kaina daimonia*), so also is
Homeric *daimōn* the precondition for Socrates' peculiar *daimonion*. The
charge thus stands in the tradition of Hesiod, while Plato's account
continues the tradition of Homer.

The plurality of Hesiodic *daimones* contrasts the characteristically
singular Homeric *daimōn*. Literary histories often begin with Homer,
yet Hesiod's writings most likely represent earlier religious beliefs.
Thus the plural Hesiodic *daimones* probably preceded the singular
Homeric *daimōn*, and Homer anticipates Plato's turn away from the
polytheistic divine apparatus. While *daimones* are spiritual entities,

---

[11]Hesiod, *The Works and Days*, in *The Homeric Hymns and Homerica* (Cambridge: Harvard University Press, 1982), ll. 121–25 and 140–42. For help with translations from
Greek texts, I am indebted to Thomas Cole and Thomas Gould. References in the
following two notes are based on current editions of the Oxford Classical Texts.

[12]Thales as cited by Aristotle, *De anima* A2, 405a19 and 411a7, and by Aetius I.7.11;
Theognis, ll. 381–82. Although Heraklitus may have opposed the myth of *daimōn* when
he asserted that "a man's character is his *daimōn*" (Diels and Kranz B119), he also
affirmed of *daimones* that "they rise up and become the wakeful guardians of the living
and dead" (Diels and Kranz B63; cp. B79); Empedocles, Diels and Kranz B112 and
especially B115.

[13]Aeschylus, *Seven against Thebes*, ll. 523, 812; *The Persians*, ll. 601–22, 825; and especially *Agamemnon*, ll. 1175, 1342, 1468, 1482, 1569, 1667. Sophocles, *Ajax*, l. 1215;
Oedipus Rex, l. 828; *Oedipus at Colonus*, l. 76. See also Thomas Gould's note to l. 34 in
his edition of *Oedipus the King* (Englewood Cliffs: Prentice-Hall, 1970); Euripides, *Hip-
polytus*, l. 832; *Alcestis*, l. 1003; *Rhesus*, l. 971; Plato, *Symposium* 202e, *Cratylus* 397e–
398c, *Laws* passim. At the end of the *Republic*, Plato's myth indicates that souls *choose*
their *daimones*. The myth thus supports a loose association of the Socratic *daimonion*
with Platonic *daimones*, both reinterpreted to the extent that they are related to individual choice. But the Socratic *daimonion* transcends individual deliberation.

[14]See Richard Heinze, *Xenokrates: Darstellung der Lehre* (Leipzig: B. G. Teubner, 1892);
Plutarch, *Isis and Osiris* 361C, *The Obsolescence of Oracles* 415B. See also Guy Soury, *La
démonologie de Plutarque* (Paris: Société d'Edition "Les Belles Lettres," 1942); Maximus
of Tyre, *Diss.* in *Philosophumena*, ed. H. Hobein (Leipzig: B. G. Teubner, 1910), chaps.
14–15; Apuleius, *De deo Socratis*, in *Opuscules Philosophiques* (Paris: Société d'Edition
"Les Belles Lettres," 1973), chaps. 3, 6–9.

guardians over men, *daimōn* only exceptionally refers to a definite spiritual entity. Homer's indefinite mode of expressing divinity is, perhaps inadvertently, a step toward monotheism.

Many classical scholars seek to define the elusive *daimōn* in Homer's poetry by fixing it according to a stable rule of meaning. Others recognize the instability of the *daimōn* as a kind of "floating signifier" (*signifiant flottant*).[15] For convenience, these may be labeled the "essentialist" and the "rhetorical" approaches.[16] The essentialist view seeks to delimit meanings as if they adhered to words; the rhetorical view emphasizes that meaning extends beyond isolated words to the functional mechanisms that govern their use. Specifically, the essentialist approach attempts to establish the core meaning of Homeric *daimōn* as a spiritual being, power, or essence; the rhetorical approach conceives *daimōn* in connection with its distinct uses, strategic force, or function. Whereas the essentialist view understands *daimōn* as a simple name, the rhetorical view understands *daimōn* in terms of the narrative configurations that represent it.[17]

The meaning of *daimōn* has always been considered in conjunction with that of *theos*, but modern scholarship has increasingly rejected the essentialist notion that *daimōn* must name a definite divine being. Nineteenth-century classicists generally view *daimōn* either as a synonym for *theos* or as the name for some inexplicable divine power. One early classicist distinguishes between three Homeric uses of the word *daimōn*: a) as an equivalent of *theos*; b) as a name for "the divine efficacy [*Wirken*] in general"; and c) as "the dark, wonderful reigning [*Walten*] of a higher power."[18] Other classical scholars compare the

---

[15]Compare M. Detienne, *La notion de daïmôn dans le pythagorisme ancien* (Paris: Société d'Edition "Les Belles Lettres," 1963), 13.

[16]Rhetorical reading attends closely to the workings of performative language, but it stands apart from the tradition that views rhetoric merely as language of persuasion.

[17]What is the extent of Plato's irony when, in the *Cratylus* 397–98, he depicts Socrates as an essentialist who traces false etymologies of *theoi* and *daimones*? Focusing on the act of naming, Socrates attempts to localize the meaning of *theoi* in terms of their "running" (*thein*) nature and explains that *daimones* are wise and knowing (*daēmones*). Since Socrates, many interpreters have attempted to specify the etymological associations of *daimōn*. Yet the search for etymologies generally discovers only what it hopes to find. F. G. Welcker, for example, writes in his *Griechische Götterlehre* (Göttingen: Dieterich, 1857): "According to the basic meaning of *daiō*, divide, separate, is also to order and to know; for we know only that which we divide, as Schiller writes to Goethe" (p. 138). Thus *daimōn* becomes a kind of guardian over efforts to discriminate among meanings, encouraging us to believe that to separate is to know.

[18]G. W. Nitzsch, *Erklärende Anmerkungen zu Homer's Odyssee* (Hannover: Hahn, 1826–40), vol. 1, pp. 89–90, and vol. 3, p. 391.

relationship between *daimōn* and *theos* to that of divine essence (*numen*) and divine persona (*persona divina*) in Latin texts.[19] At the end of the nineteenth century, Hermann Usener takes the first major step toward a rhetorical understanding when he observes that "what suddenly comes to us like a sending from above, what makes us happy, what depresses and bends us, appears to the exalted perception as a divine being. To the extent that we understand the Greeks, they possess for this the species notion *daimōn*."[20] The word *daimōn* is no longer conceived as Homer's name for a divine reality; rather, *daimōn* characterizes the vocabulary of men, who speak with limited comprehension of providence. Any occurrence that "comes to us like a sending from above" may be associated with *daimōn*, divinity or fate as it "appears to the exalted perception."

Twentieth-century scholars radicalize the rhetorical approach, for they tend to attribute different narrative roles to *daimōn* and *theos*. Rather than name indistinct or distinct divine beings, then, these words appear to characterize different modes of expression. By contrasting the speeches of Homer's characters with the Homeric narrative, recent classicists argue that while the narrator refers to the gods by their names, his epic characters express themselves more vaguely: "The poet thus distinguishes between himself and the personages that he brings in as speaking, in that these ordinarily do not recognize the personality of the intermingling divinity, while he himself constantly knows exactly whether Athena or Hera performed the miracle concerned."[21] The choice of words is determined not by an abstract difference in meaning but by differences in the speakers. Narrative principles determine whether gods are called by their proper names or by the words *daimōn* and *theos*.[22] Twentieth-century authors

---

[19]Carl Friedrich Nägelsbach, *Die homerische Theologie in ihrem Zusammenhange dargestellt* (Nuremberg: Johann Adam Stein, 1840), 68; and Eduard Gerhard, "Über Wesen, Verwandtschaft, und Ursprung der Dämonen und Genien," in *Abhandlungen der Königlichen Akademie der Wissenschaften zu Berlin* (Berlin: Besser, 1852), 238. While *daimōn* in some cases functions as the name of a divine essence, we cannot logically conclude that this function is the essence of the word.

[20]Hermann Usener, *Götternamen: Versuch einer Lehre von der religiösen Begriffsbildung* (Bonn: Friedrich Cohen, 1896), 291–92.

[21]Ove Jörgensen, "Das Auftreten der Götter in den Büchern i–m der Odyssee," *Hermes*, 39 (1904), 364.

[22]Erland Ehnmark, in *The Idea of God in Homer* (Uppsala: Almquist and Wiksell, 1935), takes the rhetorical approach further when he suggests that *daimōn* is a "special stylistic device" (p. 65). As Ehnmark observes, "the vague terms employed by the ordinary man in attempting to describe the gods are due to his limited knowledge of their real

thus decline to limit *daimōn* to definite meanings and instead concentrate on its force. *Daimōn* operates like natural forces, both within the narrative world and as a narrative practice: "An essential characteristic of *daimōn* is, on the whole, the *actual* power, the power being exerted, the *dynamic* power."[23] *Daimōn* and *theos* suggest two different conceptions of power. The initial distinction between *daimōn* and *theos* as the "divine efficacy" and the "divine persona" turns into a distinction of mechanisms in two disparate rhetorical modes.[24]

One specialized rhetorical function of *daimōn* pertains to the interpretation of Socrates' *daimonion* from the standpoint of the Latin *genius*: "The hypothesis that *daimōn* might signify *a spirit* or *a génie* . . . appears acceptable in *Il*. XV, 468, *Od*. V, 421 and XIX, 201; it even imposes itself in *Od*. XI, 587, where we see a supernatural power that

---

nature" (p. 70). In contrast, it was Homer's "right and duty as a poet to supply definite information on those points that were left vague and indefinite in the popular conception of the gods" (ibid.). But Ehnmark does not explain the different uses of *daimōn* and *theos*. Gerald F. Else's "God and Gods in Early Greek Thought," in *Proceedings of the American Philological Association*, 80 (1949), also refers to "differences in usage" between *theos* and *theoi*: "They arise not from differing opinions as to the basic assumption, but from different kinds and degrees of knowledge in the speaker. The gods know each other and each other's names and activities and have no occasion for the indefinite *theos* or *theōn tis* except when talking to men. Neither does the poet, whose knowledge is accredited as coming from the gods. Both the gods and the poet, then, are correctly polytheistic in their language. And so are men when they have the guidance of cult or prophecy. But they are not always so precise. Not only do they not always know what god or gods they are dealing with, and whether it is one or more; it does not always matter very much" (p. 28). Indefinite expressions may thus arise from the ignorance of men as to what divinity influences their lives. Represented characters refer to mysterious powers as *daimōn*; gods and Homer, whose knowledge is supposed to be divine, do so only rarely. Else argues, furthermore, that the use of *daimōn* instead of *theos* may be determined by metrical considerations (p. 30). Indeed, *daimōn* does frequently occur either at the end of a line or in fixed phrases such as *daimoni isos*. Greek theology apparently develops in conjunction with stylistic compulsions, including the demands of oral composition.

[23]Elisabeth Brunius-Nilsson, *DAIMONIE: An Inquiry into a Mode of Apostrophe in Old Greek Literature* (Uppsala: Almquist and Wiksell, 1955), 133. Brunius-Nilsson lists the number of occurrences of *daimōn* in Homer, as follows: nom. sing., 40; gen. sing., 3; dat. sing., 11; acc. sing., 3; nom. pl., 0; gen. plur., 0; dat. plur., 2; acc. plur., 1. *Daimōn* is thus clearly linked to the singular form, unlike *theos*, which occurs more frequently in the plural.

[24]More comprehensive accounts of Greek *daimōn* are: Friedrich August Ukert, "Über Dämonen, Heroen, und Genien," in *Abhandlungen der Königlichen Sächsischen Gesellschaft der Wissenschaften*, 2, *Philologische-Historische Klasse* 1 (Leipzig, 1850), 137–219; Gerhard, "Über Wesen, Verwandtschaft, und Ursprung," 237–66; Georg Wissowa et al., "Daimon," in *Paulys Realencyclopädie der Classischen Altertumswissenschaft*, supp. vol. 3 (Stuttgart: Alfred Druckenmüller, 1918). See also Martin P. Nilsson, *Geschichte der griechischen Religion*, 2d ed. (Munich: C. H. Beck, 1955), Vol. 1, pp. 216–21.

applies itself to drying up the lake in which Tantalus wishes to quench his thirst."[25] Several Homeric passages, including those that involve the agency of Athena, constitute prototypes for the guardian spirits that attend to men in later literature.[26] Yet Socrates' *daimonion* should not be equated with a familiar spirit, for it has no stable identity and only acts to oppose certain false steps.

The relationship between Hesiodic and Homeric daemonology is in part that of the plural to the singular. In Hesiod's writings, *daimones* are guardians (*phylakes*), like Athena in the *Odyssey*, but they number in the thousands. These protecting spirits recur significantly both in Heraklitus' fragments and in the account of *daimones* ascribed to Diotima in the *Symposium* 202e. Homer's sixty-odd uses of *daimōn* include only three instances in the plural.

By what transformation does *daimōn* displace *daimones*? Twentieth-century secondary literature encourages the view that through rhetorical change, the plural form cedes to the singular. No critic has yet pressed the point to its logical conclusion and asserted that Greek polytheism was displaced by abstract monotheism by means of transformations in the use of narrative modes.

Socrates' New *daimonia*

Like Homer in his narratives of *daimōn*, Plato swerves from the Greek polytheistic tradition through his representations of the Socratic *daimonion*. But while *daimonion* is the singular form of the divinities (*daimonia*) that Socrates is accused of importing, both this "something divine" and these "divine things" remain obscure.

Plutarch, Maximus of Tyre, and Apuleius project current Roman beliefs onto Socrates and regard his *daimonion* as a kind of guardian

---

[25]Gilbert François, *La polythéisme et l'emploi au singulier des mots "theos," "daïmôn," dans la littérature grecque d'Homère à Platon* (Paris: Société d'Edition "Les Belles Lettres," 1957), 333–34. Compare Walter Otto's "Iuno," in *Philologus*, 64, 18 (1905): "A remarkable circle of ideas ascribes a genius to every Roman man, a semi-divine spiritual being which . . . stands in such a close connection to the visible human being, as only the soul is thought in connection with the body" (pp. 178–79). See also A. Brelich, *Die geheime Schutzgottheit von Rom*, trans. V. von Gonzenbach (Zürich: Rhein-Verlag, 1949), and Thaddeus Zielinski's "Marginalien," in *Philologus*, 64, n.s. 18 (1905), 20.

[26]See, for example, the encounter in book 13, esp. ll. 296–99; and compare Aeschylus' *Eumenides*, passim.

spirit.[27] Christian interpreters follow their example. The decisive battle between theological and psychological interpretations takes place in the eighteenth century, when critics increasingly view the *daimonion* as Socrates' innate genius, according to the modern usage of this term. In his *Sokratische Denkwürdigkeiten*, for example, Hamann explicitly links theological *Genius* with aesthetic or psychological *Genie*.[28] Responding to this introjective tendency in the late eighteenth century, Robert Nares writes a monograph in defense of the *daimonion* as a form of divination.[29] But Edward Young's epithet describing genius as "that god within"[30] apparently satisfied most readers.

What is Socrates' *daimonion*? A rhetorical approach raises the more exact question: how does the word *daimonion* operate in Plato's dialogues? Since Schleiermacher's commentary, modern interpreters doubt that the *daimonion* is rightly conceived as a guardian genius.[31] What must the *daimonion* be if it is linked to Meletus' charge that Socrates is guilty of "not believing in the gods whom the state supports, but in other new divinities" (*kaina daimonia*) (*Apol.* 24b)?[32] According to Plato's account, contemporary Athenians thought that Socrates held novel theological beliefs. Thus Meletus' condemnatory mention of "new divinities" (*kaina daimonia*) is of central importance even if the accusation against Socrates is not directly based on ac-

[27]Plutarch, "On the Sign of Socrates," in the *Moralia*, vol. 7, trans. Phillip H. Lacy and Benedict Einarson (Cambridge: Harvard University Press, 1959), chaps. 10–12, 20; Maximus of Tyre, *Diss.*, chaps. 14–15; Apuleius, *De deo Socratis*, chaps. 17–19. Compare Jane Chance Nitzsche's *The Genius Figure in Antiquity and the Middle Ages* (New York: Columbia University Press, 1975), 36.

[28]In *Hamanns Schriften*, vol. 2, ed. Friedrich Roth (Berlin: Reimer, 1821), 38.

[29]Robert Nares, *An Essay on the Demon or Divination of Socrates* (London: T. Payne, 1782). Nares opposes a contemporary translation of *daimonion* as "internal consciousness" (p. 42).

[30]"Conjectures on Original Composition" (1759), in *The Works of Edward Young* (Edinburgh: C. Elliot, 1774).

[31]See Plato, *Werke*, pt. 1, vol. 2, pp. 432–33. As Eduard Zeller argues in *Die Philosophie der Griechen*, 4th ed. (Leipzig: Fues, 1889), vol. II, pt. 1, the *daimonion* of Socrates was "no *Genius*, no personal being, but rather only indefinitely a daemonic voice, a higher revelation" (p. 78).

[32]Plato's version of the charge is slightly milder than that given by Xenophon in the *Memorabilia* I.1.i and by Favorinus (*Diog. Laert.* ii.5.40). According to Plato, the *graphē* reads: "Socrates is guilty of corrupting the youth, and of believing not in the gods whom the state supports but in other new divinities [*kaina daimonia*]" (*Apol.* 24b). Xenophon and Favorinus report that the Athenians accused Socrates of publicly importing (*eispherōn*) or introducing (*eisagoumenos*) novel "divine things"; Plato's version mentions only a private belief in or observance of (*nomizein*) these *daimonia*. Much rests on this subtle difference, because the guilt of Socrates derives from public action, not from the private occurrence of the *daimonion*.

counts of the *daimonion*. How does Plato present the relationship between Socrates' *daimonion* and its plural form, *daimonia*? To what extent does the accusation against Socrates mistake his conceptions?

The *daimonion* occurs in only six Platonic dialogues and in one pseudo-Platonic work, the *Theages*. Two of the most extensive discussions, in the *Apology*, are the basis for any rigorous interpretation. The other instances show that Socrates' experience of the *daimonion* is distinct from contemporary forms of prophecy and that it can serve a narrative function in Plato's dialogues.

Euthyphro, in the Platonic dialogue that bears his name, encourages an association of Socrates' *daimonion* with the "new divinities" of the indictment. When Socrates refers to the writ against him, however, he apparently misquotes: Meletus "says that I am maker of gods [*poiētēn einai theōn*] and so he prosecutes me, he says, for making new gods [*kainous poiounta theous*] and for not believing in the old ones" (*Euthyphro* 3b). Perhaps to make the claim against him appear even more *atopos*, Socrates replaces the vague new "divinities" (*daimonia*) by new "gods" (*theoi*). In any case, Euthyphro understands the indictment as referring to Socrates' *daimonion* and responds, "It is because you say that your *daimonion* always occurs to you" (ibid.). The implication is, then, that Socrates is to be prosecuted for novelties concerning divinity (*peri ta theia*). Furthermore, Euthyphro notes that the multitude is unreceptive to all talk of the gods, even when Euthyphro himself tells of them and prophesies. For Euthyphro, then, the Socratic *daimonion* is indistinguishable from his own experiences of prophecy. But Plato does not represent Socrates as a prophet like contemporary prophets, and Socrates' *daimonion* probably has little in common with the prevailing daemonic beliefs and practices. In the *Republic* 496c, for example, Socrates considers that his *daimonion* (*to daimonion sēmeion*) has occurred to few others.

The *Euthydemus* and *Theaetetus* briefly refer to the *daimonion* in connection with Socrates' activities as educator. In the *Euthydemus* 272e, "as I was standing up, there came the customary divine sign [*to eiōthos sēmeion to daimonion*], so I sat down." As a result, he remains and discourses with a group of students. In the *Theaetetus* 151a, Socrates describes the *daimonion* as forbidding him to accept certain students: "These, when they come back requesting association with me and behaving in an incredible fashion, with some of these the *daimonion* that comes to me forbids [me] to associate." The *Theages*, a pseudo-

Platonic work, exaggerates this aspect of the *daimonion*. When Socrates explains the grounds of his competence as a teacher, he includes the fact that his *daimonion* helps him to prevent his acquaintances from acting wrongly. But this positive approach to the *daimonion* denies Socrates his characteristic irony.[33]

In the *Phaedrus*, Socrates again refers to the *daimonion* as something that prevents him from making a false step. While delivering his speech, Socrates had already sensed something wrong, and he ascribes this sense to the power of prophecy (*mantikon*) of the soul. But when he is about to leave the place, "crossing the river, the *daimonion*, that is, the sign that customarily comes to me [*to daimonion te kai to eiōthos sēmeion moi gignesthai*] occurred" (*Phaedrus* 242b). This *daimonion*, the customary sign, manifests itself to Socrates as a voice: "On any occasion it holds me back from what I am about to do, and I seemed to hear a certain voice thence, which now does not allow me to depart before I purify myself." As the reason for this manifestation, Socrates suggests that he has "committed some fault toward the god [*eis to theion*]" (242c). Although the soul's prophetic power had already disturbed Socrates, his uneasy sense of having erred is not identical with the voice of the *daimonion*. As Hegel asserts, then, the *daimonion* is not simply "the voice of conscience." The *daimonion* operates as something beyond Socrates' awareness and shows itself within the represented setting of the dialogue as a voice that warns. There remains a subtle interaction between the external activity of the *daimonion* and the soul's interpretive efforts.[34]

These passages suggest two preliminary observations concerning the *daimonion*. First, contrary to Hegel's belief, there is no explicit connection between the *daimonion* and Socrates' trancelike states described in the *Symposium*. One might interpret Socrates' crossing of the river in the *Phaedrus* as a symbolic passage to something rational, away from the enchanted spot in which the dialogue takes place and to which his *daimonion* calls him back, but there is no compelling reason to associate the *daimonion* with accounts of his trances. Second,

---

[33]Compare Hermann Gundert's "Platon und das Daimonion des Sokrates," in *Gymnasium: Zeitschrift für Kultur der Antike und humanistische Bildung*, 61 (1954), 522. Gundert emphasizes the ironic component of Socrates' discussions of the *daimonion*. Far from prompting us to dismiss the figure of the *daimonion*, however, this irony may only suggest Socrates' or Plato's doubts about the limited notion of divinity they accept.

[34]See Gundert, pp. 519–20.

the *daimonion* is neither determinately adjectival nor substantive in form.[35] Resisting grammatical fixity, *daimonion* can function either as an adjective or as a noun. Euthyphro mentions *to daimonion* without any qualification, but generally it is called "customary" (*eiōthos*) and is linked to a sign (*sēmeion*). Furthermore, it can be like a voice when it occurs to Socrates. Søren Kierkegaard describes the elusive grammatical form of the "something divine":

> The word *to daimonion* . . . is not simply adjectival so that one might render it complete by implying function, deed (*ergon*), or sign (*sēmeion*), or something of the kind; nor is it substantive in the sense that it describes a particular or unique being. . . . this word signifies something abstract, something divine, which by its very abstractness is elevated above every determination, unutterable and without predicates, since it admits of no vocalization.[36]

If not even the grammar of *daimonion* can be firmly established, we should not expect to be able to localize its "essential" meaning. Aware of the impossibility of establishing the essence of the *daimonion*, Kierkegaard identifies it with the unutterable Hebrew name of God (YHWH). But how does the *daimonion* function in Socrates' life, and what is the strategic place of the word *daimonion* in Plato's theology?

While passages in Plato's *Laws*, written in a less philosophical vein, repeat the Hesiodic tradition of *daimones*, Socrates characteristically reverts to the singular form. As he states in conversation with Euthyphro, he is being prosecuted "because I find it hard to accept such stories people tell about the gods" (*Euthyphro* 6a). Yet Socrates is not simply an atheist, and the *daimonion* represents some part of his own religious conviction, even if this is suffused with irony. For the polytheism of anthropomorphized gods, Socrates substitutes a vague divine power that acts only to warn him against errors.

Socrates refers to his religious innovation in the context of his trial. He offers diverse arguments, but against the religious accusation he ultimately has no defense: "The Platonic *Apology* vindicates Socrates

---

[35]Following Schleiermacher, who notes that Socrates did not conceive the *daimonion* substantially, as "a particular being of a higher kind," Paul Friedländer writes in *Platon* (Berlin: Walter de Gruyter, 1954), vol. 1: "One already obstructs access for oneself, if one says, 'the daemonion,' as if it were a thing, instead of naming it in the neutral mode of the Greek expression, 'the daemonic' " (p. 35).

[36]*The Concept of Irony with Constant Reference to Socrates*, trans. Lee M. Capel (Bloomington: Indiana University Press, 1968), 186.

triumphantly on the scores of 'atheism,' but silently owns that he was guilty on the real charge of unlicensed innovation in religion."[37] One should not hastily deny all importance to the *daimonion* in Socrates' trial, for the problem remains: how does the accusation misconceive the innovation it names?

The decisive moment occurs in chapter fifteen of the *Apology*, when Socrates calls upon Meletus to explain his *graphē*. At this point Socrates shifts the burden of his defense to the irrelevant demonstration that he is not an atheist. Socrates asks: "Do you mean that I teach the young to believe in some gods, but not in the gods of the state? . . . Or do you mean that I do not believe in the gods at all myself, and that I teach other people not to believe in them either?" (*Apol.* 27bc). Socrates may be guilty of the first charge, but Meletus exaggerates his claim and responds, "I mean that you do not believe in the gods in any way whatever" (*Apol.* 27c). After this overhasty assertion, Socrates easily shows that Meletus' charge is self-contradictory.[38] Socrates' refutation runs as follows: whoever believes in "divine things" (*daimonia*) must also believe in *daimones*, and whoever believes in *daimones* also believes in gods. If, therefore, as claimed in the indictment, Socrates believes in new "divine things," he also believes in gods (*Apol.* 27ce).[39]

Thus free of the charge of atheism, Socrates does not confront the problematic *novelty* of the "divine things" he acknowledges. Even to the Athenians, the relationship between Socrates' *daimonion*, Hesiodic *daimones*, and Homeric *daimōn* was unclear. Like *daimōn* in the *Iliad* and *Odyssey*, *daimonion* appears as an "indefinite mode of expression," with a vague divine referent. How, then, can the *daimonion* be labeled an "innovation"?

The *daimonion* is one decisive source of trouble, at least to the fictional Socrates in Plato's narratives. Euthyphro's opinion supports this view; and when Socrates first refers to the *daimonion* in the *Apology*, he says that it is what Meletus "satirized" (*epikōmōdōn*) in his indictment (*Apol.* 31c). This passage is Socrates' most extensive dis-

---

[37]A. E. Taylor, *Varia Socratica* (Oxford: James Parker, 1911), 9.

[38]Compare Antonio Camarero, *Socrates y las creencias demónicas griegas* (Bahia Blanca: Cuadernos del Sur, 1968): "It is quite clear that in the Socratic defense, Plato did not consider the *daimonion* a personal being, when in an ironic manner Socrates makes the accuser Meletus recognize that whoever believes in 'the daemonic' by force believes in 'daemons' and, therefore, in the gods" (p. 27).

[39]Compare Aristotle, *Rhetoric* 1398a.

cussion of the *daimonion*. Whereas Socrates elsewhere only mentions it in passing, here he gives an explanation: "Something godly [*theion*], that is divine [*ti kai daimonion*], comes to me. . . . this is a kind of voice [*phōnē*] that came to me beginning when I was a child, which whenever it comes, always turns me away [*apotrepei*] from what I am about to do but never turns me toward [*protrepei*]. This is what stands in the way of my participating in public life" (*Apol.* 31cd). Overtly, Socrates is here concerned to justify his abstention from politics. But at the same time, he suggests his theological and political convictions. He generalizes the importance of avoiding politics in a way that threatens the "democratic" foundations of Athens: "It is necessary for him who is really going to fight on behalf of what is right, if he is going to survive for even a short period of time, to act privately [*idiōteuein*] and not publicly [*dēmosieuein*]" (*Apol.* 32a). This is a strong expression of the individualistic origins that Hegel finds in Socrates. The modern quest for an "idiolect" may also originate in an interpretation of Socrates' wish to concern himself with private things [*idia*] rather than with things political [*dēmosia*] (*Apol.* 31c).

Throughout the *Apology*, Socrates emphasizes his theological commitments. Not only is he in great poverty as a result of his skeptical "service to the god" (23c); he is concerned with what is "pleasing to the godly" (*tō theōi philon*) and acts according to the god's interest (*to tou theou*) (21e). He asserts that only the god is wise (23a). He considers himself as a "gift of the god" (30d), "stationed by the god" (28a) to preserve Athens; for the good of Athens, "the god attached me to the state" (30e). Christian interpreters have observed that Socrates' statements concerning "the god" may suggest a monotheistic tendency. But Socrates' singular "god" (*theos*) resists personification and instead points to a vague divine power, or an indefinite way of referring to the divine, like *daimōn* and *daimonion*. Following the command of "the god," then, Socrates claims that it is his duty to act as a gadfly and arouse Athens, a sluggish horse (*Apol.* 30e–31a). In contrast to Hegel's conception of the *daimonion* as "something unconscious," Socrates conceives of a god that leads him to awaken heightened consciousness in others.

Some commentators believe that Plato represents a Socrates who exaggerates his piety in order to defend himself. More likely, Plato includes this strong theological dimension to vindicate Socrates, who may or may not have held the views that Plato attributes to him.

Whether or not Socrates actually spoke of the *daimonion* as he does in Plato's *Apology*, the theological turns of phrase ascribed to Socrates are literary constructs. To achieve its vast influence, the Platonic turn did not require a real Socrates at all.

Socrates' final words in the *Apology* are not part of his legal defense. Already condemned to death, Socrates addresses his judges. To those who voted to acquit him, Socrates explains "an amazing thing" that has occurred. Now Socrates takes the *absence* of the *daimonion* to be significant:

> The customary prophecy of the *daimonion* was quite frequent through-out my entire life until now, and has opposed me even on very minor matters, if I was on the point of doing something improperly. And now, as you yourselves perceive, there have befallen me these things which a man would think to be, and which are reckoned, the most extreme of evils. But neither as I was going out in the morning from my home did the god's sign oppose me, nor when I came up here to the court, nor at any point in my speech when I was on the point of saying something. In other speeches in other places, however, it would hold me back in the midst of speaking. But as it is, at no point concerning this matter, in no deed or word has it opposed me. [*Apol.* 40ab]

For the first time, the *daimonion* appears to offer positive information, yet only by virtue of its absence: "The chances are that this thing that has befallen me has come as something good . . . , because it is not possible that the customary sign would have failed to oppose me, were I not about to do something good" (40bc). Does the *daimonion*'s failure to occur mean that Socrates' death is not an evil? Socrates is aware that the *daimonion* has diverted him from evils, but he cannot reason with any certainty that the *daimonion* will warn him whenever anything evil is about to happen. Socrates knows that, if the *daimonion* occurs, he is endangered, but it does not follow that whenever he is endangered, the *daimonion* will occur. In connection with the *daimonion*, Socrates' beliefs reveal illogic.

We can neither stabilize nor even identify the divine nature of the *daimonion*, which never advises a course of action. For Socrates, the meaning of the *daimonion* is that he must establish his own principles of self-determination while acknowledging that rational ideas of the good and of oneself are ultimately insufficient for this purpose. Reason may retrospectively confirm the validity of what the *daimonion* motivates; where self-determination falls short, the *daimonion* takes its place, or acts as its corrective.[40]

Modern thought strives to reduce this extrarational "voice" to the workings of conscience or of the superego, but for Socrates the *daimonion* is indeed "something divine." Socrates' piety involves a moment of rectification from beyond the immanence of reason, a turn that, reinterpreted as the call of conscience, profoundly influences the Christian tradition of self-correction. If the subject is unable to decide adequately, something divine, manifesting itself as voice or sign, may give negative counsel. For Plato, reason becomes the basis of subjectivity, but Socrates denies that he is master of himself, and his *daimonion* transcends the workings of conscience.

The *daimonion* has no substantial existence, yet it acts as a double-edged turn in the life of Socrates as Plato represents it. When Socrates is on the verge of error, the *daimonion* turns him away (*apotrepei*). For the later history of genius, this turn is a decisive trope: Socrates, despite extreme rationalism, cannot master all situations. The *daimonion* is a mysterious, extrarational force that opposes false steps. For Socrates, politics appears as one such false step, and so the *daimonion* acts to *turn* Socrates *inward*. What Hegel terms a "turning back of consciousness into itself" is the decisive meaning of Socrates as moment in the development of subjective self-determination. To the extent that the *daimonion* is Socrates' own customary sign (*eiōthos sēmeion*), it also represents his individuality as a swerve from customs of the *dēmos*. Socrates' *daimonion* makes his life a prototype of mystical transcendence and of a modern master trope, the idiolect. *Daimonion* is a trope that turns inward; Hegel exaggerates this turn and makes it appear pathological.

The *daimonion* also acts as Plato's turn away from his precursors' *daimones*. While the *daimonion* does not explicitly stand at the center of Plato's theological statements, it performs a decisive revision of previous daemonology. Hovering between grammatical forms, the

---

[40]Even Socratic reason is unable to guide all action. See Edward Zilsel, *Die Entstehung des Geniebegriffs* (Tübingen: J. C. B. Mohr, 1926): "The completely irrational way in which, for the otherwise so rational philosopher, the daemonic voice separates itself from all rational considerations, easily became a point of contact when the advancing Renaissance went about emphasizing the irrational nature of poetic production, even exalting it into the supernatural" (p. 12). According to Thomas Meyer, in *Platons Apologie* (Stuttgart: W. Kohlhammer, 1962), the *daimonion* stands "in exact logical opposition to Socratic self-discovery" (p. 73).

daimonion eludes all hierarchy of divine beings and suggests a theological belief based either on vague divine power or on vague intuitions. Plato's Socratic allegory suggests that this innovation threatens contemporary Athenians and contributes weight to Meletus' accusation, which associates his *daimonion* with "new divinities" (*kaina daimonia*).

If the *daimonion* subverts coherent theological systems, how can Socrates be so certain that, when the customary sign does not occur, his death is not an evil? And what convinces him that "no evil can happen to a good man" (*Apol.* 41d)? Socrates' conception of fate, developed elsewhere in Plato's dialogues, excludes the elements of irrationality and futile destruction that characterize the Homeric universe. The absence of the *daimonion* during the trial cannot, however, secure the positive assurance Plato sought. When there is no certainty that divinity governs the world, the execution of Socrates is as potentially threatening to theology as Job's suffering or the command that Abraham sacrifice his son.

Plato's Socrates is the victim of an inevitable conflict between theological systems. In general terms, the figure of Socrates is the place in Plato's work where competing beliefs vie for domination. Greek myth depends on the plurality of gods, while Socrates' *daimonion* enhances the monotheistic tendencies at which the *Iliad* and *Odyssey* have already hinted. Abstract *daimōn* displaces plural *daimones*; the Socratic *daimonion* unsettles any recourse to the established divinities. The Athenians condemn Socrates for "importing new gods" only because they do not grasp his more radical challenge that questions the plurality of the gods.

2 Hebrew Angels, *satan*, and Philo's *logoi*

If Greek theology develops from the plural to the singular, Hellenized and Babylonian Judaism move in the opposite direction. For whereas the abstract Socratic piety challenges Greek polytheism, the Hebrew traditions of angels (*malachim*) drift away from radical monotheism.[1] The Book of Genesis represents angels as God's messengers, existing only in their fulfillment of this function, but the Book of Job, apocryphal writings, and various commentaries all multiply the manifest forms of divinity and give increasing independence to *satan*, an adversary or opposing angel. This intertextual development exposes conflicts within the diverse Hebrew traditions, conflicts that find expression in dualistic tensions at virtually every stage of Jewish thought.

Philo of Alexandria's writings exemplify the confrontation between theological systems that are based on radically monotheistic belief and those that refer to divine intermediaries. The Greek *logoi* characterize Philo's revision at the margins of rabbinic tradition. Despite strict prohibitions against representing the ineffable Tetragrammaton (YHWH), Talmudic commentaries on biblical narratives also slip toward hypostases of secondary divine beings. Postbiblical versions of

---

[1]Yehezkel Kaufmann, in *The Religion of Israel: From Its Beginnings to the Babylonian Exile*, trans. and ed. Moshe Greenberg (Chicago: University of Chicago Press, 1960), convincingly argues—against Julius Wellhausen and nineteenth-century biblical criticism—that monotheism is the earliest stage of Israelite belief.

the *akedah*, the binding of Isaac, exemplify modes of expansion that turn mysterious passages of Scripture into more comprehensible narratives of divine intervention. The images of angels and *satan* may indicate literal polytheistic tendencies or only an enhanced metaphorical element.

At the same time that Hellenized Jewish thought magnifies the role of divine intermediaries in versions of scriptural narrative, a Stoic distinction affirms God's dual transcendence and immanence. Retaining the notion of an inexpressed thought (*logos endiathetos*) that is analogous to divine mind, Philo adds instances of externalized language (*logos prophorikos*) to representations of the heavenly court. Christian scholars have demonstrated that Philo's wisdom has affinities to the Gospel of John; Jewish mystics have been reluctant to acknowledge Philo as a forerunner.

The *malach YHWH* and *satan*

Malach, the Hebrew word for "angel," apparently derives from the root, to send (*lach*).[2] Like Greek *angelos*, Hebrew *malach* is primarily a "messenger" and can refer to human messengers (as in Gen. 32:4). But God's *malachim* are essentially linked to the divine Word, or *Logos*, and are inseparable from the messages they bear from God to men. God speaks with individuals through the mediation of *angeloi*, or *logoi*. The biblical Genesis and Exodus grant no independent existence to these divine emissaries.[3]

The angel of God (*malach YHWH*) first appears in Genesis 16:7–12. God has already promised Abraham an heir, but the childless Sarah offers him her servant girl, Hagar. After Hagar conceives, Sarah treats her harshly, and she flees. At this point, God's angel finds Hagar in the wilderness and echoes God's promise to Abraham: "The angel of YHWH said to her, 'I will greatly multiply your seed. . . . Behold, you are with child and will bear a son, and you will call his name Ishmael, because YHWH has heard your affliction' " (Gen. 16:10–11). God's

---

[2]See Solomon Mandelkern's *Veteris Testamenti Concordantiae Hebraicae atque Chaldaicae* (Berlin: F. Margolin, 1925), 625–26.

[3]Compare Alexander Kohut, *Über die jüdische Angelologie und Dämonologie in ihrer Abhängigkeit vom Parsismus* (Leipzig: F. A. Brockhaus, 1866), 1–2. See also J. B. Frey's "L'angelologie juive au temps de Jésus-Christ," in *Revue des Sciences Philosophiques et Théologiques*, 5 (1911), 75–76.

angel is primarily the bearer of His message; Ishmael's name derives
from the fact of God's having heard (*shama*) through the angel. When
Hagar and Ishmael are turned out into the wilderness together, God
hears Ishmael's cry and again announces, through the voice of His
angel, "I will make him a great nation" (Gen. 21:18). The first-person
form indicates that, as in the previous passage, the angel is in some
way identified with God; when the angel hears and blesses, God
hears and blesses. The angel exists primarily to convey God's Word.

Genesis 22 also suggests a conflation of God with His angel. Ini-
tiating the command to sacrifice Isaac, God calls "Abraham" (Gen.
22:1); when He annuls the command, His angel calls, "Abraham,
Abraham" (Gen. 22:11). The angel serves to communicate God's blessing: "The angel of YHWH called to Abraham a second time out of
the heavens, and said, By Myself I have sworn, says YHWH, because
you have done this thing, and have not withheld your son, your only
son, that in blessing I will bless you and in multiplying I will multiply
your seed as the stars of the heavens . . . because you have listened
to My voice" (Gen. 22:15–18). Later interpreters find a problem in the
shift from God's initial command to the angel's subsequent retraction.
But as the angel of God exists in order to express God's Word, there
is no discrepancy.

Jacob's dream (Gen. 28:12–15) further implies the significance of
angels as divine words (*logoi*). Rather than describe *malachim* inde-
pendently, as Hesiod describes *daimones*, this passage makes God's
words the essence of their manifestation: "He dreamed, and behold
a ladder set up on the earth, and the top of it reached to the heavens;
and behold the angels of God ascending and descending on it. And
behold, YHWH stood beside him and said, 'I am YHWH, the God of
Abraham your father, and the God of Isaac. I will give the land on
which you lie to you and to your seed' " (Gen. 28:13–14). The dreamed
vision of angels is essentially linked to God's revelation. Following
the Septuagint, Philo suggests that God's *angeloi* are analogous to
logoi.

In Genesis, then, the angel of God is inseparable from God's Word,
speech, or message.[4] The angels in Exodus are similarly subordinate
to God: if the angel of God appears to Moses in the burning bush
(Ex. 3:2), it is God who calls "Moses, Moses" (Ex. 3:4) and who reveals

---

[4]Difficult passages in Gen. 18–19 and 32 lie beyond the scope of this analysis.

the future of "My people." Furthermore, concerning the angel of God's presence that accompanies the Jews out of Egypt (Ex. 14:9 and Ex. 23:20), God announces, "My name is in him." Philo's Greek usage indicates, then, that *angeloi* may be understood as representations of God's *logoi*.

Later versions and commentaries hypostatize the communicative agency of God. Rather than conceive *malachim* as figures for the sendings of ineffable divinity, some postbiblical commentators literally conceive them to be semidivine beings in an elaborate cosmology. Acute tensions result from increasingly dualistic explanations of evil in terms of fallen angels.

The word *satan*[5] probably derives from the verb meaning, "to act as an adversary," though some scholars trace it to *shut*, "to go about or deviate"; *satan*, an adversary or force of opposition, deviates and causes others to deviate.[6] In the Pentateuch, the word *satan* occurs only once. When Balaam departs to speak against Israel, "the angel of YHWH placed himself in the way as an adversary [*l'satan*] against him" (Num. 22:22). To express God's anger and to correct Balaam's course, the angel appears to block Balaam's path. Far from opposing God's will, this *satan* is an angel that directly fulfills God's Word.

In the Book of Job, *satan* becomes an explicit heavenly adversary.[7] The opening chapters represent a heavenly court to which "the sons of God [*b'nai Elohim*] came to present themselves before YHWH" (Job 1:6). This representation raises the classical problem of theodicy, the existence of evil in God's world, along with other insoluble problems of interpretation. The visual aspect of God's court is reminiscent of 1 Kings 22:19: "I saw YHWH sitting on His throne, and all the host of heaven standing beside Him on His right and on His left." But the reference to "the sons of God" ultimately echoes Genesis 6:2 and the associated accounts of "fallen angels."

[5]The italicized *satan* refers to the ancient Hebrew word, and is thus differentiated from the English Satan.

[6]See N. H. Tur-Sinai (H. Torczyner), *The Book of Job: A New Commentary* (Jerusalem: Kiryath Sepher, 1957), 38–45. Other works associate *satan* more closely with a power of accusation, as does Rivkah Schärf Kluger's *Satan in the Old Testament*, trans. Hildegard Nagel (Evanston: Northwestern University Press, 1967), 25–34.

[7]1 Chronicles 21:1 and Zechariah 3:1–2 also show that *satan* has assumed a new role but with less drastic consequences for men. See Edward Langton's *Satan: A Portrait* (London: Sheffington, 1945). For a general overview, see Jeffrey Burton Russell, *The Devil: Perceptions of Evil from Antiquity to Primitive Christianity* (Ithaca: Cornell University Press, 1977).

At the start of the story of Job, God speaks with *satan*. The adversary's first words explain his name in terms of his activity: "Where do you come from?" God asks, and *satan* responds: "From going about [*m'shut*] on the earth" (Job 1:7). Like Hesiodic *daimones*, *satan* wanders the earth and weighs the actions of men. To some extent, *satan* already takes on a more independent function than that of angels. More than the vehicle of God's communications, *satan* retains an identity as a heavenly being that searches out evil.[8] In a sense, the explicit adversary of men shifts the problem of evil away from God, taking the blame for the ills of life. But in this biblical narrative, *satan* is only able to act insofar as God permits his action.

The "outside books" of Enoch and of the Jubilees (the Little Genesis) exemplify later additions to the canonized image of *satan*.[9] In 1 Enoch 6–11 there appears a seminal account of angelic origins in the form of an expanded retelling of Genesis 6:1–4. Fallen angels have intercourse with the daughters of men, who give birth to giants. The Book of Jubilees substantially agrees with this version.[10]

The Manual of Discipline, recovered from the Qumran caves, substantiates the traditional view that Jewish angelology shows traces of Persian influence. According to Edward Langton, the Persian dualism is first expressed in *Yasna*: originally "there were two primeval spirits, also called *principles* or *things*, a better and a worse."[11] Similarly, the Manual of Discipline informs that God "created man to rule the world, and appointed for him two spirits after whose direction he was to walk until the final inquisition. They are the spirits of truth and of perversity."[12] While this document clearly expresses a dualistic con-

---

[8]Yet *satan* may only represent human doubts that result from the human inclination toward evil. As the Babylonian Talmud, Baba Batra 15b, suggests, *satan* is the evil impulse (*yetzer hara*) of men.

[9]Edward Langton discusses the apocryphal literature regarding angels and *satan* in his *Essentials of Demonology* (London: Epworth, 1949), 107–44.

[10]Compare Bernard J. Bamberger's *Fallen Angels* (Philadelphia: Jewish Publication Society, 1952), 26–30, and Michel Testuz's *Les idées religieuses du "Livre des Jubilés"* (Paris: Librairie Minard, 1960), 75–86. But in the Book of Jubilees, God sends the angels to earth, where they are corrupted, while in 1 Enoch they already lust in heaven and descend in order to mate with women. Both versions clearly threaten the more abstract Mosaic representations of God and heaven.

[11]*Essentials of Demonology* (London: Epworth, 1949), 65.

[12]*The Dead Sea Scriptures*, trans. Theodor H. Gaster (New York: Doubleday, 1956), 43. Compare Jacob Licht, "An Analysis of the Treatise on the Two Spirits in DSD," in *Scripta Hierosolymitana*, vol. 14 (Jerusalem: Magnes Press, 1958), 88–100. If, as Licht maintains, one of the "two spirits" is assigned to each individual at birth, then this dualism closely parallels the Roman doctrine of good and evil guardian geniuses.

ception of good and evil, and gives them the name of "spirits," God creates this opposition. The Manual of Discipline, often attributed to the Essenes, appears to synthesize Persian and Jewish sources.

As several scholars have written detailed accounts of the Talmudic angelology, there is no need to reproduce their findings.[13] Versions of biblical narratives supply many instances in which Talmudic and Midrashic legends develop toward increasingly dualistic expressions.

The Divine *logoi*

The Greek tradition of *daimones*, the Stoic tradition of *logoi*, and the Hebrew tradition of *malachim* come together in Philo's writings; although Philo never profoundly influences Jewish orthodoxy, his synthesis parallels the transformations that occur elsewhere in the diaspora. While the Pentateuch refers to *malachim* as mere extensions of God, the later traditions develop toward dualistic beliefs in the evil agency of *satan* and demons (*mazziqim, shedim*). Within early Christianity, which rejects such hints at polytheistic belief, *daimones* irreversibly become demons.[14] Philo stands in a more complex relationship to both Judaic and Hellenic sources.

Logos, mediating between the transcendent God and immanent world appearances, is one key word in Philo's scriptural interpretations. Following Stoic terminology, Philo also refers to intermediary *logoi*, similar to the *daimones* of Plato's *Symposium* 202e. In fact, Philo explicitly identifies biblical *angeloi* with *daimones* and *logoi*.

But while *logos* is the term that links transcendence and immanence, it also gives rise to dualistic antitheses. The singular *Logos* stands opposite plural *logoi*; divine *Logos* contrasts human speech; God's reason is distinct from though associated with human reason; God's abstract *Logos* contrasts the more concrete forms of God's *angelos*. For

---

[13]See Ferdinand Weber, *Jüdische Theologie auf Grund des Talmud und verwandter Schriften gemeinfasslich dargestellt*, ed. Franz Delitzsch and George Schnedermann (Hildesheim: Georg Olms, 1975), sec. 54; Alan F. Segal, *Two Powers in Heaven: Early Rabbinic Reports about Christianity and Gnosticism* (Leiden: E. J. Brill, 1977); Peter Schäfer, *Studien zur Geschichte und Theologie des rabbinischen Judentums* (Leiden: E. J. Brill, 1978). In his *Rivalität zwischen Engeln und Menschen* (Berlin: Walter de Gruyter, 1975), Schäfer writes of a "constantly expanding angel-conception" (*sich immer weiter entfaltende Engelvorstellung*) (p. 73).

[14]See, for example, Augustine's *De civ. dei* VIII, 14 and X, 9.

the tradition of Christian interpretations of Philo, dispute centers around the question: is God's *Logos* impersonal or personal?[15] In connection with Socrates' *daimonion*, a more central question concerns the relationship between *Logos*, *angelos*, and conscience.[16] But as some interpreters recognize, the crux of Philo's synthesis is his use of the Stoic opposition between *logos endiathetos* and *logos prophorikos*.[17] Rather than rigorously define these terms, Philo employs them loosely, in ways that can only be translated inadequately into the English-language oppositions of "internalized thought" and "expressed word," meaning and utterance. The dualistic tensions within *logos* derive from this most basic opposition.

Jordan Bucher, one of Philo's most decisive interpreters, takes the antithesis within the *logos* as his starting point. In the context of nineteenth-century German scholarship, his work entitled *Philonische Studien* inevitably considers the tension between impersonal and personal meanings of *logos*. He seeks a resolution, however, by establishing both sides of the *logos* together.[18]

Bucher recognizes, furthermore, that the dispute does not revolve around two different meanings of the word *logos* but rather results from two different types of linguistic expression. His concise work thus begins by asking "whether Philo's *logos* be merely personification or actual hypostasis" (*PS* 1). Rhetorically, the question is whether *logos* takes part in a mode of naming or functions as a personifying trope. Rather than decide in favor of either alternative, Bucher follows a "historical-pragmatic path," pointing to the necessity of both rhetorical aspects of the *logos*. After reviewing the critical literature on

[15]See August Gfrörer, *Philo und die alexandrinische Theosophie* (Stuttgart: Schweizerbart, 1831), pt. 1, chap. 8; Edward Zeller, *Die Philosophie der Griechen*, 3d ed. (Leipzig: Fues, 1881), vol. III, pt. 2, pp. 378–81; and Joseph Buschmann, *Die Persönlichkeit des philonischen Logos* (Aachen: M. Ulrichs Sohn, 1873). This last inquiry is obviously, and at times explicitly, motivated by the wish to find an analogue to the Gospel of John.

[16]See Gfrörer, pp. 211–12; Friedrich Keferstein, *Philo's Lehre von den göttlichen Mittelwesen* (Leipzig: Wilhelm Juranz, 1846), 70; and Max Heinze, *Die Lehre vom Logos in der griechischen Philosophie* (Oldenburg: Ferdinand Schmidt, 1872): "Here the Logos plays the role of conscience, is also called precisely an examiner [*elengchos*], and is as such the divine angel that leads us" (p. 275).

[17]See Emile Bréhier, *Les idées philosophiques et religieuses de Philon d'Alexandrie* (Paris: Vrin, 1925), bk. 2, chap. 2; and see also Austryn Wolfson, *Philo* (Cambridge: Harvard University Press, 1947), vol. 1, chap. 4.

[18]Jordan Bucher, *Philonische Studien* (Tübingen: Zu-Guttenberg, 1848), 5 (henceforth cited as *PS*). According to its subtitle, this monograph is an "effort to resolve the question concerning the personal hypostasis of the *Logos* in Philo's writings in a historical-pragmatic way."

Philo, Bucher comments that, despite a general recognition that Philo's speculation moves within the categories of thinking and speaking, no previous interpretation of Philo adequately grasps the *logos* in these terms (*PS* 19).

Bucher thus begins anew by noting a linguistic distinction: "The external word (whether it be spoken or written) carries a doubleness in itself: on the one hand, something internal, the thought, which shall come to expression and representation; but on the other hand, also an external and sensuous form, in which every inner thought sees the light of day" (*PS* 19–20). In order to achieve a reinterpretation of Philo's thought, Bucher sets theological and cosmological beliefs aside, concentrating instead on a basic dichotomy in language. The realm of the internal thought is that of sense; the external form is an audible or visible sign. This verbal antithesis becomes the model of Philo's cosmology: "Completely analogous are also the appearances of the visible world, external signs, so to speak a grand sequence of letters, behind which a secret sense, the divine world of ideas, is concealed" (*PS* 20). Because the visible world is analogous to a sequence of letters (*Buchstaben*), an education in reading these signs is required for the recognition of the divine world of ideas behind external appearances. The externalized forms of word and world reveal and conceal the divine Word and world of ideas. *Logos* permeates the opposition. Like kabbalistic authors, Bucher writes, Philo understands the world as "a divine expression" (*ein göttlicher Ausspruch*) (*PS* 21). Thus the dialectics of *logos* must be realized, not simply reconciled.

Sense (*Sinn*) and written sign (*Schriftzeichen*) correspond to interiority and exteriority, thought and sensuous form, ideas and appearances, divine speaking and the divinely spoken. In other words, *logos* is the mediating unity of active and enacted speech, God's *legōn* and *legomenon* (*PS* 24–26). While *logos* is the mediating term between divine and worldly spheres, it is identified with both poles of the opposition.

Philo's central dialectic consists of *logos endiathetos* and *logos prophorikos*. Just as men may precede speech by thought, so God's speech, the world, is preceded by God's thought, the ideas. Bucher recognizes no essential difference between these two aspects of *logos*: "What a person speaks aloud, he has previously spoken inwardly. . . . But a distinction between *external* and internal speaking is grounded on the observation that thinking is an inner speaking, an inward-turned speaking; for we do not think without words, and there is no clear, complete thought without word" (*PS* 29). Bucher observes that thinking is basically an inner speech, or an "inwardly turned speaking" (*ein inwendiges Sprechen*). Philo and Bucher follow the Platonic definition of thinking as "the internal dialogue of the mind with itself" (*Sophist* 263e). One might speculate on relationships between this inward dialogue and Socrates' *daimonion*.

Bucher opposes the view that a conception of the doubled divine *Logos* gave rise to the belief in a doubled human *logos* (*PS* 30). According to Bucher, the distinction is originally present in human languages such as Greek, which employs *logos* in contexts referring to both "thinking" and "speaking." Philo allegorizes the opposition of *logos endiathetos* and *logos prophorikos* and infers a distinction in the "sphere of the absolute" (*PS* 32). Personifications of the divine *Logos* should thus be understood allegorically; for Philo, *angeloi* synthesize Stoic forces and Platonic ideas (*PS* 42).

Because Philo's works are structured primarily as scriptural interpretations, not as theoretical treatises, his thought has a fragmentary character. Yet he returns often to certain biblical figures: Adam and Eve, Cain and Abel, the Nephilim, Abraham and Isaac, Hagar, Jacob, Joseph, Moses and Aaron, Balaam. Philo conceives these diverse personalities as externalizations of God's activity and hints at systematic meanings through allegorical interpretations. Similarly, the word of God (*rhēma theou*) contains a tension between *logos endiathetos* and *logos prophorikos*. While Philo presents himself as an interpreter of texts, he seeks to demonstrate that God's transcendence and immanence are equivalent to mind and appearance, divine thought and letter.

But *logos* does not always appear in the singular form. In connection with the biblical account of Jacob's dream, Philo associates *logoi* with the angels that ascend and descend; *logoi* are like ambassadors to God. In turn, Philo notes that *logoi* and *angeloi* are different names for what "other philosophers call *daimones*."[19] *De gigantibus* 6 similarly

---

[19]*De Somn.* I, 141–42. I have consulted and modified translations of Philo's works that appear in F. H. Colson's and G. H. Whitaker's *Philo*, 10 vols. (London: William Heinemann, 1929–42). Philo is one of Heidegger's most striking unacknowledged predecessors. Not only does Philo base his work on a distinction between onto-theological and ontic-existential *logos*; he asserts that *logos* is "the house of God" (*De Mig. Abr.* 2–4) and discusses God's *Lichtung* as the archetype of visible light. As Bucher (*PS* 21) and others have recognized, Philo's teaching shares images of light with kabbalistic mysticism. Furthermore, like the later kabbalistic sources, Philo writes that "a garment

explains that "those which other philosophers call *daimones*, Moses customarily calls angels." Philo both follows the tradition of Hesiodic *daimones* and suggests the Platonic myth of the *Symposium* 202e, when he adds that God has given to the *logos* "the chosen right to stand on the boundary and distinguish the Creator from the created. This same *logos* both acts as suppliant to the immortal for afflicted mortality and as ambassador of the ruler to the subject" (*Quis Rer. Div.* 205). Philo moves in the direction of visual representation when he describes the role of the *logos* as an ambassador.[20] At the same time, Philo insists on the final unity of God's *Logos* with the *logoi* that are active as divine power, God's emanations. Though he returns to the Hesiodic and Platonic *daimones*, Philo gives them a new allegorical form in scriptural contexts.

God's relationship to his *Logos* and *logoi* thus parallels the opposition between *logos endiathetos* and *logos prophorikos*. Ethical questions arise when Philo illustrates this dialectic by means of biblical types: Abel and Cain, Moses and Aaron, Adam and Eve (*Quod Det.* 35–37, 126–27). Philo associates greater perfection with the *logos endiathetos*, which explains his special interest in ascetic Jewish sects. The two modes of *logos* correspond to two human types: "Many reason [*logizontai*] flawlessly but are betrayed by bad interpretation, that is, by bad *logos*. . . . Others, however, have been most formidable in interpretation but most foul in giving advice, such as the so-called sophists" (*De Mig. Abr.* 72). Sophistry accounts for Abel's defeat by Cain: Abel, "though he had the advantage of a faultless understanding, yet through lack of training in speaking is worsted by Cain" (ibid., 74).[21]

The doubleness of *logos* thus suggests an inevitable conflict between perfection and imperfection, good and evil. To account for the existence of worldly evil, Philo has recourse to a sharper separation of *Logos* from *logoi*, and of God's *angelos* from *angeloi*. When God creates

---

is a symbol of *logos*" (*De Somn.* I.102). God is like an architect whose blueprint, the *logos*, informs the world (*De Opif.* 17–20). Compare Genesis Rabbah on Gen. 1:1.

[20]Conceived abstractly, this boundary *logos* is analogous to Heidegger's "ontological difference" between Being and beings.

[21]Outward expression is not merely an evil. Other passages insist that, just as Cain and Abel are brothers, so the body is brother of the soul; expressed language (*prophorikos logos*) is "closest kin to mind [*nous*]" (*De Fug.* 90). Moses requires the assistance of Aaron to express the perfect *Logos*. For the sake of human understanding, there must occur a kind of fall from divine mind to *logos prophorikos*.

man, His work is partially performed by angels; scripture states, "Let
us make man" (Gen. 1:26) in order that "man's right actions might
be attributed to God, but his sin to others" (*De Conf. Ling.* 179). Philo
simplifies his analysis, however, by avoiding discussion of evil angels.
Instead, he focuses on the work of God's angel as an *elengchos*, an
examiner, appearing to oppose Balaam.

What does it mean for the divine *Logos* to enter a human soul? Philo
wavers between the tradition of Mosaic revelation on Mount Sinai
and the Platonic tradition of abstract revelation through wisdom (*so-
phia*). A *logos* comes to Philo at difficult moments of interpretation:
"But I have sometimes heard an even more authoritative *logos*, from
my own [*eiōthuias*] soul, which is often god-possessed and gives
prophetic utterance concerning things of which it can have no knowledge" (*De Cher.* 27). The god-possessed (*theolepteisthai*) soul is at the
origin of inspiration, en-thusiasm. Philo insists that God "speaks"
without voice; personifications of God are falsifications that only heu-
ristic ends justify: "the *logos* [= *hieros Logos*?], longing to educate those
whose lives are without knowledge, likened Him to man. . . . For this
reason it has ascribed to Him face, hands, feet, mouth, voice, anger
and indignation, and even armour, arrivals and departures, movements up and down" (*De Somn.* I.234–35). Representations are useful
only to dull people who are "not able to conceive of God at all without
a body, people whom it is impossible to instruct otherwise than in
this way, saying that as a man does so, God arrives and departs, goes
down and comes up, makes use of a voice" (ibid., 236). Such comments imply that the educated could entirely avoid the metaphorical
prophorikos, and thus Philo allies himself with an asceticism of language.

But Philo constantly reverts to the deceptive illusions he condemns.
For instance, when God gave the ten commandments (*logous, chrē-
mous*), He expressed Himself without the medium of voice: "I think
that on this occasion God created a miracle most appropriate to the
holy by summoning an invisible sound to be constructed [*dēmiurges-
thenai*] in the air, more marvelous than all the instruments [*organon*]
and fitted with perfect harmonies . . . , a rational soul [*psychēn logikēn*]
full of clearness and distinctness" (*De Dec.* 33). A new personification
enters the description: "The power [*dynameis*] of God drove forth the
newly created voice [*phōnē*], breathing on it [*epipneusa*], kindling it,
and spreading it far and wide, and made it more luminous at the end
[*telos*] by placing another hearing far better than that which works

through the ears in the souls of every man" (ibid., 35). The figure of an "invisible sound" carries Philo's account beyond the range of the senses, creating for the reader a novel kind of hearing. Prototype of the ordinary *logos*, the ten commandments are expressed by divine mind and impressed on human reason without undergoing the distorting effects of air. God's *Logos* appears to communicate directly with the internal *logos endiathetos* of men.

Philo writes as an enemy of figuration and of the *logos prophorikos* in general. His writings abound in visual imagery and are grounded on methods of allegorical interpretation, however, and he cannot maintain his distance from the ways in which language bears (*prophero*) meaning. If "inappropriate" figuration is inescapable, Philo can only encourage a strict distinction between allegorical and literal interpretation. Writing errs, and reading can only seek to swerve again and again from error. Philo ultimately succumbs to the *logos* that carries his words beyond the asceticism he wishes to proffer.

Encounters with *satan*

Postbiblical retellings of the story of Abraham and Isaac also move beyond the univocal divine call to representations of diverse angelic and satanic interventions. The increasing predominance of *satan* in later accounts suggests that, as Blake commented concerning Milton, many an exegete "wrote in fetters when he wrote of Angels and God, and at liberty when of Devils."[22] We need not draw Blake's conclusion that they were "of the Devil's party without knowing it," but the question remains: How did *satan* penetrate the canonical tale of Abraham's last trial?

The *akedah*, the story of the binding of Isaac, is "fraught with background [*hintergründig*],"[23] and postbiblical commentators repeatedly add to the minimal details of the original. Because these additions take the form of *aggadah*, or legend, they are not bound to the stricter constraints of *halakhah*, normative law.[24] Retellings that date from

[22]William Blake, "The Marriage of Heaven and Hell."
[23]Erich Auerbach, *Mimesis*, trans. Willard Trask (Princeton: Princeton University Press, 1953), 12.
[24]Alexander Kohut, *Über die jüdische Angelologie und Daemonologie in ihrer Abhängigkeit vom Parsismus* (Leipzig: Brockhaus, 1866), 15. On the complex relationship between

about 200 B.C.E. to 700 C.E. reveal the changing attitudes of their distinct contexts. The interpreters obviously rely on preexisting notions of the heavenly court and revise the narrative according to their angelological assumptions. These versions of the *akedah* also respond directly to each other and embody a complex tradition of intertextual relations.

Three versions of the binding of Isaac illustrate the developing traditions of Jewish angelology and demonology: the Book of Jubilees 17–18, Sanhedrin 89b, and Midrash Tanchuma, Vayirah 22–23.[25] With the exception of the early Book of Jubilees, these works are central to the rabbinic canon.

The Book of Jubilees suggests some of the earliest major additions to Genesis 22. This pseudepigraphic work claims to be an angel's revelation to Moses on Mount Sinai; as a result, the retelling of Genesis occurs in the first-person form. Genesis 22 thus becomes part of the angel's narrative, as when "I called to him from the heavens, saying: Abraham, Abraham" (chap. 18).

The shift to an angel's narrative is accompanied by additions to the role of an accusing spirit. According to the the Book of Jubilees, the Prince of Mastema[26] inspires Abraham's last trial: "the Prince Mastema came and said before God: Behold, Abraham loves Isaac his son, and delights in him above all things else. Bid him offer him

---

halakhah and aggadah, see also: Leo Baeck, "Der alte Widerspruch gegen die Haggada," in Aus drei Jahrtausenden (Tübingen: J. C. B. Mohr, 1958), 176–85; and Abraham Joshua Heschel, God in Search of Man (New York: Farrar, Straus and Giroux, 1955), 322–47. For a fuller bibliography on Midrash, see the notes to David Stern's "Rhetoric and Midrash: The Case of the Mashal," Prooftexts, 1 (1981), 261–91.

[25]I will also refer to the parallel passages in Genesis Rabbah 55–56 and Midrash Vayosha. Citations are modified from the following translations: The Book of Jubilees or, The Little Genesis, trans. R. H. Charles (New York: Macmillan, 1917); Sanhedrin, in The Babylonian Talmud, Seder Nezikin, vol. 3, trans. H. Freedman and ed. I. Epstein (London: Soncino Press, 1961) (henceforth, "Sanh."); Midrash Rabbah, 1, trans. H. Freedman and Maurice Simon (London: Soncino Press, 1939). For help with the translations of Midrash Tanchuma (henceforth cited as "Tanch.") and Midrash Vayosha, I am indebted to James Ponet and Michael Lozenik. I have also consulted the translations of Vayosha contained in the collections: Bet ha-Midrasch: Sammlung kleiner Midraschim, ed. Adolph Jellinek (Jerusalem: Wahrmann, 1967); and Aus Israels Lehrhallen, trans. August Wünsche, vol. 1 (Leipzig: Eduard Pfeiffer, 1907).

[26]In the Ethiopian text, this evil spirit is at various points called the "Prince Mastema," the "Prince of Mastema," and the "Prince of the Mastema." The name derives from the Hebrew root meaning "to accuse." The dark prince is thus a prince of accusation, or prince of the accusations, perhaps leader of a group of evil spirits.

as a burnt offering on the altar, and You will see if he will do this command, and You will know if he is faithful in everything wherein You try him" (chap. 17). In Genesis 22, only God is named as initiator of the command; here Mastema follows the *satan* of the Book of Job and provokes the test. This alteration makes God's action more comprehensible: in response to evil powers that doubt Abraham, God resolves to demonstrate Abraham's piety by means of a test. Yet as in the Book of Job, the acknowledgment of evil powers has a subversive tendency to relativize God's mastery over the world.

In this early revision, the Prince of Mastema is clearly subordinate to God. He can only propose the test and later suffer humiliation when Abraham is strong: "And the Prince of the Mastema was put to shame" (chap. 18). Mastema's "shame" indicates the presence of an extensive heavenly court.

Sanhedrin, one of the sixty-three tractates of the Babylonian Talmud, retells the story of Abraham and Isaac in the traditions of the Book of Jubilees and the Book of Job: "*Satan* spoke before the Holy One, blessed be He: Master of the Universe! You graced this old man with the fruit of the womb at the age of a hundred, yet of all the banquet he prepared, he did not have one turtle-dove or pigeon to sacrifice before You" (Sanh. 89b). *Satan*'s intervention appears as an explanation of Genesis 22:1.[27] Its purported origin is an oral tradition based on the words of Rabbis Johanan and Jose b. Zimra, but the Book of Job and the Book of Jubilees are written precedents.

Sanhedrin adds a further event that significantly extends *satan*'s range of activity. Previously, the evil instigator had appeared before God's assembly, as in the Book of Job: "Now there was a day when the sons of God came to present themselves before YHWH, and *satan* also came among them" (Job 1:6). In the second part of Sanhedrin's revision, *satan* comes to earth and speaks directly to Abraham. Many of *satan*'s words are citations from the speech of Eliphaz in Job 4, and as a result, the human or superhuman nature of this accuser remains ambiguous:

> *Satan* anticipated him on the way and said to him, "If one attempts a word [*davar*] with you, will you be weary? [. . .] Behold, you have instructed many, and you have strengthened weak hands. Your words

[27]Compare Genesis Rabbah 55:4, where the accusation is alternatively attributed either to Abraham himself or to God's ministering angels.

have upheld a stumbler.[. . .] But now it has come upon you, and you
are weary" [Job 4:2–5].
He [Abraham] said to him, "I will walk in my integrity" [Ps. 26:1].
He said to him, "Is not your fear of God your foolishness [*kislatecha*]?"
[Job 4:6].
He said to him, "Remember, who that was innocent ever perished?"
[Job 4:7]. [Sanh. 89b]

In this contest of scriptural citations, the accuser could be a false friend
like Eliphaz, or a satanic manifestation, or both. The *satan* ultimately
claims to possess inside information, "from beyond the partition,"
God's inner secrets, but Abraham repulses him with the rejoinder:
"It is the penalty of a liar, that even if he tells the truth, he is not
listened to" (ibid.). The Talmudic account brings *satan* down to earth
and places him in direct confrontation with Abraham. Transformed
from an accuser within God's court into a tempter among men, *satan*
is on the way to becoming an independent force of worldly evil. Of
course, the interpreters introduce *satan* to emphasize his spectacular
failure: despite all efforts to spoil the fulfillment of God's command,
Abraham remains unmoved.[28]

Quotation is the primary rhetorical device of Sanhedrin's revision.
In the new context, words from Job and Psalms become *satan*'s accusations and temptations. *Satan* undermines Abraham by revealing
hidden meanings, as in the question, "Is not your fear of God your
foolishness?" In Job 4:6, this question signifies, "Is not your fear of
God your strength?" *Satan* uncovers and exploits a further meaning
of the Hebrew *kislatecha*.

The *satan* of Tanchuma, a fuller expansion of the *akedah*, frees himself from his subservient origins in the divine assembly. This account
does not mention the initial accusation against Abraham; instead, it
represents *satan*'s independent work as deceiver and tempter. Tanchuma follows the pattern of Sanhedrin, but without the scriptural
allusions:

Satan anticipated him on the way and appeared to him [Abraham] in
the form of an old man.
He said to him, Where are you going?
He said to him, To pray.

[28]In Genesis Rabbah 56:4, however, *samael* (another name for *satan*) succeeds in partly
unsettling Isaac. Here the demonic agency oversteps the purported goal, to test Abraham's piety.

> He said to him, And someone who is going to pray, why does he [carry] fire and a knife in his hand and wood on his shoulder?
>
> He said to him, In case we stay a day or two and we slaughter, cook, and eat. [Tanch., Vayirah 22]

Whereas Sanhedrin leaves *satan*'s form mysterious, Tanchuma specifies that *satan* appears "in the form of an old man." To Abraham, then, the tempter seems to be merely another human being.

Tanchuma's *satan* plays a devious trick of disparate voices, in order to suggest that the trial has been commanded, and not merely provoked, by the tempter: "He [*satan*] said to him [Abraham]: Old Man, wasn't I there when the Holy One, blessed be He, said to you, 'Take your son'? And an old man like you will go and lose a son that was given to him at the age of a hundred! Haven't you heard the parable of one who lost what he had in his hand, and begged from others? And if you answer, I will have another son, then listen to the tempter [*masteen*], destroy a soul, and you will be guilty" (ibid.). Abraham is aware of the deception and responds: "Not the tempter, but rather the Holy One, blessed be He, Himself, said to me, 'Take now your son.' " But while Abraham thus affirms the authenticity of God's command, his encounter with the tempter (*masteen*) suggests dualistic tendencies.[29]

The sequence of satanic interventions outlines a development toward increasingly dualistic speculation. Not only do the later interpreters give special importance to *satan*'s efforts; they also hint that *satan* may not be entirely subordinate to God. At the same time that stories about demons flourished, suspicions also increased. When God's angel calls from heaven to annul the command, Tanchuma represents Abraham in the position of demanding a dialogue with God. The mediated call now appears insufficient:

> An angel of YHWH called to him from the heavens, saying:
>> Abraham, Abraham!
>
> Why twice? Because he was hurrying and was going to kill him.
> And he said to him:

---

[29]In a moment of supreme deception, the *satan* of Vayosha also ascribes the trial, not to God, but to the tempter: "Unfortunate one! Wasn't I there when the tempter [*masteen*] said to you, 'Take your son, your only one, whom you love, and offer him up to me as a burnt offering'? And an old man like you will lose such a sweet son, a youth whom the Holy One, blessed be He, gave you at one hundred years of age?" At the same time that he conceals his identity, *satan* maintains that he commanded the sacrifice.

Do not stretch forth your hand to the lad.
He said to him, Who are you?
He said to him, An angel.
He said to him, When He said to me, "Take now your son," the
Holy One, blessed be He, Himself, spoke to me. And now, if He wishes,
let Him speak to me. [Tanch., Vayirah 23]

At this late stage of Midrashic development, the distinction between
God and His angel has been established; Abraham no longer recognizes God's will in an angel's call. The terrible fear is, of course, that
Abraham may confuse the voice of God with the voice of *satan*. This
latter-day Abraham was perhaps the first to express dissatisfaction
with God's angel and to demand an audience with God Himself.

The mystery and "background" of Genesis 22 reflect the theology
of the Hebrew Bible. "After these things, God tested Abraham": despite all efforts of later interpreters, the reason for the test eludes our
understanding. The true YHWH cannot be known, and no divine
motives can be established as the reason for Abraham's last trial. Later
aggadic versions of Genesis 22 remove aspects of its mystery, when
"after these things" comes to mean "after the words of *satan*," who
accuses Abraham before God, and the three days' journey include
satan's temptations.

The successive expansions of the *akedah* thus manifest increasing
modifications of the initial, radically monotheistic account. The ineffable God becomes more accessible when represented in form similar to a Persian king who sits enthroned before his court. Instead of
attributing the test to a negative aspect of God, of course, postbiblical
retellings introduce *satan* to take the blame. At first Mastema must
present his accusations before God and must receive approval in order
for the trial to begin; later, *satan* appears to achieve virtual independence and is capable of entering into subversive dialogue with Abraham and Isaac. To some extent, the expanded *akedah* reflects the
demonology that had developed during the time of its successive
revisions. Postbiblical versions of the *akedah* justify their existence
through their vivid representation of scenes, but they also drift away
from the strictest monotheism of YHWH.

The propensity to believe in "two powers in heaven" has always
been perceived as a threat to rabbinic Judaism. Thus Philo's double
logos and the legends of angels and *satan* have never been comfortably
accepted by the rationalistic strands of Jewish religious thought. Yet

the ascetic practices of the Essenes and Therapeutai found expression in Christianity, and the *logos endiathetos*, a figure of inward-turned language and prototype of confession, is the distant forerunner of modern *mono-logos*. Skeptical of proffered speech and inclined to solitary study of Scripture, the ascetic Jewish sects developed belief in the God within, a *logos* partaking of the divine.

The representation of angels as God's messengers, to the extent that it gives concrete forms to aspects of God, is unacceptable from the standpoint of the most literal interpretation of Jewish law. An ascetic component of Judaism consequently turns theological language "inward" toward *logos endiathetos*. The radical expression of Philo's linguistic asceticism is his neo-Platonic polemic against the sophists; the conflict with dualistic tendencies centers around the anthropomorphic views of *satan* and angels. Like Socrates' *daimonion*, *satan* is a figure of turning, deviation. The *daimonion* turns Socrates away from false steps; the *satan* turns men away from God by causing them to deviate from the strictest monotheism. But the real error is to read *satan* literally, as a metaphysically existing evil angel, rather than as a figure for the worldly evil that confronts men. *Avodah zarah*, idol worship, thus appears as a problem of mistakenly literal interpretation. Postbiblical commentaries containing the word *satan* are not intrinsically suspect; rather, overliteral interpretations of this *satan* (and of God's manifestations) lead men astray.

Despite ascetic leanings, then, Philo and many Hebrew sources show a double interest in stories of angels and *satan*. The *logos* of Judaism is at war within itself, retaining its secrets while concealing its concealment by pretending to proffer what it cannot give.[30]

---

[30]The decision of modernity has been to read *angeloi* and *satan* in an allegory that empties these words of spiritual content. Eighteenth-century English aesthetics illustrates the displacement of spiritual *daimōn* and radical monotheism by psychological *genius* and radical monologue.

3 The Eighteenth-Century Introjection of Genius

"Genius" has a spectacular history, and eighteenth-century England is the scene of its most dramatic metamorphoses. In the writings of Anthony Shaftesbury, and until mid-century, "genius" runs roughly parallel to the German *Geist*, and retains traces of its Latin heritage; all individuals have a genius (spirit or mind) of some sort. Afterward, despite occasional efforts to recover classical meanings, a new range of signification takes control. While Joseph Addison anticipates this result as early as 1711, the eighteenth century fully appropriates Addison's use of the word only after Edward Young's conjectures of 1759. Beginning in the 1750s, a craze of theoretical writings urges that the inspired need not *have a genius*; instead an inspired author *has genius* or *is a genius*.

English usage has never shaken off this powerful introjection. The gods have fled, or we have buried them within ourselves by means of a verbal turn. The eighteenth century is both the meeting ground of genius and monologue and the scene of a decisive battle between the languages of theology and psychology. When Young writes of genius as "that god within," theological genius symbolically cedes to subjective monologue.

In retracing certain pathways in the eighteenth-century discussions of genius, this chapter is suggestive rather than comprehensive, and the present context excludes all analysis of the related theories of wit and imagination. Lord Shaftesbury and Joseph Addison sketch the

66

early model for modern genius. Henry Fielding, Alexander Gerard, Edward Young, and William Duff propose improvements, often in the form of elaborate scenarios. Immanuel Kant, by importing their invention, reveals limitations in the English product. Viewed collectively, these authors' expressions of "genius" exemplify ways in which verbal transformations predetermine intellectual history.

Characteristics and Authors of Genius

The modern turn to subjectivity and monologue is signaled by Shaftesbury's identification of Greek *daimōn* and Latin *genius* with soliloquy: the influence of an externalized guardian spirit becomes indistinguishable from effects of individual intelligence. In Shaftesbury's usage, "genius" is a vague term like the German *Geist* and roughly equivalent to "spirit," "mind," or "intellect." If individuals have genius to varying degrees, Shaftesbury's "Miscellaneous Reflections" can refer without redundancy to "the free Spirits and forward Genius's of Mankind."[1] As a spirit may be free, so a genius may be forward. Comfortable with applying the word "genius" to individuals, Shaftesbury writes of what modernity calls geniuses as "the better *Genius's*" (*Char.* III, 273). Shaftesbury also refers to "*divine* Men of a transcending Genius" (*Char.* III, 136). Because "genius" no longer names a transcendent being or power, certain men may be said to possess "a transcending Genius"; another may be only a "popular Genius" (*Char.* III, 4). As an individual has a personality, so individuals are characterized by a certain kind of genius.

"Genius" does not refer only to the mind of men in general; it also denotes a special capacity. Shaftesbury anticipates Addison's discussion when he writes of authors "who have a *Genius* for *Writing*" (*Char.* III, 272). Like Addison after him, he censures authors who "wou'd be *all Genius*" (*Char.* III, 258). Every man and woman has a genius of some kind, and only rare authors have genius of the forward variety; yet "genius" can also signify a particular quality of writing that should not be exaggerated.

In his "Soliloquy; or, Advice to an Author" (1710), Shaftesbury

[1]Anthony Shaftesbury, *Characteristicks of Men, Manners, Opinions, Times* (London, 1711), vol. 3, p. 2 (henceforth cited as *Char.*). I have italicized words originally printed all in capital letters.

further revises the notion of genius. When Shaftesbury explicitly associates soliloquy with the notions of "Daemon, Genius, Angel or
Guardian-Spirit," the transcendent genius vanishes and is replaced
by monologue as a kind of internal dialogue. If such "beings" did in
fact accompany us, their existence would support his argument, "for
it wou'd be infallibly prov'd a kind of Sacrilege or Impiety to slight
the Company of so Divine *a Guest*, and in a manner banish him our
Breast, by refusing to enter with him into those secret Conferences
by which alone he cou'd be enabled to become our *Adviser* and *Guide*"
(*Char*. I, 168–69). But Shaftesbury disputes the belief that these spirits
were ever independent of men and prefers to read them figuratively.
The ancient authors meant that, through soliloquy, "we could discover a certain *Duplicity* of Soul, and divide our-selves into *two Partys*"
(*Char*. I, 169). A genius is no supernatural agency but rather our "self-
dissecting" partner in "this Home-*Dialect* of *Soliloquy*" (*Char*. I, 170).

On September 2, 1711, a long and productive Sunday, "genius"
was transformed. The printers rested from their labors on *The Spectator*, and readers were at leisure to contemplate the mysterious fiction
of the day before. In Saturday's issue, number 159, Addison had
pretended to translate the "first Vision" of an obscure "Oriental Manuscript" entitled *The Visions of Mirzah*.[2] The narrator of this extended
allegory approaches "the Haunt of a Genius": "I drew near with that
Reverence which is due to a superior Nature; and as my Heart was
entirely subdued by the captivating Strains I had heard, I fell down
at his Feet and wept. The Genius smiled upon me with a Look of
Compassion and Affability that familiarized him to my Imagination,
and at once dispelled all the Fears and Apprehensions with which I
approached him" (*Spec*. 323). This is both a fictional tale of encounter
with a divine being and Addison's account of his own approach to
the classical term *genius*. The narrator first approaches fearfully, but
his reverence is soon replaced by familiarity. (In the following paper,
Addison shows how familiar genius has become to his imagination.)
Addison's narrator has apparently read Shaftesbury's "Soliloquy,"
and thus his guide "lifted me from the Ground, and taking me by
the Hand, *Mirzah*, said he, I have heard thee in thy Soliloquies, follow

---

[2]*The Spectator* (henceforth *Spec*.), nos. 159–60, is quoted from *Selected Essays from "The
Tatler," "The Spectator," and "The Guardian,"* ed. Daniel McDonald (New York: Bobbs-
Merrill, 1973). There are interesting echoes of Addison in Alexander Pope's "Preface
to the Iliad."

me" (ibid.). As the allegory proceeds, the Genius shows a vision of human life as a bridge and reveals islands of eternity reserved for men after death. "Despite the immense popularity of this Mirzah paper," a modern editor notes, "no others were published" (*Spec.* 326n): the allegorical bridge stretches, not only from mundane life to eternity, but also from the classical to the modern genius. A Genius fades from view at the close of number 159, and when the following number appears on Monday, "genius" makes its debut under a new guise.

Addison's decisive statement on genius, in *The Spectator*, number 160, opens with an epigraph from Horace:

> —Cui mens divinior, atque os
> Magna sonaturum, des nominis hujus honorem.
>
> [*Satires* I. iv. 43-44]
>
> —Honor him with this name [of poet],
> Who has a divine mind and a great voice.

This citation from the *Satires* is aptly ambiguous, for the *mens divinior* signals both divine intervention and introjected divinity. But the *absence* of the opening words of the excerpted lines is especially suggestive. The passage from Horace reads: *Ingenium cui sit, cui mens divinior, atque os / Magna sonaturum, des nominis hujus honorem*, which may be translated: "To whom there is genius [*ingenium*], who has a divine mind and a great voice, / Honor him with this name [of poet]." Addison omits the crucial word *ingenium* from the passage he cites. He will discuss a form of genius that derives from nature and chooses not to acknowledge that Horace employs the difficult word *ingenium*, rather than the familiar *genius*. Addison's innovation depends on his simultaneous usurpation of both ranges of meaning and denial of their difference. Addison makes English "genius" signify as does the Latin *ingenium*, at the same time displacing the spiritual notion of a guardian genius.[3] He conceals the Latin origins of "genius" and shifts the emphasis to mental capacity without acknowledging its separate origins in *ingenium*. The guardian spirit steals away in silence.

[3] To this day the German language preserves the difference between *Genius* (from the Latin *genius*) and *Genie* (from seventeenth-century French *génie*, which bears traces of both the Latin *genius* and *ingenium*). After Addison's rather French usage, this distinction has remained unclear in English. Compare "Génie" in Diderot's *Encyclopédie* (1751) and "Genie" in the Grimm brothers' *Wörterbuch* (1854).

In the opening words of his article in *The Spectator*, number 160, Addison soberly maligns the genius of his contemporaries: "There is no Character more frequently given to a Writer, than that of being a Genius. I have heard many a little Sonneteer called a *fine Genius*. There is not an Heroick Scribler in the Nation, that has not his Admirers who think him a *great Genius*; and as for your Smatterers in Tragedy, there is scarce a Man among them who is not cried up by one or other for a *prodigious Genius*" (*Spec.* 327). By fusing two notions of genius, Addison innovates (with a French accent) and at the same time gives his invention the appearance of age. Genius is indeed ascribed to all people, in the sense that every individual has a mind or mental capacity; by means of an implicit synecdoche, Addison pretends that "genius" must mean "great Genius." Addison exerts control over linguistic development by shifting the application of "genius" while retaining the fact of its frequent, former usage. Shaftesbury repeatedly refers to diverse types of "genius"; Addison moves toward the modern sense of "genius" as an extraordinary mind. Yet Addison also writes of "great Genius's," which is not redundant if "genius" retains the older sense of mental faculty in general. In his discussion of "great natural Genius's," then, Addison both retains an established sense and innovates, along the lines of contemporary French *génie*.

Solomon, Homer, Pindar, and Shakespeare are Addison's examples of "great natural Genius's, that were never disciplined and broken by Rules of Art" (*Spec.* 328). A second class consists of "those that have formed themselves by Rules and submitted the Greatness of their natural Talents to the Corrections and Restraints of Art" (*Spec.* 329–30). Addison discerns a "great Danger in these latter kind of Genius's," for they may "cramp their own Abilities too much by Imitation, and form themselves altogether upon Models, without giving full Play to their own natural Parts" (*Spec.* 330). According to Addison, genius is a natural gift; the forces of genius have precedence over the forces of art, so that a genius is endangered by following rules and models. Despite an explicit denial, in other words, Addison prefers geniuses of the first, natural class: "An imitation of the best Authors, is not to compare with a good Original; and I believe we may observe that very few Writers make an extraordinary Figure in the World, who have not something in their Way of thinking or expressing themselves that is peculiar to them and entirely their own" (ibid.). Addison's *Spectator* essay unveils a fully formed mythology of an "extraordinary Figure," the "original Genius." At the same time that he expresses hostility toward convention, Addison favors peculiarity in a manner that is decisive for later expositions.

Fielding revives Addison's "genius" and may have provoked Young's formulations. The narrator of *Tom Jones* mentions characters of "great Genius," of *a* "great Genius," and of "the greatest Genius."[4] If it is still possible to refer to a person's "vast Strength of Genius" (*TJ* 159) without redundancy, then "genius" does not yet carry its modern signification. To speak of a "great Genius" is like speaking of a great mind or, in German, like speaking of a *grossen Geist*.

Whereas Addison's narrator tacitly takes leave of the archaic and exotic Genius in *Visions of Mirzah*, Fielding explicitly renounces all spiritual guidance. He notes, "The *Arabians* and *Persians* had an equal Advantage in writing their Tales from the *Genii* and *Fairies*, which they believe in as an Article of their Faith," yet adds: "We have none of these Helps. To natural Means alone are we confined" (*TJ* 676). Nevertheless, Fielding is not beyond referring to genius in mock epic invocation. In his skeptical age, Fielding asks for the assistance of "Genius; thou Gift of Heaven; without whose Aid, in vain we struggle against the Stream of Nature" (*TJ* 525). Here genius is a gift and not a "Geist" of heaven, for heaven gives a mental capacity, not a mythical attendant. Thus genius requires an education: "And thou, O Learning, (for without thy Assistance nothing pure, nothing correct, can Genius produce) do thou guide my Pen" (*TJ* 526). Although this passage is fraught with irony, Fielding apparently does believe that genius is a "Gift of Nature." His empirical definition of genius is a forerunner of Gerard's theories: "By Genius I would understand that Power, or rather those Powers of the Mind, which are capable of penetrating into all Things within our Reach and Knowledge, and of distinguishing their essential Differences. These are no other than Invention and Judgment; and they are both called by the collective Name of Genius, as they are of those Gifts of Nature which we bring with us into the World" (*TJ* 372).[5] Fielding disputes the notion that

---

[4]Henry Fielding, *Tom Jones*, ed. Sheridan Baker (New York: W. W. Norton, 1973), 86, 160, 249 (henceforth cited as *TJ*).

[5]Compare John Locke, *An Essay Concerning Human Understanding* (London, 1706/1690), bk. 2, chap. 11, on "the difference of wit and judgment." See also Addison's article in *Spec.*, no. 62.

invention is "a creative Faculty," instead arguing that it involves "a quick and sagacious Penetration into the true Essence of all the Objects of our Contemplation." Consistently opposed to mystification, Fielding anticipates the cautious theoreticians of the following decades when he adds that invention "can rarely exist without the Concomitancy of Judgment" (*TJ* 372–73). Hence Fielding follows Addison, although he does not support the trope that equates "genius" with "a great Genius." At the same time, Fielding disputes the less rationalistic hints contained in *The Spectator*, number 62. The discussion of genius in terms of invention and judgment recurs in the writings of Gerard and thus indirectly influences the entire tradition after Kant.

Following Addison's prodigious leap from September 1 to September 3, 1711, almost fifty years pass before expressions of the new genius advance further. By synecdoche, Addison writes "genius" and signifies "a great Genius." When this trope comes into its own, it captures the theoretical imagination of the 1760s.

Alexander Gerard's *Essay on Taste* appears in the same year as Edward Young's "Conjectures on Original Composition," and although they represent opposing traditions, both rely on elaborate images to represent the workings of genius. Gerard is especially indebted to the associationism of Locke, whereas Young's reputation is founded on his poem entitled "Night Thoughts."

Gerard concurs with Fielding when he asserts that "the first and leading quality of genius is *invention*," but he conceives this as "a readiness of associating the remotest ideas that are any way related."[6] Like a magnet, invention first collects materials and then "by its magical force ranges them into different species." Genius distinguishes itself by its design of "a regular and well-proportioned whole" (*ET* 164).

---

[6]Alexander Gerard, *An Essay on Taste* (1759), 3d ed. (London: T. Cadell, 1780), 163 (henceforth cited as *ET*). In his *Dissertation on Genius* (London, 1755), William Sharpe tersely expresses Gerard's associationist assumptions. If a tabula rasa theory of the mind is assumed, what explains the difference between one person's mind and another's? Considering a hypothetical pair of brothers, Sharpe asks: "why is *Richard's* Genius brighter than *Bill's*? You answer, because the *tabula rasa* of *Richard's* Genius is more susceptible of ideas than that of *Bill's* is: allowed indeed that his Genius is, but this superiority of it is not founded upon any innate difference between the *tabula rasa* of his and that of his brother's understanding; rather upon the different means and opportunities he has had of arriving at ideas between this period of his age, and the minute of his birth" (p. 11). Furthermore, Sharpe explicitly rejects all inspiration theories of genius; no "divine energy" impinges on the mind (pp. 16–17).

Gerard's characterization emphasizes classical order and makes genius into "the grand architect which not only chuses the materials, but disposes them into a regular structure" (ibid.). For the perfection of its structure, however, genius requires the assistance of taste. The greatest tragic poets combined genius and taste: "The vigour of their imaginations led them into unexplored tracks; and they had such light and discernment, as, without danger of error, directed their course in this untrodden wilderness" (*ET* 168). Landscape imagery reappears throughout the tradition, for genius is typically in danger of straying into forests of wild figuration and of eluding the rigorous systematization Gerard seeks.

Meanwhile, some "forward Genius's" attempt to impose order. Samuel Johnson's *Dictionary* (1755) provides the clearest summary of previous applications of the word "genius." Johnson lists five senses:

1. The protecting or ruling power of men, places, or things
2. A man endowed with superior faculties
3. Mental power or faculties
4. Disposition of nature by which any one is qualified for some peculiar employment
5. Nature; disposition.

The first sense corresponds roughly to the archaic usage (still present in Shakespeare's *Macbeth* III.i). The second sense derives from Addison's article of 1711. Senses 3, 4, and 5 chronologically precede Addison's usage and are the basis on which he can write of geniuses of diverse types. Johnson's *Dictionary* entry expresses the eighteenth-century tensions between theological and psychological interpretations; the writings of Young and Duff exemplify two distinct paths of speculation within the new humanistic traditions.

Landscapes of Genius

Edward Young's "Conjectures on Original Composition" (1759) and William Duff's *Essay on Original Genius* (1767) both emphasize the originality or peculiarity of genius. At the same time, they blur the origins of originality, for how can original genius originate in men? If Addison demonstrates that a genius is a man of great "natural Parts," does it follow that original genius is really original nature?

Although Young explicitly discusses Addison, his essay conceals the link between their "original" conceptions.

The "Conjectures on Original Composition" are framed by an e-pistolary convention. Subtitled "a letter to the Author of Sir Charles Grandison," referring to the novel published by Samuel Richardson in 1753–54, Young's essay is initially concerned with age, and the tone is apologetic.[7] Young's immediate concern is to *justify* the production of his text. Because he values original composition, Young fears that a writer who is old may have no justification for his activity of writing. An elderly author, Young implicitly writes his essay to explain how, by virtue of genius, his mind may "enjoy a perpetual Spring."

The predominant imagery of the "Conjectures" is that of landscape. After describing his letter as "miscellaneous" and "somewhat licentious in its conduct," he notes that he has "endeavoured to make some amends, by digressing into subjects more important." *Digression* takes on special significance, both in the progress of the essay and in the content of Young's aesthetic theory. Young compares the movement of his essay to an extended scenario: "A serious thought standing single among many of a lighter nature, will sometimes strike the careless wanderer after amusement only, with useful awe: as monumental marbles scattered in a wide pleasure-garden (and such there are) will call to recollection those who would never have sought in a church-yard walk of mournful yews" (Conj. 67). The reader of Young's letter is, then, like a "careless wanderer after amusement only" who will be affected by "useful awe" in confrontation with scattered, serious thoughts. Landscapes are central to the figuration of the essay, and at this point the entire essay is figured as "a wide pleasure-garden" in which "monumental marbles" are scattered. Genius and originality, like monuments in a garden, are the more serious thoughts to which Young wanders. Young continues his landscape imagery when he describes the "Conjectures" as a kind of voyage leading to a "hidden lustre." This natural scene provides the ground for Young's essay; Addison is the luminary he uncovers, but in fact the true goal of the "Conjectures" is Young's own revision of Addison's "genius." In terms of genius and originality, the remainder of the essay con-

---

[7]"Conjectures on Original Composition" (henceforth cited as "Conj."), in *The Works of Edward Young* (Edinburgh: C. Elliot, 1774), 67.

siders the difference between compositions that shine brightly and those that are extinguished.

Young further develops his version of genius by means of a series of natural images. He connects problems of linguistic originality and genius with processes of natural aging, for example, when he states that "it is with thoughts as it is with words, and with both as with men; they may grow old, and die" (Conj. 72). In contrast to this process of decay, Young writes that "the mind of a man of genius is a fertile and pleasant field; pleasant as Elysium, and fertile as Tempe; it enjoys a perpetual spring" (Conj. 70). References to Elysium and Tempe gesture in the direction of an explicit paradise myth of genius, associated with a supernatural nature. Defying the processes of deterioration that would make him imaginatively old, Young finds a way to defeat time by positing that genius is endowed with "a perpetual spring." Two kinds of growth, originals and imitations, arise from that spring; if not all fruits of genius are originals, an aging man of genius may have reason to doubt the merits of his writing. This complication leads to a more aggressive turn in the figuration.

With a hint at the world of exploration, Young shifts from the figure of natural growth to that of territorial conquest: originals "are great benefactors: they extend the republic of letters, and add a new province to its dominion" (ibid.). Behind this presentation stands a powerful myth that writing can (dis)cover *new ground*. On the other hand, an imitator is ultimately weak because he always "builds on another's foundation" (Conj. 71). When genius appears as conqueror, the artist begins to stand at a distance from the art he masters. Young leaves ambiguous whether the original author *is* nature or only has special powers like those of nature. Insisting on natural imagery, Young conceives genius as a spontaneous growth: "an original may be said to be of a vegetable nature; it rises spontaneously from the vital root of genius; it grows, it is not made" (ibid.). "Genius" names the magical place of creation ex nihilo, or rather, "out of a barren waste."

This mystification does not long retain its full force. After all, even a "barren waste" may have to be wrested from previous settlers, and a "new province" is not so easily annexed. "Why are originals so few?" Young asks. According to the previous account, a dearth of originals should result from a lack of genius or of new terrain, but Young explains that in fact "illustrious examples engross, prejudice, and intimidate" (Conj. 73). Obstructive presences, not a scarcity of genius, impede the creation of originals. Poetic originality demands both the natural power called "genius" and an avoidance of excessive exposure to previous examples. Overwhelmed by prior authors, we are inclined to "bury our strength."

Before acknowledging that a more radical move is necessary, Young returns to a naturalistic solution in answer to the problem, "Must we then (you say) not imitate ancient authors?" He responds: "Imitate them, by all means, but imitate aright. He that imitates the divine Iliad, does not imitate Homer; but he who takes the same method which Homer took, for arriving at a capacity of accomplishing a work so great. Tread in his steps to the sole fountain of immortality; drink where he drank, at the true Helicon, that is, at the breast of nature" (Conj. 74–75). But it is not enough to insist that the original author must drink "at the breast of nature." Young supplements this natural myth by suggesting that an author must turn away from his predecessors: "As far as a regard to nature and sound sense will permit a departure from your great predecessors; so far, ambitiously, depart from them: the farther from them in similitude, the nearer are you to them in excellence: you rise by it into an original" (Conj. 75). At this crossroad, the departure from predecessors, rather than spontaneous growth, appears to constitute originality: "All eminence, and distinction, lyes out of the beaten road; excursion and deviation are necessary to find it, and the more remote your path from the highway, the more reputable" (ibid.). Deviation replaces natural growth as the determining mark of the original. Images of travel or errancy undo the initial, natural myth and necessitate deviation rather than straightforward growth.

After the publications of Young and others, William Duff's situation is far more difficult. Although he does not refer to contemporary writers, in an "Advertisement" to the *Essay on Original Genius*, Duff shows his awareness that the field is already crowded. Speaking of himself in the third person, Duff writes that "he is at the same time well aware, that in an *Essay on Original Genius*, Originality of Sentiment will naturally, and may, no doubt, justly be expected; and where this is altogether wanting, no other excellence can supply the defect."[8] Whereas Young displaces his fears to the problems associated with

[8]William Duff, *An Essay on Original Genius and Its Various Modes of Exertion in Philosophy and the Fine Arts, particularly in Poetry* (London: Edward and Charles Dilly, 1767), x (henceforth cited as *EOG*).

old age, Duff directly confronts the necessity of justifying his text, recognizing that his *Essay on Original Genius* must itself proceed in the manner of original genius. Duff is "not a little apprehensive of the issue of a strict examination" (*EOG* x–xi) when readers employ originality as their criterion of merit.[9]

Duff's landscapes resemble Young's figures for imaginative activity, although he dispenses with the "perpetual spring." Instead of conceiving original genius as a natural growth, Duff immediately identifies it as an errant traveler: "To explore unbeaten tracks, and make new discoveries in the regions of Science; to invent the designs, and perfect the productions of Art, is the province of Genius alone" (*EOG* 5). Again, "it is the peculiar character of original Genius to strike out a path for itself whatever sphere it attempts to occupy" (*EOG* 90). In Duff's treatise, literary landscapes are the only sites of divergences and divagations by genius. Later, however, Duff admits that precursors may represent serious obstacles: "A Poet of real Genius, who lives in a distant uncultivated age, possesses great and peculiar advantages for original composition." Like Young, Duff prefers new imaginative ground. The genius in an "uncultivated age" is free to uncover treasures without restraint, "the mines of Fancy not having been opened before his time" (*EOG* 265).

Duff emphasizes that *deviation* characterizes original genius by noting that imagination, left to itself, has a tendency to deviate: "*Imagination* . . . perpetually attempting to soar, is apt to deviate into the mazes of error" (*EOG* 9). As if to excuse the aberrations of genius, Duff carefully transforms these deviations into positive effects: "The objects he has, or ought to have in view, are, to bring into open light those truths that are wrapped in the shades of obscurity, or involved in the mazes of error, and to apply them to the purpose of promoting the happiness of mankind" (*EOG* 92). Duff's subsequent turn away from the errant conception of genius occurs by mediation of "mazes of error": those mazes by which the genius was endangered become those that genius illuminates for the benefit of all.

---

[9]Duff's apology revolves around a distinction between what he calls "derived" and "original sentiments" (*EOG* xi). No sooner does Duff set up this opposition, however, than he calls it into question. Again the problem of *justice* arises, and Duff is perhaps too quick to allow certain claims of originality "where not the least imitation was intended." Writing after Young, Duff attempts to separate himself from the class of blameworthy, intentional imitators, and he implies that "a casual coincidence" will sometimes occur, although he does not "intend" to imitate Young.

As Duff would have it, then, the brightness of original genius serves to illuminate obscure paths. Yet he cannot fail to acknowledge that genius is at times the source of confusions. Duff discusses imagery as a distinctive mark, an elevated style that corresponds to the flights characteristic of genius (*EOG* 143–45). Elevated above "ordinary modes of speech," a poet's language attains "a peculiar dignity." Images, however, do not always shed light, or rather may blind by shedding too much light at once: "An original Author indeed will frequently be apt to exceed in the use of this ornament, by pouring forth such a blaze of imagery, as to dazzle and overpower the mental sight; the effect of which is, that his Writings become obscure, if not unintelligible to common Readers; just as the eye is for some time rendered incapable of distinguishing the objects that are presented to it, after having stedfastly [*sic*] contemplated the sun" (*EOG* 145–46). As excessive light produces darkness, an excess of metaphor obscures. If writings of an original genius are too extreme in their figuration, they overpower readers' abilities and cause pseudoblindness. Duff prefers to close his eyes to the danger that must consequently attach to creations of original genius.

Both Young and Duff acknowledge that original genius is known, not simply for what it is, but for what it is not; the lights of genius shine in contrast to other lights, and flights of genius astound in contrast to the motions of those who crawl. When Young considers the subject of words old and new, he returns to the theme that opens the "Conjectures": "It is with thoughts as it is with words, and with both as with men; they may grow old, and die. Words tarnished, by passing through the mouths of the vulgar, are laid aside as inelegant and obsolete; so thoughts, when become too common, should lose their currency; and we should send new metal to the mint; that is, new meaning to the press" (Conj. 72). Genius must take care to select proper currency, for the original genius is known by its "new metal." Young does not wish to lose the ground of original composition by undermining its supposed origins in genius, yet the subsequent passage suggests a need for new schemes: "So few are originals, that, if all other books were to be burnt, the lettered world would resemble some metropolis in flames, where a few incombustible buildings, a fortress, temple, or tower, lift their heads, in melancholy grandeur, amid the mighty ruin" (Conj. 73). The ambitious author might perhaps wish for such a conflagration; the blaze of genius returns as a burning of previous authors' works. Is the success of an original genius akin to the "melancholy grandeur" of ruins amid a charred city? What is the temple Young imagines still standing after the destruction of a city?

Genius, Introjected Divinity

Young and Duff elaborate myths of genius because, without this figure, originality could threaten to subvert all grounds. To justify and explain innovations, genius must supply the ground and the new harvest of literary creation: as Young writes, "an original may be said to be of a vegetable nature; it rises spontaneously from the vital root of genius; it grows, it is not made" (Conj. 71). Similarly, Duff conceives original genius as a power that frees an author from the need to imitate:

> A Poet endued with a truly original Genius, will however be under no necessity of drawing any of the materials of his composition from the Works of preceding Bards; since he has an unfailing resource in the exuberance of his own Imagination, which will furnish him with a redundance of all those materials, and particularly with an inexhaustible variety of new and splendid imagery, which must be regarded as one distinguishing mark of original poetic Genius. [*EOG* 148]

"New and splendid imagery" is supposed to derive from genius, especially in happier, freer moments when there is no necessity to deviate. Duff strives to make original genius the ultimate ground, whereas Young draws from the Roman tradition to intimate divine origins of genius. Young and Duff rely on much of the same naturalistic figuration; their difference arises from Duff's suppression of the theological dimension.

Young interprets the origins of originality through a myth of divine inspiration. But this genius is not analogous to the *daimonion* of Socrates nor to any of the guardian spirits suggested by tradition. Instead, Young radically introjects the divine spark: "With regard to the moral world, conscience; with regard to the intellectual, genius, is that god within" (Conj. 78). Young's "genius" does not descend to man but rises with him; he advises the aspiring author: "let thy genius rise (if a genius thou hast) as the sun from chaos; and if I should then say, like an Indian, Worship it, (though too bold), yet should I say little more than my second rule enjoins, (*viz*.) Reverence thyself" (Conj. 87). Young thus proposes a secularized religion of self-realization. Unfortunately, our genius does not necessarily present itself directly: "Genius, in this view, is like a dear friend in our company under disguise; who, while we are lamenting his absence, drops his mask, striking us, at once, with equal surprise and joy" (Conj. 86). Originals are the products of divinity in man, but divine epiphany occurs in a peculiar scene of self-demasking. To recognize our own genius, we must wait for the moment when the disguise is dropped.[10] Our disguise presumably consists of "figures" borrowed from previous authors, and which we in rare moments escape—unless the "dear friend" whose absence we lament turns out to be, not our own genius, but a feared precursor. The Christian exorcism of "daemons" (Conj. 96–97) is a figure for the pseudoreligious turn Young proffers, the passage from multiple precursors to an original persona.

The theological framework of Young's "Conjectures" becomes most explicit at its close. Raising the subject of Addison's genius, Young considers Addison's final words that "taught us how to die." If "the mind of a man of genius" is like "a perpetual spring" that assures eternal life, these dying words that "spoke human nature not unrelated to the divine" (Conj. 109) perform a similar function.

Young's final three paragraphs return to the image drawn by the initial two. He prefaces his remarks by writing of a wish to reveal the "hidden lustre" concealed in some monument. Now he refers again to "the sacred deposit, which by Providence was lodged in my hands." At the same time that he reflects the Roman tradition of a *genius* that passes on a torch to man, Young passes on his revised conception of genius. Addison, a Christian man of genius, turns out to be the "sepulchral lamp" mentioned earlier; Young has led us to "the long hidden lustre of our accomplished countryman, who now rises, as from his tomb, to receive the regard so greatly due to the dignity of his death; a death to be distinguished by tears of joy; a death which angels beheld with delight" (Conj. 109). Why is Young so concerned to praise Addison? In his praise, of course, he chooses to ignore Addison as a forerunner in the theory of genius. While Young asserts

---

[10]Compare Shaftesbury's "Soliloquy": "Thus *Dialogue* is at an End. The Antients cou'd see Their own Faces; but we can't" (*Char*. I, 205).

his wish to restore Addison's reputation, he simultaneously proclaims his own mission, to eulogize Addison, a "sacred deposit, which by Providence was lodged in my hands." To pronounce Addison's genius is for Young to become a divine messenger, to mediate between heavens and earth, to transform the light of the sun into sparks of thought and the blaze of imagery: to write with genius, as genius.

One striking absence from Duff's account is the theological ground that Young retains for genius. Young's original composition appears to "rise from the vital root of genius," and genius, in turn, "is that god within" (Conj. 71, 78). Duff curtails the theological dimension and implies, firmly within the empiricist tradition, that genius is an independent power of mind. Although Young's "genius" prevails in the poetic tradition of the nineteenth century, his rival Gerard, whose associationist theory in some ways parallels Duff's, finds double-edged expression in modern aesthetics.

Eighteenth-century aesthetics culminates in the writings of Immanuel Kant, whose *Kritik der Urteilskraft* (1790) and the *Anthropologie in pragmatischer Hinsicht* (1798) present central statements on genius (*Genie*) in the tradition begun by Shaftesbury. Both brief passages begin by conceiving genius in connection with a theory of talented artistic creation. Section 46 of the third *Kritik* and section 47 of the *Anthropologie* attempt unified expositions of genius following the associationism of Gerard, but hints of the theological conception destabilize Kant's definitions.

Kant explicitly links the German *Genie* with French *génie* rather than with Latin *genius*—because he discusses genius as an inborn capacity of the artist, that is, he traces the word to Latin *ingenium* and keeps the Latin *genius* at a distance. The genius of the artist is the product of nature, not of divine agency. In a parenthesis, however, Kant acknowledges the buried etymology of genius: "For presumably the word *Genie* is derived from *genius*, from the peculiar guiding, guardian spirit that is given to a person at his birth, and from whose inspiration these ideas were supposed to come forth."[11] The recognition of a double etymology allows Kant (like Addison) to emphasize the meaning of "Genie" as a mental capacity (*ingenium*) while retaining the mythological overtones suggested by the notion of a guardian *genius*.

---

[11]Immanuel Kant, *Kritik der Urteilskraft*, ed. Karl Vorländer (Hamburg: Felix Meiner, 1924), 182-83 in the original pagination. In English, see Immanuel Kant, *Critique of Judgment*, trans. J. H. Bernard (New York: Macmillan, 1951), 151.

But Kant (again like Addison) does not acknowledge the difficulties associated with combining psychological and mythological conceptions. The discussion in the *Anthropologie* also becomes more complex when Kant seeks to explain the reason for using a "mystical" name, *Genie*, to mean "the exemplary originality of talent":

> But the reason why the exemplary originality of talent is called by this *mystical* name, is that the one who has it cannot explain its outbursts to himself; nor can he make comprehensible to himself how he comes upon an art, which he could not have learned. For *invisibility* (of the cause of an effect) is a collateral idea of a spirit [*Geist*] (a genius [*Genius*], which accompanied the talented already at his birth), whose inspiration, so to speak, it only follows.[12]

At the close of a century of dispute between theological and psychological explanations, Kant observes the final similarity between the notion of talent and the idea that a spirit accompanies a man from the time of his birth. The "exemplary originality of talent" that creates beautiful art cannot be explained, even by its possessor.

According to Kant's later analysis, then, *Genie* derives from Latin *genius*, but this guiding spirit appears essentially in the capacity of Latin *ingenium*. Although Kant directly acknowledges the work of Alexander Gerard, his efforts to equate *genius* with *ingenium* ultimately ally him with Addison and Young. Yet the palimpsest of "genius" asserts itself when Kant finishes by recognizing its etymology: a slippage from *Genie (ingenium)* to *genius* occurs in both the *Kritik der Urteilskraft* and the *Anthropologie*.

Whereas Greek *daimōn* names a vague transcendent power, and Latin *genius* refers to a transcendent being, modern English "genius" characteristically signifies an immanent, self-sufficient mental activity. As the eighteenth century opens, Shaftesbury casts "genius" in the role of "mind," or "human spirit." This genius is not transcendent, and thus Shaftesbury mentions unusual "*divine* Men of a transcending Genius." Soliloquy, in Shaftesbury's terminology, names the independence of human genius; yet theorists of genius never agree con-

---

[12]*Anthropologie in pragmatischer Hinsicht* (1800/1798), in Kant's *Werke in sechs Bänden*, vol. 3 (Frankfurt am Main: Insel, 1964), 545. The major passage on genius is section 54 in the second edition and section 57 in *Kants gesammelte Schriften* (1907). In English, see Immanuel Kant, *Anthropology from a Pragmatic Point of View*, trans. Victor Lyle Dowdell and ed. Hans H. Rudnick (Carbondale: Southern Illinois University Press, 1978), 125. This translation is based on Oswald Külpe's edition of 1907.

cerning the origins of originality. "Transcending (original) genius," or mind that steps beyond established paths, uneasily seeks to usurp the place of transcendent guidance. Addison gives a radical turn to English "genius" by means of the synecdoche that equates it with "great Genius." All genius comes to be great though nontranscendent. In the wake of Locke's associationism, Fielding understands genius as a power of mind, a gift of nature that must be combined with learning. Gerard similarly writes of genius as a natural faculty of mind, closest to invention.

When Young persists in ascribing divine origins to genius, he simultaneously creates an introjected divinity, "that god within." An unnamed friend is like the Christian emperors who "expelled daemons, and dedicated their temples to the living *God*." The new "genius" suggests a religion of the self that purges itself of precursor-demons. Yet the notion of originality displaces transcendent origins, for the pre-Romantic genius strives to become its own originator. In a complex natural scenario, however, self-origination appears as a necessary deviation from overtrodden paths.

Despite their search for a sound basis of originality, then, eighteenth-century English authors represent originality as a swerve away from origins. The poet, who can no longer claim a transcendent muse, relies on natural talents that permit him to explore new paths. Genius turns inward, transformed from the status of an externalized divine guide into the role of a mundane wanderer in aesthetic realms. The new humanistic genius fails to replace spiritual guidance by soliloquy, however, for new forms of transcendence emerge.

4 The Transcendence of Monologue

"Transcendence" is an inheritance from Kant, who displaces transcendent concepts, or the transcendent use of concepts, by writing of transcendental knowledge. Twentieth-century philosophers have, however, repeatedly modified the rhetoric of transcendence to suit their particular ends. Edmund Husserl "reduces" the transcendent and implicitly bases his phenomenology on an experiential, immanent monologue, while Martin Heidegger turns back toward a preexperiential, ontological transcendence. In consequence, phenomenology has wavered between epistemological and metaphysical projects. Husserl's phenomenological method primarily seeks to secure a field of absolute certainty by grounding its theses in the immanence of monadic consciousness, but Heidegger's ontology questions all assumed philosophies of immanence, from Descartes to the neo-Kantians, and points to the essential transcendence of Dasein.

Jacques Derrida carries Heidegger's deconstructive project further and attempts to show that Husserl relies on an unexamined notion of monologue. *La voix et le phénomène* and *De la grammatologie* represent the crux of his project to deconstruct the monological "metaphysics of presence." From his analysis of Husserl to his readings of Rousseau, Derrida systematically shows that voice, monologue and autoaffection are infiltrated by writing and difference. Derrida questions the effort of Husserl's *Logische Untersuchungen* to ground consciousness in the supposedly pure presence of monologue or undifferentiated autoaffection. Analysis of Rousseau's *Confessions* further reveals the absence that haunts even the most intimate passion for immediacy.

Heidegger's later works implicitly restore the transcendent meaning of monologue. No longer the interiority of a subject, *mono-logos* becomes the ultimate reality of language. Heidegger's later philosophy grants special status to poetry, as an "authentic" response to the essence of language. In a sense, then, Heidegger strives to recover ancient origins by reclaiming a spiritual *Logos* as transcendent genius.

Husserl and the Immanence of Consciousness

The role of immanence in Husserl's philosophic method may be understood in connection with Kant's distinction between the transcendental and the transcendent. Explaining the character of transcendental knowledge, Kant asserts, "Not every a priori cognition should be called transcendental, but rather only that through which we recognize that and how certain ideas (intuitions or concepts) are employed solely or are possible a priori" (A56/B80).[1] Knowledge is "transcendental" when it concerns the possibility or modes of cognition, our "manner of cognition [*Erkenntnisart*] of objects insofar as this should be possible a priori" (A11/B25). The error of "transcendent use" involves a faulty application of concepts, which seeks to "step beyond [*überschreiten*]" the bounds of experience (A296/B352–53). In contrast to the transcendent use of concepts, then, immanent use "limits itself solely to possible experience" (A327/B383). Immanent use of reason refers to nature only through possible experience; transcendent use of reason involves a "connection [*Verknüpfung*] of the objects of experience, which transcends [*übersteigt*] all experience" (A845/B873).

Kant expresses his scorn for the transcendent use of principles by means of an image. Both *transcendental* and *transcendent* principles "transcend" experience; but while the former are grounded a priori, the latter deceptively pretend to ground themselves only by denying

[1]Immanuel Kant, *Kritik der reinen Vernunft*, ed. Raymund Schmidt (Hamburg: Felix Meiner, 1956). I henceforth refer to the first (A) and second (B) editions. In English, see Immanuel Kant, *Critique of Pure Reason*, trans. Norman Kemp Smith (New York: St. Martin's, 1965). The *use* of an idea, not the idea itself, is immanent or transcendent (A643/B671). Translations are my own.

that they step beyond the evidence of experience. *Transcendent* principles are those "that encourage us to tear down all those boundary-
posts and claim for ourselves a completely new ground, which no-
where recognizes demarcation" (A296/B352). The transcendent use of
principles threatens rational boundaries and fraudulently annexes a
new territory.[2] Enemy of adventure, Kant clings to his island of pure
reason and warns against false hopes aroused by the illusion of new
lands.

In his lecture at a Kant Festival in 1924, Husserl directly acknowledges his debt: during the development of phenomenology, Husserl
has recognized "a manifest, essential relationship between this phenomenology and the transcendental philosophy of Kant."[3] He discusses "metaphysical transcendence" and finds a similarity between
the Kantian "transcendental attitude" and the "natural attitude" spoken of by phenomenology (ibid., 248, 254). Husserl neglects to mention his equal debt to Kant's conception of the transcendent, which
phenomenological method will attempt to "bracket out."[4]

In his *Ideen zu einer reinen Phänomenologie und phänomenologischen
Philosophie*, Husserl uses the words "transcendent" and "immanent"

---

[2]This anarchic rejection of property rights is especially distasteful to Kant, who
describes his own work by means of the figure of colonization: "We have now not
merely traveled through the territory of pure understanding, and carefully observed
every part of it, but have also measured it across, and determined the place of every
thing on it. But this territory is an island, and enclosed by nature itself in unchangeable
boundaries. It is the territory of truth (an enticing name), surrounded by a wide and
stormy ocean, the real place of illusion, where many a fog-bank and many a quickly
melting iceberg give the appearance of new lands, which ceaselessly deceive the fa-
natical sea-traveler with empty hopes, and involve him in adventures, which he can
neither desist from nor bring to an end" (A235–36/B294–95).

[3]Edmund Husserl, "Kant und die Idee der Transzendentalphilosophie," in *Husserliana: Erste Philosophie 1923/24*, ed. Rudolf Boehm (The Hague: Martinus Nijhoff, 1956),
230.

[4]On occasions other than the Kant Festival, Husserl denies the fullest acknowledg-
ments by observing that Kant never took possession of the promised land of phenom-
enology, though he was the first to sight it. See Edmund Husserl, *Ideen zu einer reinen
Phänomenologie und Phänomenologische Philosophie*, ed. Karl Schuhmann (The Hague:
Martinus Nijhoff, 1976), sec. 62. In citing *Ideen* below I note the page numbers in the
1950 edition, which the English edition retains: Edmund Husserl, *Ideas Pertaining to a
Pure Phenomenology and to a Phenomenological Philosophy*, 2 vols., trans. F. Kersten (The
Hague: Martinus Nijhoff, 1982). Compare *Die Krisis der Europäischen Wissenschaften und
die Transzendentale Phänomenologie* (The Hague: Martinus Nijhoff, 1962), sec. 26–27. For
a more detailed exposition of the relationship between Husserl's phenomenology and
Kant's transcendental philosophy, see Iso Kern's *Husserl und Kant* (The Hague: Martinus
Nijhoff, 1964); and Walter Hoeres' *Kritik der transzendentalphilosophischen Erkenntnis-
theorie* (Stuttgart: W. Kohlhammer, 1969).

to describe different types of perceptions, or intentional acts.[5] Rather than speak of "outer" and "inner" perception, Husserl cautiously notes two modes of directedness. Immanently directed acts "have as their essence, that their intentional objects, if they exist at all, belong to the same stream of experience as they themselves. That is therefore always the case, e.g., where an act is related to another act (a cogitatio to a cogitatio) of the same I" (*Ideen* 68). The intentional objects of an immanently directed act belong to the same experiential unity as the intentional act, for "consciousness and its object form an individual unity, produced purely through experiences [*Erlebnisse*]" (ibid.). Immanent acts constitute a unity of perceiver and perceived, as when a speaker asserts, "I speak." How far this realm of immanence extends is a difficult problem of Husserlian phenomenology. Thus the delimitation of transcendent acts, as those which exceed immanence, is equally problematic: "intentional experiences for which that is not the case are transcendentally directed; as, e.g., for all acts directed to essences, or to intentional experiences of other I's with other streams of experience; and equally for all acts directed to things" (*Ideen* 68). "Transcendence" and "immanence" characterize two kinds of intentional acts or modes of "givenness" to consciousness (*Ideen* 77).[6] While Husserl does at times discuss the "transcendence of the thing," his distinction is essentially epistemological rather than ontological.

Husserl's later discussion of transcendence and immanence emphasizes the certainty of the immanent and the doubtfulness of the transcendent perception. Immanence is the foundation of Husserl's phenomenology, because "every immanent perception necessarily guarantees the existence of its object" (*Ideen* 85). Husserl's discussion of immanent perception leads, however, to the transcendental ego.

[5]Here words associated with "intentionality" are used in the technical sense, referring to the directedness by which consciousness constitutes, or "intends," an object.
[6]J.-P. Sartre's "Une idée fondamentale de la phénoménologie de Husserl: L'intentionalité," in *Situations* 1 (Paris: Gallimard, 1947), 29–30, misconstrues Husserl's discussion of transcendence and immanence in the *Ideen*. Thus, according to Sartre, the idea of intentionality should put an end to philosophies of immanence. In Sartre's version, a philosophy of immanence conceives knowledge in terms of "contents of consciousness," whereas Husserl views knowing as a going out toward (s'*éclater vers*) its object. Sartre misrepresents Husserl by suggesting that the idea of intentionality implies a "philosophy of transcendence" at odds with all "philosophy of immanence." Intentionality is indeed central to Sartre's philosophy of transcendence, but Husserl deals with both immanence and transcendence in an epistemological context that is virtually unrelated to Sartre's usage.

The unique evidence of the *cogito* means that "only for the I and for the stream of experience in relation to itself does this distinguished state of affairs exist, only here is there something like immanent perception" (*Ideen* 85–86). Husserl describes this pure "I" as "a peculiar, nonconstituted transcendence, a transcendence in immanence" (*Ideen* 110). According to Husserl, all other forms of transcendence must, as unreliable constructs, be "bracketed out"; Husserl conceives only the transcendental ego to be immanent.

In one sense, then, Husserl sets up a philosophy of transcendence: in relation to the transcendental ego. The *Cartesianische Meditationen* are not directly concerned with the distinction between transcendence and immanence, yet Husserl's discussion of the transcendental ego proceeds from one interpretation of this opposition. An experienced "transcendence in immanence" suggests that the pure "I" of the *cogito* is transcendental: "I am no longer the one who finds himself in the natural attitude as a human being. . . . Through the phenomenological *epoché* I reduce my natural human I and my inner life—the realm of my psychological self-experience—to my transcendental-phenomenological I, the realm of the transcendental-phenomenological self-experience."[7] In the *Pariser Vorträge* and *Cartesianische Meditationen*, however, Husserl subordinates even this transcendence to immanence: "Transcendence is an immanent character of being, which constitutes itself inside the ego" (*CM* 32; cf. *CM* 117). Husserl does develop a philosophy of transcendental subjectivity, but it involves a methodological reduction to the sphere of immanence in which both the transcendence of the world and of other egos are constituted in the immanence of transcendental subjectivity. As a skeptic in relation to the transcendent, and in support of a philosophy of monadic consciousness, Husserl asserts that we should accept nothing except "what we can make essentially visible to ourselves in consciousness itself, in pure immanence" (*Ideen* 113). The unsettling consequence of Husserl's philosophy of immanence finds expression in the repeated question, "How do I escape from my island of consciousness?" (*CM* 32,

---

[7]Edmund Husserl, *Cartesianische Meditationen und Pariser Vorträge*, ed. S. Strasser (The Hague: Martinus Nijhoff, 1973), 64–65 (henceforth cited as *CM*). In English, see Edmund Husserl, *Cartesian Meditations: An Introduction to Phenomenology*, trans. Dorion Cairns (The Hague: Martinus Nijhoff, 1960).

116).[8] The secure island of Kantian reason turns into a prison for consciousness when phenomenology constructs a transcendental theory of knowledge by reduction to the "sphere" of immanence.

Derrida and the Impossibility of Monologue

La voix et le phénomène marks both Derrida's turn away from phenomenology and his development toward deconstructive method in the traditions of Heidegger and Nietzsche. Derrida argues that Husserl's theory of language privileges voiced speech and relies on an impossible ideal of monologue: the meanings "given" to the phenomenologist in an originary presence allegedly occur as, or are secured by, internalized discourse.[9]

Derrida focuses on the *Logische Untersuchungen*, section 8, entitled "The Expressions in the Solitary Inner Life." Determined to lay bare Husserl's hidden metaphysical presuppositions, Derrida makes this incidental passage stand for the broader tendencies in Husserl's philosophy. According to Derrida, this section reverts to an internalized voice in order to preserve both the bodily and ideal aspects of sound linked to meaning. Derrida's third chapter, then, entitled "Meaning as Soliloquy" (*Le vouloir-dire comme soliloque*), implies that Husserl's theory of meaning is grounded on monologue.[10] As Derrida recognizes, Husserl's discussion denies the creative power of monologue and assumes an undifferentiated presence to oneself. Husserl concludes his discussion of solitary speech with a scenario in which

> someone says to himself: You did that badly, you can't go on like that. But in the genuine, communicative sense one does not speak in such

[8]Heidegger's *Sein und Zeit*, 4th ed. (Tübingen: Max Niemeyer, 1977), 60, clearly responds to Husserl's mode of questioning. I shall henceforth cite *Sein und Zeit* as *SZ*.

[9]To some extent, Derrida discloses a hidden metaphysical assumption only by exaggerating the monological aspect of Husserl's theory of signs. Rather than exalt monologue to a position of supreme importance, Husserl dismisses it from the domain of truly significant communication. Yet while Husserl repudiates "expressions in the solitary inner life" (*Ausdrücke im einsamen Seelenleben*), he implicitly depends on a monological level of thought as the basis of phenomenological evidence.

[10]But Husserl argues the reverse: monologue has meaning only because meanings are intuited prior to their linguistic expression. Husserl bases his phenomenology on a prethematic meaning-intention; monologue appears pointless to him, because it communicates nothing new to the speaker.

cases, nor does one tell oneself anything; one merely imagines oneself
as speaking and communicating. In monological speech, words cannot
perform the function of indicating the existence of mental acts, because
such indication would be completely purposeless here. For the acts in
question are experienced by us in the same moment.[11]

Monologue is futile if its meaning is simultaneously experienced and
if no real communication occurs because the speaker always already
knows what he "means." Husserl consequently discredits the signifying function of dreams and other unconscious bearers of meaning,
and further excludes gestures, in order to focus on expressions with
"intended" meanings. According to Husserl's analysis, which denies
that solitary discourse produces anything new, monological speech
falls short of the realm of genuine communication. Yet Husserl under-
estimates the role of "expressions in the solitary inner life" because
he assumes that a prelinguistic level of meaning precedes whatever
we tell ourselves. The generative function of monologue fades in the
light of logical meanings that are supposed to ground linguistic
utterances.

Derrida paraphrases Husserl's statement of the limits of monologue: "If the subject indicates nothing to himself, it is because he
cannot do this, and he cannot do this because he does not need to.
As the lived [le vécu] is immediately present to oneself in the mode
of certitude and of absolute necessity, the manifestation of oneself to
oneself through the delegation or representation of an indicator is
impossible because it is superfluous."[12] Husserl grants the possibility
of solitary speech but denies that it exerts a significant communicative
function. Derrida questions the supposed presence to oneself and
thus takes a more radical step toward the undoing of monologue.
Reading the Logische Untersuchungen, section 8, in conjunction with
the Cartesianische Meditationen, Derrida suggests that monologue is

---

[11]Edmund Husserl, Logische Untersuchungen, vol. II, pt. 1 (Tübingen: Max Niemeyer, 1913), 36–37 (henceforth cited as LU). In English, see Edmund Husserl, Logical Investigations, trans. J. N. Findlay (New York: Humanities Press, 1970), II, 279–80.
[12]Jacques Derrida, La voix et le phénomène: Introduction au problème du signe dans la phénoménologie de Husserl (Paris: Presses Universitaires de France, 1967), 65. In English, see Jacques Derrida, Speech and Phenomenon and Other Essays on Husserl's Theory of Signs, trans. David Allison (Evanston: Northwestern University Press, 1973), 58. I shall henceforth cite this work as VP, using a slash to separate page numbers for the French edition from those for the English translation. But all translations cited here are my own.

impossible, just as no ultimate reduction to the monadic sphere can be performed.

At issue is not whether one can talk to oneself but whether the self of such a conversation is ever truly monadic. In other words, can a solitary speaker retain a coherent and pristine realm of immanence? Husserl denies that inner voice is the last resort of his reduction of the "immanent sphere" by asserting the primacy of prelinguistic intuitions. But Derrida recognizes that Husserl requires the fiction of a monological voice, in order to assure the existence of a "mental corporality" (*geistige Leiblichkeit*).

Derrida's subversion of the supposedly monadic phenomenological voice ensues from an awareness of difference within language. Conceived as a stream of language, conciousness can never insulate itself against otherness: monadic consciousness turns nomadic. Derrida notes that "the sign is originarily wrought by [*travaillé par*] fiction" (*VP* 63/56). The fictionality or rhetoricity of signs introduces difference where previously a solitary sameness was assumed. Derrida consequently disturbs the facile distinction between internal and external language. He maintains that solitary speech is never entirely pure, purged of the shared language of others. The conventional occurrences of dialogue are preconditions of monologue; the "I" observes and questions "itself" in the medium of the "they."[13]

Thus Derrida perceives a "non-identity to oneself of the supposedly originary presence" (*VP* 76/68). Solitary speech shows itself as a dubious autoaffection that denies its inevitable reference beyond itself. "Autoaffection" is the particular object of Derrida's attack against self-originatory myths: "Is not the concept of pure solitude—and of a monad in the phenomenological sense—impaired by its own origin, by the very condition of its presence to itself: 'time' reconceived starting from the *différance* within autoaffection?" (*VP* 77/168). To indicate the internal difference within language, Derrida alters the spelling of this key word: *différance* strikes at the illusion of a stable, unchanging self. Derrida further undermines the phenomenological monad by

---

[13]Compare L. S. Vygotsky's attack on Piaget's discussion of "egocentric" speech, in *Thought and Language*, trans. Eugenia Hanfmann and Gertrude Vakar (Cambridge: MIT Press, 1962), chap. 2. See also Emile Benveniste's analyses of man in language, in *Problèmes de linguistique générale* (Paris: Editions Gallimard, 1966); and, of course, Mikhail Bakhtin's *Problems of Dostoevsky's Poetics*, trans. Caryl Emerson (Minneapolis: University of Minnesota Press, 1984).

showing the impossibility, not only of monologue, but of autoaffection in general.

"Voice" appears as a kind of autoaffection that establishes presence,
"a medium which at once preserves the *presence of the object* before
the intuition and the *presence to itself* " (*VP* 85/76). Thus the illusion
of an isolated subject arises. Without leaving the immanent sphere,
a subject appears to affect itself through language: "the subject can
hear itself or speak to itself, allow itself to be affected by the signifier
which it produces without any detour through the instance of exteriority, of the world, or of what is not one's own in general" (*VP* 88/
78). This monological autoaffection commands a privileged position:
"Every other form of autoaffection must either pass through what is
not one's own or renounce universality. When I see myself, whether
this is because a limited region of my body offers itself to my look or
because it is reflected in a mirror, what is not my own has already
entered into the field of this autoaffection which from then on is no
longer pure" (*VP* 88/78–79). Only the internal voice is experienced as
"absolutely pure autoaffection," such that "the operation of hearing
oneself speak," the autoaffection of the voice, gives rise to subjectivity. Derrida pushes this analysis one step further and concludes that,
according to the tradition, "voice *is* consciousness" (*VP* 89/79).

Derrida undoes this statement of the "metaphysics of presence" by
reference to problematics of repetition and inscription. He finds a
tension within Husserl's work, because "the possibility of writing
inhabited the inside of speech" (*VP* 92/82). Difference, which produces the transcendental subject, asserts itself despite Husserl's wish
to preserve a pure presence: "Autoaffection is not a modality of experience characterizing a being that would be already itself (*autos*). It
produces sameness as a relation to itself in the *différance* from itself,
the same as the non-identical" (ibid.). Both monologue and autoaffection thus reveal their illusory character, erroneously posited as
prior to what in fact produces them. Passing through Heidegger's use
of the related term *Selbstaffektion*, in *Kant und das Problem der Metaphysik*
(especially section 34), Derrida arrives at a statement of the impossibility of pure autoaffection, as a result of the movement of temporal
difference: "The theme of a pure interiority of speech or of 'hearing
oneself speak' is radically contradicted by 'time' itself. The going-out
'into the world' is also, itself, originarily implied by the movement

of temporalization" (*VP* 96/86). Derrida interprets Husserl, then, by following the lead of Heidegger's revision.

Just as there are dramatic soliloquies and scenes of writing, there is necessarily a scene of monologue. The supposedly pure inner voice is infected by rhetoricity; "the 'presence' of sense and of speech has already begun to be missing from itself" (*VP* 97/87). Derrida generalizes from a linguistic observation—that all "mono-logos" is permeated by dialogue—to the argument that the subject or "I" is incapable of pure presence to itself, even in the form of a self-addressed proposition of self-knowledge.[14] The supposedly pure autoaffection of monological voice is already divided by *différance* or writing (*VP*, chaps. 6–7). The incursion of writing, associated with the indicator (*Anzeichen*), thus pronounces the death of all idealized monological purity.

Derrida continues his subversion of monologue by interpreting the scene of autoaffection in *Les confessions*. The text of Rousseau represents an autoeroticism that undergoes an analogous play of presence and absence. Even more intricate than phenomenological efforts to secure the presence of an object to a subject by means of voice, *Les confessions* constitute a scene in which Rousseau manipulates the presence and absence of his love object by means of masturbation. While the phenomenological autoaffection supposedly ensures the self-presence of the "intended" object to the subject, Rousseau's autoeroticism similarly aims at the imaginary presencing of an absent other. Derrida finds a connection in the shared futility of these projects, for voice is as much a phantom as is the imagined object of autoeroticism.

Thus *De la grammatologie* describes "the age of Rousseau" in familiar terms. Consciousness is grasped as an experience of autoaffection: "The *logos* can be infinite and present to itself, it can *produce itself as autoaffection*, only through *voice*: an order of the signifier by which the subject goes out from itself in itself, does not borrow outside of itself the signifier which it emits and which affects it at the same time. Such at least is the experience—or consciousness—of voice: of hearing oneself speak."[15] Husserl appears as a latecomer in the era of metaphysics

---

[14]On this vast and differentiated subject, see *VP* 105–6; *L'écriture et la différence* (Paris: Editions du Seuil, 1967), 139, 153, 171–72, 265; and *De la grammatologie* (Paris: Editions de Minuit, 1967), 23, 33, 94 (henceforth cited as *Gram.*).

[15]*Gram.* 146. In English, see Jacques Derrida, *Of Grammatology*, trans. Gayatri Chak-

since Descartes, characterized by "phonologism." With Rousseau the situation is more complex, however; for him, "this motif composes and organizes itself with its opposite: a ceaselessly reanimated mistrust with respect to speech that is called full." For Rousseau knows the failure of voice, inasmuch as "we are dispossessed of the coveted presence in the gesture of language by which we seek to seize it" (*Gram.* 203–4/141); he both condemns "writing as the destruction of presence" and gives priority to "writing as the restoration, by a certain absence and by a sort of calculated effacement, of the disappointed presence of oneself in speech" (*Gram.* 204/142).

Writing thus emerges as a "dangerous supplement" that both adds and supplants. Rousseau's *Confessions* represent this supplement as a writing parallel to masturbation; Rousseau himself refers to "that dangerous supplement which deceives nature."[16] According to Derrida, this deception of nature is like the operation of writing, because it turns away from nature into the imaginary. Whereas Husserl requires monologue to assure self-presence, Rousseau needs masturbation to secure desired, absent feminine presences. But like the voice that suffers contamination by writing, autoeroticism must acknowledge its self-delusion: "The presence that is thus delivered to us in the present is a chimera. Autoaffection is a pure speculation" (*Gram.* 221/154).

Masturbation and monologue share in the effort to obtain illusory presence. But autoaffection extends beyond the activity of masturbation and includes other attempts to procure an absent presence. Since the immediacy of *jouissance* appears unattainable, pure presence must cede to differentiated absence, the play of transference or chain of supplements. As monologue is infected by meaningless indicators and writing, severed from the "meaning-intention" of the subject, so masturbation is plagued by the absence it must posit while seeking to overcome distance. Derrida's reading of Rousseau retrospectively demonstrates the impossibility of pure monologue.

Derrida traces a path from voice and autoaffection, impossible dreams of pure presence, through autoeroticism and writing, as ges-

---

ravorty Spivak (Baltimore: Johns Hopkins University Press, 1976), 98. Page numbers in the English edition appear after the slash in the citations below; all translations are, however, my own.

[16]Jean-Jacques Rousseau, *Les confessions* (Paris: Garnier-Flammarion, 1968), vol. 1, p. 146. Cited in *Gram.* 215.

tures toward a recuperated presence in confrontation with inevitable absence. The ultimate undoing of the voice/writing dichotomy means that not only monologue but also writing appears in an autoerotic light: "within the chain of supplements, it was difficult to separate writing from onanism" (*Gram.* 235/165). And voice remains a form of autoaffection that denies its internal contradiction and difference: "Voice and consciousness of voice—that is to say in short, consciousness as presence to oneself—are the phenomenon of an autoaffection lived as suppression of *différance*" (*Gram.* 236/166).

While monologue affords a delusion of presence by suppression of absence, writing *is* the delusory making-present in absence. Derrida's "preference" for writing reflects his choice of explicit mediation as opposed to pretended immediacy. Monologue seeks to elude the inevitable play of presence and absence, of *différance*; masturbation enters into this play; writing sets up the conditions of possibility for presence and absence, "transcendental" conditions of mediated immediacy. In a way that requires further scrutiny, Derrida's writing aims toward a new transcendentalism. Language, or figuration, becomes the precondition of all possible experience. Heidegger chooses a different turn on the same path.

Heidegger and the Transcendence of Dasein

Heidegger's reinterpretation of Kant is most apparent in his use of the word "transcendence" (*Transzendenz*). Many critics have questioned Heidegger's discussion of transcendental philosophy as fundamental ontology, and even Heidegger admits that Kant became an "advocate for the question of Being I had raised."[17] But apart from the immediate problems relating to the interpretation of Kant's first *Kritik* as a grounding of metaphysics rather than as a theory of knowledge, Heidegger clearly projects the terminology of *Sein und Zeit* onto Kant's text.

In *Kant und das Problem der Metaphysik*, Heidegger's exposition of transcendental knowledge begins by subtly replacing the adjectival

---

[17]Martin Heidegger, *Kant und das Problem der Metaphysik*, 4th ed. (Frankfurt am Main: Vittorio Klostermann, 1973), p. XIV (henceforth cited as *KPM*). In English, see Martin Heidegger, *Kant and the Problem of Metaphysics*, trans. James S. Churchill (Bloomington: Indiana University Press, 1962).

form "transcendental" by the substantive form "transcendence": "transcendental cognition investigates not beings themselves but rather the possibility of the prior understanding of Being, i.e. at the same time: the constitution of the Being of beings. It concerns the stepping beyond (transcendence) of pure reason to beings, so that reason can now in the first instance take on experience as a possible object" (*KPM* 16).[18] Heidegger initiates his ontological turn away from Kant's inquiry into a mode of cognition (*Erkenntnis*) by substituting "transcendence" for the Kantian "transcendental." That is, he subsumes the epistemological terms of transcendental cognition and transcendental use of ideas under an ontology involving transcendence. The Kantian schematism becomes inseparable from "the most inner happening [*Geschehen*] of transcendence," and transcendental philosophy becomes equivalent to an "essential uncovering [*Wesensenthüllung*] of transcendence" (*KPM* 105, 120). Heidegger concludes that "if Kant calls this mode of cognition 'transcendental,' from this may be inferred that it has transcendence as its theme" (*KPM* 128). Heidegger argues that Kant was concerned to make transcendence visible (*KPM* 159), but contrary to Heidegger's claim, Kant never abstracts from "transcendental cognition" to thematize transcendence. Without marking any discontinuity between the exposition of Kant's thought and his own philosophical work, Heidegger grafts the language of *Sein und Zeit* onto Kant's *Kritik der reinen Vernunft*: "The existential analytic of everydayness . . . should show that and how transcendence—being-in-the-world—is already at the basis of all intercourse with beings" (*KPM* 228). As in Heidegger's other works of this period, transcendence appears as the ontological essence of Dasein.

   After the publication of *Sein und Zeit*, Heidegger writes several works that give special emphasis to transcendence. As if to provide a previously neglected key to his thought, "Was ist Metaphysik?" and "Vom Wesen des Grundes" insistently return to this term. Furthermore, the Marburg lectures of 1928 culminate in a discussion of "the transcendence of Dasein." What roles does transcendence play in Heidegger's philosophy?[19]

---

[18]Despite reservations, I follow the usual translation of *Sein* and *Seiende* as "Being" and "beings." Because the distinction has more to do with temporality than with a difference in number, "Being" and "the existing" (or "the existent") are in some cases preferable.

[19]In tracing the uses of "transcendence" from *Sein und Zeit* to "Vom Wesen des

"Transcendence" is seldom named by *Sein und Zeit*, but it functions under various guises throughout. A footnote to "Vom Wesen des Grundes" can thus assert that "what has until now been published of the researches concerning *Sein und Zeit* has as its task nothing other than a concretely disclosing project [*Entwurf*] of transcendence (cp. sections 12–83, especially section 69)."[20] Heidegger's note refers to virtually all of *Sein und Zeit*, from section 12 to the end. In other words, *Sein und Zeit* deals with transcendence insofar as it explicates "being-in-the-world," the necessary precondition or ground of experience.[21] Because only section 69 explicitly discusses transcendence, Heidegger indicates that it appears in diverse forms without being named.

A substantial footnote in "Vom Wesen des Grundes" further explains the centrality of transcendence by recalling the title of what was then the "First Part" of *Sein und Zeit*: "The Interpretation of Dasein in terms of Temporality and the Explication of Time as the Transcendental Horizon of the Question of Being."[22] Spatial metaphors proliferate. According to the footnote, the transcendence of Dasein indicates that Dasein exists "ec-statically" or "ec-centrically" (*ekstatisch*, *'exzentrisch'*). This interpretation recurs at several stages of the analysis of Dasein. As Heidegger shows in the Marburg lectures, then, the ontological difference repeats itself within transcendence. In addition to the transcendence that must always already have taken place, as a precondition of existence, another transcendence continues to occur, as in the form of intentionality. *Sein und Zeit* never acknowledges this doubleness of transcendence, and Heidegger's unresolved relationship to Husserlian phenomenology complicates its disparate uses.

Grundes," the essential problem is not to establish definitions but to clarify the functioning of this key word in Heidegger's texts. From this point of view the Marburg lectures are especially instructive because they make explicit the role Heidegger gives transcendence in his revision of the philosophical tradition.

[20]Martin Heidegger, "Vom Wesen des Grundes," in *Wegmarken*, 2d ed. (Frankfurt am Main: Vittorio Klostermann, 1978), 160n (henceforth cited as "WG").

[21]*KPM* makes clear that Heidegger regards his writings as constituting a fundamental ontology in the sense that they deal with "conditions of possibility": "the ontological, i.e. here always pre-ontological cognition is the condition of the possibility that something like the existing itself [*Seiendes selbst*] can stand opposite a finite being in general" (p. 67).

[22]*SZ*, pp. ix, 41. The original pagination is reproduced in the English edition: Martin Heidegger, *Being and Time*, trans. John Macquarrie and Edward Robinson (New York: Harper and Row, 1962).

After section 12 of *Sein und Zeit* establishes being-in-the-world as the ground of all encounter with beings in space, section 13 begins the redefinition of transcendence. This revision follows from Heidegger's overcoming of the epistemological tradition of subject-object relation. False questions arise from the traditional approach, for example: "how does this cognizing subject come out of its inner 'sphere' into an 'other, external one,' how can cognition in general have an object, how must the object itself be thought, so that finally the subject knows it, without needing to risk a leap into another sphere?" (*SZ* 60). In contrast, his version of phenomenological method strives to raise the more fundamental question by understanding cognition as "a mode of being of Dasein as being-in-the-world" (*SZ* 61).

Sein und Zeit attempts to ground the presumed "transcending of the subject" in a more fundamental, ontological transcendence. Heidegger argues that "being-there" (*Da-sein*) is always already being-in-the-world (*In-der-Welt-Sein*):

> In directedness to . . . and comprehending, Dasein does not first go beyond its inner sphere, so to speak, in which it first is encapsulated, rather it is in its primary mode of being always already "out there" with an existent [*Seienden*] that encounters it in an already discovered world. And the determinative openness for beings to be cognized is not anything like a departure from the inner sphere, but rather Dasein is, in this "being-out-there" with the object, in the rightly understood sense, "inside," i.e., it is itself as being-in-the-world, that cognizes. [*SZ* 62]

Heidegger writes in reaction against contemporary works of epistemology, such as Nicolai Hartman's *Metaphysik der Erkenntnis* (1921). Yet his interpretation of transcendence also involves a radicalization or revision of Husserl's phenomenology. If the terms "directedness to" and "comprehending" replace Husserlian intentionality, the question arises: to what extent does Heidegger ground intentionality as described by Husserl, and to what extent does he modify it?

Heidegger's analysis of discourse (*Rede*) repeats the inner-outer problematic of transcendence. Heidegger argues that Dasein is always already "in the world," and in regard to expression Heidegger maintains that Dasein is always already "outside," beyond itself: "All speech concerning . . . , which communicates in that of which it speaks [*in ihrem Geredeten*], has at the same time the character of a speaking-itself-out [*Sichaussprechen*]. Speaking, Dasein speaks itself *out*, not because it first of all is encapsulated as something 'inner' in opposition to something outer, but because it is already 'out there' as being-in-the-world" (*SZ* 162). At this stage of the work, Heidegger has characterized Dasein as "being-in-the-world" in the mode of *Verstehen*. Thus language, as the expression (or as the actuality) of understanding, is another form of transcendence. To the extent that it takes part in the constitution of "world," then, language is implicitly another aspect of transcendence, or of the transcendental horizon of experience (*SZ* 160–61).

In section 69, *Sein und Zeit* explicitly grounds the "transcendence of Dasein" in the "transcendence of the world": "In order for the thematization of the present-at-hand . . . to be possible, *Dasein must transcend* the thematized existent [*das thematisierte Seiende*]" (*SZ* 363). A footnote to this passage hints at Heidegger's relationship to Husserl: "That and how the intentionality of 'consciousness' is *grounded* in the ec-static temporality of Dasein, the following section will show" (*SZ* 363n). Without contradicting his teacher, Heidegger puts "intentionality" in its place, derivative in relation to Heidegger's own "transcendence."

Section 69c contains the fullest reinterpretation of transcendence, in connection with certain directional modes of Dasein (*Um-zu, Wozu, Dazu, Um-willen*). Without considering the relationship between these terms and intentionality, Heidegger turns to an ontological interpretation of temporality. Again, ontological transcendence serves to displace the subject-object model: "The 'problem of transcendence' cannot be brought down to the question: how does a subject come out to an object, whereby the totality of objects is identified with the idea of the world. It is to be asked: what makes it ontologically possible for a being to be encountered in the world and objectified as such? The return to the ec-static, horizontally founded transcendence gives the answer" (*SZ* 366). Later texts show, however, that Heidegger cannot strictly maintain the ontological difference within transcendence.

Until the recent publication of the Marburg lectures, "Vom Wesen des Grundes" was the seminal explication of Heidegger's "transcendence." In its condensed restatement of the problematics of *Sein und*

Zeit, as of the ontological difference, this text employs "transcendence" to mark the difference between Being and beings (*Sein* and *Seiendes*). Heidegger refers to the ground of the ontological difference as the transcendence of Dasein, and his search for the essence of rational grounds becomes a study in transcendence: "If the essence of the ground has an inner connection to the essence of truth, then the *problem* of the ground can also only have its home where the essence of truth creates its inner possibility, in the essence of transcendence."[23] At the same time that he points to a truth founded in transcendence, Heidegger enacts a gentle philosophical *Destruktion* by asserting that his project is more fundamental than Husserl's: "If one characterizes all *conduct* in relation to beings as intentional, then *intentionality* is only possible *on the ground of transcendence*, but neither identical with this nor, on the other hand, that which makes transcendence possible" (WG 31/29).

Heidegger accepts the traditional meaning of transcendence as "a step beyond," but he tries to avoid describing it as something that can happen. Nevertheless, he initially explains transcendence in terms of its inherent spatial metaphor: "The step beyond may be formally grasped as a 'relation' that reaches 'from' something 'to' something. That to which the step beyond accedes, which for the most part is inappropriately called the 'transcendent', is included in the step beyond. And finally, in the step beyond, *something* is always stepped beyond" (WG 33/35). Taking the etymological origins of the word as his pre-text, Heidegger seeks to rule out aspects that are inappropriate for his purposes. "Stepping beyond" retains a disturbing residue of spatial imagery, and Heidegger tries to eliminate what he considers its unsuitable metaphorical content. He concedes that "the human Dasein" has the possibility of going beyond concrete spatial limitations, but he hopes to keep this "step beyond" separate from his purportedly more fundamental transcendence as the step beyond that makes existence possible (WG 34/37).

After Heidegger purges transcendence of its spatio-temporal meanings, he suggests paradoxically that it is a going beyond that neither "goes" nor goes "beyond." Heidegger's transcendence cannot occur but rather must always already be: "With the fact of Da-sein the step

---

[23]WG 31/29. Numbers after the slash refer to pages in the bilingual edition: Martin Heidegger, *The Essence of Reasons*, trans. Terrence Malick (Evanston: Northwestern University Press, 1969). All translations are my own.

beyond is already there." Thus "beings themselves" (*das Seiende selbst*) must be transcended, which means defining Dasein as an ontological being and linking transcendence with "being-in-the-world" (WG 35/ 39–41). But "transcendence" functions in Heidegger's texts as more than a synonym for "being-in-the-world," although in some contexts the terms appear to be interchangeable. In fact, ontological transcendence is the more fundamental term, without which there could be no construction of "world."

The Marburg lectures of 1928 further reveal the strategic place of transcendence in Heidegger's overcoming (*Überwindung*) of the tradition. As in *Sein und Zeit* and "Vom Wesen des Grundes," Heidegger employs "transcendence" both to undermine the epistemological tradition based on a subject-object dichotomy and to distinguish his philosophical project from that of Husserl. The text is contained in volume 26 of the *Gesamtausgabe*.[24] Entitled by Heidegger's editors "The Transcendence of Dasein," section 11 is apparently an earlier version of the text that became section 2 of "Vom Wesen des Grundes" and begins similarly, with an interpretation of the word "transcendence."

Heidegger observes that the philosophical tradition has viewed the transcendent in opposition to the immanent. The immanent, then, "is that which remains within, meaning: what remains in the subject, in the soul, in consciousness,—the transcendent is then that which does not remain within but is rather outside: that which lies *outside* of the soul and of consciousness" (*MAL* 204). Heidegger caricatures the "capsule-conception of the subject" (*Kapselvorstellung des Subjekts*) that is implied by this version of transcendence: "What thus lies outside the barriers and the enclosing wall of consciousness therefore has, when one speaks from the most intimate court of this consciousness, stepped beyond the enclosing wall and stands outside" (ibid.). Consciousness appears as a fortress, perceiving the world as if from inside a walled courtyard. Heidegger believes that this transcendence involves a false ontology of the subject, in which "the subject is represented as if it were a capsule, with an inside, a capsule-wall, and an outside . . . a barrier between inner and outer must be stepped

[24]Martin Heidegger, *Metaphysische Anfangsgründe der Logik im Ausgang von Leibniz*, in the *Gesamtausgabe*, vol. 26, ed. Klaus Held (Frankfurt am Main: Vittorio Klostermann, 1978), henceforth cited as *MAL*. Heidegger's editors have made it impossible to be certain of the accuracy of these transcripts. In English, see *The Metaphysical Foundations of Logic*, trans. Michael Heim (Bloomington: Indiana University Press, 1984).

beyond" (*MAL* 205). Heidegger calls this the "epistemological concept of transcendence" because it raises questions about the knowledge a subject can have of a transcendent object.

At a safe distance from Freiburg, Heidegger argues that Husserl's phenomenology also relies on this "ontic transcendence." Heidegger maintains that Husserl did not understand intentionality radically enough, and in consequence his intentionality is "a narrow conception, insofar as it is understood to mean a relation to what is present at hand" (*MAL* 168). Heidegger insists that Husserl's conception is less fundamental than his own: "The problem of transcendence in general is not identical with the problem of intentionality. This is, as ontic transcendence, only possible on the ground of the original transcendence: *being-in-the-world*" (*MAL* 170). In Heidegger's view, the problem of transcendence points beyond theories of knowledge to an ontological inquiry. A passing comment suggests that "the vulgar phenomenon of transcendence is the transcendence in which Dasein essentially and immediately moves" (*MAL* 169).

Heidegger can thus assert that his more fundamental transcendence is "the original constitution of the *subjectivity* of a subject" (*MAL* 211). This transcendence must always already be, as a precondition for subjective existence: "The subject transcends as subject; it would not be a subject if it did not transcend. Being a subject means transcending" (ibid.). Dasein does not occasionally involve itself in a movement of going beyond; rather, Dasein itself is the step beyond. If transcendence is not a particular behavior of Dasein in which a mundane obstacle is exceeded, then "what is stepped beyond is rather the existent itself, which can become manifest to the subject, and indeed on the ground of its transcendence" (*MAL* 212). Dasein transcends, not by perceiving objects, but through its "being-in-the-world" that grounds all potential experience.

Heidegger employs "transcendence" in his overcoming of the epistemological tradition. He displaces the subject-object model of cognition by reference to a transcendence that undermines the "capsule-conception of the subject," and even the intentionality of Husserl appears derivative in relation to Heidegger's ontological transcendence. But a contrary interpretation has tacitly intervened. Heidegger cannot entirely purge transcendence of the spatial metaphor it contains. Ontic transcendence reasserts itself when Heidegger writes of "the transcendence, in which Dasein essentially and immediately

moves" (*MAL* 169). While Husserl does not write fundamental ontology, Heidegger grants that he does account for the transcendence
familiar to everyday Dasein. From a Heideggerian standpoint, Husserl
perhaps deals with an inauthentic transcendence or with a transcendence of Dasein in the mode of inauthenticity.[25]

Logos as Genius

Early in *Sein und Zeit*, Heidegger anticipates his subsequent turn
toward the *logos*. Section 7B translates *logos* as discourse (*Rede*), a
"letting see" (*Sehenlassen*) (*SZ* 33). In turn, understanding is seeing
"something as something" (*Etwas als Etwas*) (*SZ* 149). Metaphoric
"seeing-as" combines with metonymic "seeing-for." Though Heidegger does not explicate the modes of understanding in rhetorical
terms, several of his texts reencounter the *logos*.

Heidegger's early philosophy culminates in silence because the call
of conscience does not open up a "conversation with oneself" (*Selbstgespräch*) (*SZ* 273), while "in anxiety words fail us" (*die Angst verschlägt
uns das Wort*).[26] Skeptical of everyday language, Heidegger refers to
an ontological level of "discourse" (*Rede*); Heidegger believes that
discussions of signs generally neglect the grounding of language in
ontological modes of Dasein. In contrast, Heidegger asserts that discourse is "existentially equiprimordial with finding oneself and understanding" and the basis of language: "That *only now* language
becomes a theme, shall indicate, that this phenomenon has its roots
in the existential constitution of the resoluteness of Dasein. *The ex-
istential-ontological foundation of language is discourse*" (*SZ* 60). An earlier
passage similarly discusses the foundation of meaning and language
in the "resoluteness" of Dasein involved in understanding (*SZ* 87).
But Heidegger later questions this approach that places the understanding of Dasein at the origin of language. In a marginal comment

[25]Heidegger ultimately approaches transcendence in relation to problems of self. Thus
in a Marburg lecture of 1927 he asserts: "The *selfhood* of Dasein *grounds itself in* its
Transzendenz," *Gesamtausgabe*, vol. 24, ed. Friedrich-Wilhelm von Herrmann (Frankfurt
am Main: Vittorio Klostermann, 1975), 425. Compare Karl Jaspers' contemporaneous
work on transcendence in his *Philosophie*, vol. 3: *Metaphysik* (Berlin: Julius Springer,
1932).
[26]"Was ist Metaphysik?" in *Wegmarken*, 2d ed. (Frankfurt am Main: Vittorio Klostermann, 1978), 111.

to this passage, supplied by the fourteenth edition of *Sein und Zeit*,
Heidegger writes that Dasein and language are equally fundamental:
the earlier statement is "untrue. Language is not layered [*aufgestockt*],
but rather *is* the originary essence of truth as There [*Da*]" (*SZ* 442).
This self-correction nevertheless conceals the shift in Heidegger's terminology. Whereas *Sein und Zeit* distinguishes everyday "language"
(*Sprache*) from ontological "discourse" (*Rede*), some kind of meaningful articulation prior to explicit verbalization, Heidegger's later works
refer to language and "the essence of language" that may be approached through poetry.

Der *Ursprung des Kunstwerkes* and "Hölderlin und das Wesen der
Dichtung" (1936) initiate Heidegger's later reflection on language. As
the essence of language, poetry "precedes" ordinary usage: "Poetry
never takes up language as a raw material that is present at hand,
rather poetry itself makes language possible. . . . the essence of language must be understood out of the essence of poetry."[27] Heidegger
gestures toward "the conversation as an authentic happening of language" (HWD 40); Hölderlin's poetry inspires Heidegger to write of
the divine mission of a poet, who stands "between these—the gods,
and those—the people" (HWD 43). Like ancient *daimones* and *malachim*, poets mediate between god(s) and men. Through poetry, the
divine Word becomes accessible; the danger is that essential language
may become perverted in becoming common: "inauthenticity" of language is linked to its daily "chatter" (*Gerede*), while "authenticity" is
the metaphysical capacity to create a world out of the essence of
language.

Heidegger reflects on language by responding to previous authors
in a "repetition and destruction" (*Wiederholung und Destruktion*) of the
tradition. His reading of Novalis is one of the most surprising and,
indirectly, one of the most decisive for his development "on the way
to language." The essay entitled "Der Weg zur Sprache," in *Unterwegs
zur Sprache*, begins with a contemplation on the metaphysical meaning
of language as monologue. Without expressing any interest in the
mundane phenomenon of a subject's inner speech, Heidegger approaches the sense in which language carries on its own monologue.
Novalis is another source of the idea that "language speaks,"[28] and

[27]"Hölderlin und das Wesen der Dichtung," in *Erläuterungen zu Hölderlins Dichtung*,
5th ed. (Frankfurt am Main: Vittorio Klostermann, 1981), 40 (henceforth cited as "HWD").
[28]At the start of Novalis' "Lehrlinge zu Saïs," a mysterious voice pronounces (in

Heidegger's discussion of Novalis' "Monolog" gives meaning to this phrase.[29] The opening lines of "Der Weg zur Sprache" cite Novalis approvingly: "To start with, let us hear an expression by Novalis. It stands in a text which he entitled *Monolog*. The title points to the secret of language: it speaks solely [*einzig*] and solitary [*einsam*] with itself. One sentence of the text reads: 'Precisely what is peculiar about language, that it is concerned merely with itself, no one knows.' "[30]

---

indirekter Rede) that "one does not understand language, because language does not understand itself, does not want to understand itself: genuine Sanskrit spoke, merely in order to speak, because speaking was its desire and its essence." Heidegger's *Ursprung des Kunstwerkes* to some extent supports the myth of an original, "authentic" language, such as Greek before its displacement by Latin translations. See *Holzwege*, 5th ed. (Frankfurt am Main: Vittorio Klostermann, 1972), 13.

[29]The original version of the obscure and profound aphorism entitled "Monolog" is contained in *Novalis: Werke, Tagebücher, und Briefe Friedrich von Hardenbergs*, ed. Hans-Joachim Mähl and Richard Samuel (Munich: Carl Hanser, 1978): "There is a really crazy [*närrische*] thing about speaking and writing; the correct conversation is a mere word-play. The laughable error is only to be wondered at, that people think—they speak for the sake of things. Precisely what is peculiar about language, that it is merely concerned with itself, no one knows. For this reason it is such a wonderful and fruitful secret,—that when one merely speaks, in order to speak, he expresses exactly the most magnificent and original truths. But if he wants to speak of something definite, moody language lets him say only the most laughable and perverse rubbish. Thence arises the hatred, which so many serious people have against language. They note its mischievousness but do not notice that the despicable chatter [*das verächtliche Schwatzen*] is the infinitely serious side of language. If one could only make comprehensible to people that it is with language as with mathematical formulae—they constitute a world for themselves—they play only with themselves, express nothing but their wonderful nature, and just for this reason are they so expressive—just for this reason do they mirror the strange play of relations of things. Only through their freedom are they parts of nature and only in their free movements does the world soul express itself and make them into a gentle measure and groundplan of things. So it is also with language—whoever has a fine feeling of its fingering [*Applicatur*], its beat, its musical spirit, whoever perceives in himself the gentle working of its inner nature, and thereafter moves his tongue or his hand, he will be a prophet; on the other hand, whoever knows it well but does not have enough of an ear and a sense for it will write truths like these but will be bested by language and mocked by men, like Cassandra by the Trojans. If I believe that I have thus indicated most clearly the essence and office of poetry, yet I know that no one can understand it and that I have said something completely absurd because I wanted to say it, and thus no poetry comes into existence. How would it be, however, if I had to speak? and if this drive to speak were the sign of the inspiration of language, of the efficacy of language in me? and if my will only willed everything that I had to, then this could after all be poetry, without my knowledge and belief, and make a secret of language comprehensible? and so I would be a writer with a calling [*ein berufener Schriftsteller*], for a writer is indeed only one inspired by language [*ein Sprachbegeisterter*]?—" (vol. 2, p. 438; translation mine).

[30]In Martin Heidegger's *Unterwegs zur Sprache* (Pfullingen: Neske, 1959), 241; and in *On the Way to Language*, trans. Peter D. Hertz (New York: Harper and Row, 1971), 11.

In opposition to all subjective interpretations of speech, Heidegger accedes that language speaks, not men; men speak "authentically" by letting language speak. But what can it mean that language speaks with itself? How does this seemingly divine autoaffection interact with human languages?

Heidegger's discussion of "the way to language" parallels Novalis' statements, which Heidegger ultimately summarizes: "Language *is* monologue. Now this implies two things: it is language *alone* [*allein*] that authentically speaks. And it speaks *solitarily*" (*US* 265/134). Despite his diffidence in relation to Novalis' version of "Monologue," Heidegger unmistakably stands in the tradition that asserts: "Man does not speak alone—the universe also *speaks*—everything speaks— infinite languages."[31] Heidegger faults his precursor "because Novalis, in the field of vision of absolute idealism, imagines language dialectically from the standpoint of subjectivity" (*US* 265/134), but Heidegger's writings merge phenomenological discourse with the antisubjectivist tendency already evident in Novalis' texts. Heidegger's later thoughts on language rejoin the powerful pathways of "pure" poetry that follow inherent possibilities of language.

Through the musical grammar of thought, Heidegger exemplifies ways in which speech responds to language: "Language speaks. Man speaks, in so far as he corresponds to language. Corresponding is hearing. It hears, insofar as it belongs to the bidding of silence."[32] Human "speaking" (*sprechen*) becomes "corresponding" (*entsprechen*) and "hearing" (*hören*) becomes "belonging-to" (*gehören*), following clues already provided by language. A further, personifying trope occurs with the mysterious "it hears" (*es hört*), in which "the corresponding'" (*das Entsprechen*) seems to hear, not man. The peculiarly passive agent in this process seems to be the "bidding of silence" (*Geheiss der Stille*). In conjunction with his antisubjectivist views of language, Heidegger allows free play to the inner music, correspondences, and hidden palimpsest of language. Because the true problem is to correspond to language, Heidegger denies all effort to achieve originality: "Nothing rests on bringing forth a new view of language.

I shall henceforth cite this work as *US*. Page numbers in the English edition appear after the slash.

[31]Novalis, *Werke*, II, 500.

[32]*US* 32–33. The essay entitled "Language" appears in Martin Heidegger's *Poetry, Language, Thought*, trans. Albert Hofstadter (New York: Harper and Row, 1971).

Everything rests on learning to live in the speaking of language" (US 33).
Heidegger works more profoundly through traditions of the *logos* in the recently published Freiburg lectures on Heraklitus (1943–44). Heidegger's analyses focus on Heraklitus' Fragment B50:

> ouk emou alla tou Logon akousantas
> homologein sophon estin Hen Panta.
>
> Not listening to me, but to the *Logos*,
> it is wise to agree that the All is One.

English editions of Heraklitus' fragments generally do not capitalize *Logos*, but Heidegger recapitulates the ontological difference (suggested by the English translations of "Being" and "beings") by distinguishing between *Logos* and *logos*. This distinction allows him to write that Fragment 50 deals with the "homological relationship of the human *logos* to the *Logos*."[33] The single *Logos* "is the originary, origin-granting col-lection that holds itself at the origin, as the essence of Being itself" (*Hera*. 292).[34] For Heidegger, then, the homology of being-there (*Da-sein*) and Being (*Sein*), or of human *logos* and divine *Logos*, means that "man can be related through his *logos* to the *Logos* in the *homologein*, but this he is not always and perhaps only seldom" (*Hera*. 306). Although man is only seldom capable of correspondence, the possibilities for this privileged moment suggest Heidegger's late revision of existentialist authenticity. The "agreement" spoken of by Heraklitus is not conformity in the opinions of men but a relationship to the *Logos*. Because man is generally "turned away from the *Logos*," the presence of human *logos* conceals the absence of the divine *Logos*:

[33]Martin Heidegger, *Heraklit*, in the *Gesamtausgabe*, ed. Manfred S. Frings (Frankfurt am Main: Vittorio Klostermann, 1979), 296 (henceforth cited as *Hera*.). Until this important volume appears in translation, English readers can only compare Martin Heidegger and Eugen Fink, *Heraclitus Seminar 1966/67*, trans. Charles H. Seibert (University: University of Alabama Press, 1979). The capitalization of German nouns would efface the difference between *logos* and *Logos*; as in his essay "Logos (Heraklit, Fragment 50)," Heidegger distinguishes these forms by referring to them in Greek.

[34]Heidegger continues with an unusual reference to metaphor: "Accordingly it looks as if Heraklitus had read off the essence of reading and gathering from human doing and from there carried it over to the Being of beings in general. Such a carryover is called, in Greek, *metapherein*. The characterization of the Being of beings as *Logos* would then be a metaphor. In this metaphor would lie the often practiced, partly conscious and partly unconscious but perhaps unavoidable procedure of carrying over the lines and forms of human manner and human conduct onto the world totality" (*Hera*. 292). If this is the case, then "divine *Logos*" is necessarily an anthropomorphizing trope.

"That, therefore, which authentically and essentially concerns the human soul in its ground, i.e., in its proper *logos*, the *Logos* as Being, just this would indeed be present for man and his dispersion on the self-seeking path, but yet at the same time absent and set aside and therefore foreign" (*Hera.* 307). Heidegger wavers between a universalized ontological assertion and a discussion of rare moments. The transcendence of the *Logos* precedes human *logos*: "The dictum of Heraklitus says that man in his essence belongs to Being and is determined to the collection of this; and that only from it does he receive his own possibility" (*Hera.* 356). A special movement of human language, poetry that responds to the essence of language, suggests a form of authenticity.

Heidegger turns back from subjective monologue toward the transcendence of divine language. Like the lightning of Zeus, *Logos* brings the world into appearance. Heidegger rediscovers or invents a myth that unites lightning (*der Blitz*), a figure of Zeus, with the *Logos* and Hen Panta:

> The lightning brings forth, at once, all that is present in the light of its presence. The lightning now named steers. It brings to each in advance the essential place that is shown to him. Such a bringing-to is at once the bringing-forth, the *Logos*. "Lightning" stands here as a name for Zeus. He is, as the highest of the gods, the destiny of the universe. Accordingly the *Logos*, the *Hen Panta*, would be nothing other than the supreme God. The essence of the *Logos* would thus give a hint into the godliness of God.[35]

While Heidegger does not claim that Heraklitus taught this union of *Logos* with Zeus, he rediscovers the meaning of transcendence in Heraklitus' *Logos*. Ultimately, Heidegger narrates a new myth of genius: in place of divine selection or talent, poetic creativity emerges as a "listening . . . to the *Logos*" (*Hera.* 371).

[35]Martin Heidegger, "Logos (Heraklit, Fragment 50)," in *Vorträge und Aufsätze* (Pfullingen: Neske, 1954), 214. In English, see Martin Heidegger, *Early Greek Thinking*, trans. David Farrell Krell and Frank A. Capuzzi (New York: Harper and Row, 1975), 59–78.

Part Two

LITERATURE OF MONOLOGUE

You know that I have long been accustomed to the art
of soliloquy. If on leaving a social gathering I return
home sad and troubled, I retire and ask: What is the
matter? . . . a mood? . . . Yes . . . Are you doing badly?
. . . No . . . I press myself; I wrest the truth from myself.
Then it seems to me that I have a gay soul, tranquil,
honest and serene, which interrogates another that is
ashamed of some stupidity it is afraid to confess.
However, the confession comes. If it is an act of
stupidity I have committed, as happens fairly often, I
absolve myself. If it is one that has been done to me,
as occurs when I have met people disposed to abuse
the facility of my character, I pardon. The sadness
dissipates; I return to my family, a good husband, a
good father, a good master, at least so I imagine; and
no one feels the effects of a disturbance that was about
to expand to all who approached me.

I will advise this secret examination to all those who
wish to write; in this way, they will at once become
more honest people and better authors.

—DENIS DIDEROT, *Discours de la poésie dramatique*

5 Pre-Shakespearean and Shakespearean Soliloquies

If there is no true solitude for the believer who conceives God to be omnipresent, then the earliest soliloquies are necessarily divine. Medieval religious dramas present God (and the rebellious angel, Lucifer) in solitary speeches, while human solitude typically involves expressions of prayer or conscience, piety or guilt. Later the anguished contemplations of Marlowe's Faustus appear in conjunction with the addresses of good and evil angels. Renaissance drama retains the connection between solitary speech and communication with divine beings.

Shakespeare's *Richard III*, *Macbeth*, and *Hamlet* introduce a vivid mode of psychological soliloquy. Malformed by nature, distanced from society, and unaware of God, Richard proclaims himself "determinèd to prove a villain." He opens as a secret schemer and does not collapse under the strain of defeat until a dream of ghostly curses condemns him. At that point, an unsettling internal dialogue disrupts his efforts to attain unswerving self-determination. Macbeth and Lady Macbeth are also destroyed by solitary hallucinations. Hamlet's soliloquies unfold as equally conflict-ridden meditations, while Ophelia's deviant monologues express the threat of madness he occasions.

Dramatic soliloquies develop together with the evolving representation of English individuality. Freeing itself from narrative uses of soliloquy, in which characters rehearse a sequence of events, drama reveals the psychological complexity or theological transcendence of

111

solitary characters. When solitary speech loses its foundation in prayer, anguished conscience and madness grip the soliloquist. Just as the subject appears on the verge of appropriating a unified discourse, monologue uncovers internal divisions.

The development of soliloquy in drama combines monological representation and performance, for the history of monologue is a monological history, a history of swerves or deviations that border on the madness of so many literary monologues. Rhetorical differences manifest themselves as intimate forms of psychological doubling, which often resemble encounters with supernatural beings.

"Alas, sinner, what have I done?"

The Anglo-Norman *Ordo Repraesentationis Adae* (or *Jeu d'Adam*) opens as a dialogue of God with Adam and Eve, followed by subversive dialogues initiated by devils. The stage direction for God, "Figura," perhaps shows an awareness of the questionable nature of representing God on stage; God's image is only a figural illusion. As traditions of monologue evolve, drama makes represented spirits into figures for psychological turns. Following a brief retelling of the biblical story of creation, God instructs Adam and Eve through dialogue:

>   Adam! *Let him respond*: Sire?
>   FIGURA   I have formed you
>   Of the earth.
>   ADAM   I know it well.
>   FIGURA   I formed you in my image[1]

The drama is at first essentially a narrative and only faintly dramatic. God observes that he has given Adam his equal (*pareil*), Eve, who also recognizes Adam as her equal. The tensions in the representation revolve around the error of this pair in attempting to become the equal of God. Adam and Eve are created for perfect dialogue, but

---

[1]References to the *Ordo Repraesentationis Adae* (which I shall cite as *ORA*) and to the *Corpus Christi Cycle* from Wakefield and Brome follow the line numbers and the inconsistent orthography retained in David Bevington's *Medieval Drama* (Boston: Houghton Mifflin, 1975). I have slightly altered his translations. I shall henceforth cite the Wakefield Master's "The Creation" as "Cr." and his "Mactatio Abel" as "MA." Brome's "Sacrifice of Isaac" I shall designate as "SI."

their first sin propels them further from the parity with God they seek and brings monologue into the world. At a distance from God, expelled from Paradise, human language takes on a new potential for solitude.

Adam's first words, "I know it well," anticipate a crucial moment of dialogue just before the Fall (*ORA* 281): all is well as long as Adam and Eve's knowledge corresponds with God's, but knowledge of the devil (*Diabolus*) soon undoes them. When the "Figura" retires to a church backstage, Adam and Eve are left to enjoy Paradise in the company of demons. The perfect dialogue turns out to be a polylogue of demonic temptations, as the Latin stage directions indicate: "Meanwhile, let demons run about the platea, making appropriate gestures; and let them come, one after the other, close to paradise, showing Eve the forbidden fruit, as if tempting her to eat it. Then let the devil come to Adam and say to him: 'What are you doing, Adam?' "(*ORA* 113). A dialogue ensues in which the devil tempts Adam with the prospect of becoming God's peer ("per," *ORA* 167, 190). Adam resists steadfastly and labels the evil being "Satan" (*ORA* 196).

The devil then gives up on Adam, walks through the audience, and comes to Eve. She also recognizes Satan, but for her the name apparently connotes no evil. Eve listens with interest while the devil tempts her by describing her and Adam as an ill-matched pair. Adam reproaches Eve for talking with Satan, recalling the tradition that this traitor sought to place himself higher than God (*ORA* 289–90). When she has eaten the forbidden fruit, Eve commits Adam to the same sin by reminding him that "you are my peer" (*per*) (*ORA* 313).

After he joins Eve in sin, Adam begins a guilty self-reflection: "Alas, sinner, what have I done? / Now I am dead without escape." The breach of God's commandment opens up a new possibility of soliloquy. Adam reflects that, through the folly that has led him to abandon his Creator, he now knows sin (*ORA* 321–28). While he complains of his distance from "my Creator," "my Lord," the "King of Glory" (*ORA* 321, 339, 348), this proliferation of names does nothing to bring God closer. The separation makes it possible for Adam to speak God's name as an expletive, without referential significance ("Deu!"). He bemoans his new solitude that results from Eve's betrayal, Eve whom "God gave me as an equal [*pareil*]."

Tempted by the devil's own wish to become God's equal, the human pair is gripped by a kind of madness. Adam both speaks of his own "madness" (*folor*) and refers to his wife as a "crazed woman" (*femme desvee*) (*ORA* 357). He turns to Eve and curses the hour "when you became my equal [*parail*]" (*ORA* 372). Because his human equal cannot help him, Adam thinks of God, but recognizes that sin has disrupted their communication:

> I will be redeemed thence by no mortal,
> Unless by God in his majesty.
> What do I say, unfortunate? Why did I name Him?
> Will He help me? I have angered Him . . .
> I don't know where to turn,
> When we have not kept faith with God.
> [*ORA* 378–84]

The drama traces the development from divine dialogue, in a Paradise before sin, to the isolated monologue that results from the Fall. The sinless Adam and Eve never appear to be alone, for they always engage in dialogues with the "Figura," with each other, and with the devil. Yet Adam receives the possibility of worldly dialogue from God only to find that this dialogue with Eve destroys him; and to deviate from the path decreed by God is to open up the possibility of monologue. Adam and Eve express their new solitude by hiding themselves, for they recognize that—by attempting to become God's equal—they have lost all rights to be His peer.

The Fall occurs in the tension between man's likeness to God and his desire to become God's equal. God has formed Adam in His likeness (*a mun semblant*), and has given him an equal (*ta femme e tun pareil*). Provoked by the devil, man deviates by seeking to become God's equal, thus striving to usurp the divine dialogue. Consequently, the devil promises Adam:

> Eat it, and you'll do well.
> You'll have nothing to fear from God;
> Instead you will be in everything His peer.
> [*ORA* 165–67]

The devil further tells Adam he will be "without a lord," freed of God's sovereignty. If Adam's fantasy is to usurp the divine *Logos*, Eve only wishes to become privy to all He says, and the devil promises, "He won't be able to hide advice from you" (*ORA* 266). From the moment of creation, Adam is God's likeness (*semblant*), but the forbidden fruit brings this figurative likeness dangerously close to an experience of literal equality. After tasting the fruit, Eve says, "I seem to be God the all-powerful" (*ORA* 308). From likenesses of God, Adam and Eve become feigners of God. Adam sees clearly that Eve is his peer, and only Eve shares his present plight. God, the "Figura," explicitly interprets their sin as the misguided effort to "be my equal" (*estre mon per*) (*ORA* 415, 443). Like poor readers, they seek to transform a metaphorical relationship into literal equivalence.

Following their attempt to become God's peer, Adam and Eve receive only "peril" and "perdition" (*ORA* 508, 574, 536). Driven out of Paradise, a place where one does not erroneously seek equality, Adam laments:

> Alas! woe is me, how evil was that hour . . . .
> Where was my sense? What became of my
>   memory,
> That for Satan I forsook the king of glory?
>   [*ORA* 519, 531–32]

To follow Satan is to attempt to displace God and also to become crazed. Loss of God's dialogue is loss of the divine *Logos* and the eternal life that accompanies it. The Fall arises from folly and gives rise to new folly, for Adam wonders where his sense has gone, and Eve appears to him as a woman bereft of reason. Opposition to divine dialogue, Satan's slander against reason, motivates the Fall of human language into solitude.

Like the *Ordo Repraesentationis Adae,* the Wakefield *Corpus Christi Cycle* opens with God's speech, an introductory address that begins "The Creation" as a divine soliloquy. Before He creates man, God alternates between the first person and the royal "we" of His heavenly court. In a striking example of soliloquy as the divine *Logos,* God narrates and creates simultaneously:

> [DEUS] *Ego sum alpha et o:*
> I am the first, the last also,
> Oone God in magesté . . . .
>   . . . . .
> All maner thing is in my thoght
> Withoutten me ther may be noght,
> For all is in my sight.

> Hit shall be done after my will;
> That I have thoght I shall fulfill
> And manteyn with my might.
>   [Cr. 1–3, 13–18]

While God's soliloquy serves a narrative function, it also indicates that the divine *Logos* is primary and that only this *Logos* is genuinely *solus*. As in the biblical account, the first-person plural form is either a royal "we" or a hint that angels are also present:

> At the beginning of oure dede
> Make we heven and erth, on brede,
> and lightys faire to se.
>   [Cr. 19–21]

The excitement of this pageant begins after the fifth day of Creation, when Lucifer presumes to usurp God's place. This competing soliloquy parodies God's speech, for while God creates light, Lucifer revels in the light he possesses:

> I am so fare and bright,
> Of me commys all this light. . . .
> And ye well me behold;
> I am a thowsandfold
> Brighter then [*sic*] is the son.
>   [Cr. 82–89]

A typical monologist, Lucifer mistakenly considers himself to be autonomous. Wakefield thus represents him as a comical fool, full of pride, who blithely sits in God's throne: "I am so semely, blode and bone, / My sete shall be theras was His" (Cr. 102–3). Evil angels debate about his presumption until suddenly they find themselves in hell with demons, foretelling man's Fall.

One moment in Wakefield's "Mactatio Abel" further reveals the development of monologue in relationship to prayer. After the Fall, Cain and Abel can only strive, by means of sacrifice and prayer, for the dialogue Adam and Eve have lost. Wakefield's comic realism makes Cain a likable rogue in contrast to his pious brother, who sermonizes:

> And therfor, brother, let us weynd,
> And first clens us from the feynd

> Or we make sacrifice;
> Then blis withoutten end
> Get we for oure service,
> Of Him that is oure saulis leche.
>
> [MA 78–83]

Cain answers as the audience may wish to answer:

> How! let furth youre geyse; the fox will preche.
> How long wilt thou me appech
> With thy sermoning?
> Hold thy tong, yit I say,
> Even ther the good wife strokid the hay!
> Or sit downe, in the dwill way,
> With thy vain carping.
>
> [MA 84–90]

As often as Abel repeats the name of "God," Cain refers to "the dwill." Unable to grasp divine relation, or confusing God with Satan, Cain commands his offering to "bren, in the dwillys name!"(MA 278). When Abel comments that "thy tend shuld bren withoutten smeke," Cain answers, figuring himself as the devil, "Com kis the dwill right in the ars!" (MA 287).

God speaks to Cain at this point, responding to his inadequate dialogue with Abel: "Cam, why art thou so rebell / Agans thy brother Abell?" Cain responds in one of his funniest blasphemous speeches, mocking the "small" voice that has addressed him:

> Why, who is that hob over the wall?
> We! who was that that piped so small?
> Com, go we hens, for perels all.
> God is out of his wit!
> Com furth, Abell, and let us weynd.
> Me think that God is not my freynd.
> On land then will I flit.
>
> [MA 297–303]

Cain misunderstands God as a "hob"(goblin) localized in space and consequently believes he can go where "God shall not me see." Intensifying the disobedience of Adam and Eve, Cain hears God's words and refuses to take them seriously. After he murders Abel, Cain first confronts his guilt only by threatening the audience in an aside: "If

any of you think I did amis, / I shal it amend wars then it is" (MA
331–32). The staged soliloquy retains an element of address to the
audience. Cain continues, however, in a new vein of conscience:

> Bot now, syn he is broght on slepe,
> Into som hole fain wold I crepe.
> For ferd I qwake, and can no rede;
> For, be I taken, I be bot dede.
>
> [MA 336–39]

This drama exemplifies the use of soliloquy in conjunction with re-
jections of God's words. Unable to pray, at a distance from God, Cain
(like the fallen Adam) breaks into solitary speech. Dialogue and monologue compete through the interaction of piety and impiety, good
and evil, relationship to God and to devils.

In contrast, the Wakefield and Brome cycles represent Noah and
Abraham in a mode of pious soliloquy. Wakefield's "Noah" first acknowledges "mightfull God veray, maker of all that is," who "maide
both night and day, beest, fowle, and fish; / All creatures that lif may
wroght thou at thy wish" (1, 3–4). Brome's "Sacrifice of Isaac" opens
similarly, combining address to God with a review of the Creation
narrative:

> Fader of hevyn omnipotent,
> With all my hart to the I call!
> Thow hast goffe me both lond and rent,
> And my livelod thow hast me sent.
> I thanke the heyly, evermore, of all.
>
> First of the erth thou madist Adam,
> And Eve also to be his wiffe.
>
> [SI 1–7]

As the story of the sacrifice of Isaac continues, Abraham speaks asides
that are essentially addresses to God: "A, Lord, my heart brekith on
twain, / This childys wordys they be so tender!" (127–28). Onstage,
however, prayer is presumably not prayer and constantly interacts
with elements of performance. The attempted dialogue with God
turns into an indirect communication with other human beings. Prayer,
when it has lost the exclusive relation to God, becomes dialogue with
the community. To separate oneself from this community is to risk
an even greater Fall. The earliest monologues are speeches of God

and of the dissenting Lucifer; Adam and Cain exclaim their solitary pangs of conscience that result from disobedience; Noah and Abraham pray to restore the dialogue. After Babel, the confusion of tongues makes uniform speech, or divine *Logos*, into a distant dream.

"Divinity, adieu!"

In later drama, soliloquy emerges as the strongest stylistic expression of guilt and madness. Christopher Marlowe's *Doctor Faustus* works through the dynamics of an individual fate in relation to divine *Logos*. Like medieval dramas that represent the Fall and Cain's murder, Marlowe's play explicitly presents the soul's choice between heaven and hell, God and Lucifer. This metaphysical stage is set by Faustus' decision to cut himself off from God and to communicate with Mephostophilis. But Marlowe advances beyond the medieval tradition both by individualizing Faustus and by adding to the psychological significance of the supernatural beings he confronts. *Doctor Faustus* stages the human potential to perform vastly different roles and to receive or refuse guidance from a conscience that is figured by debates between good and evil angels.

Marlowe's play opens with Faustus' renunciation of the God he seeks and never successfully finds. For Adam, monologue is a consequence of the Fall; for fallen humanity, solitude is a given, and Faustus first appears in the self-address of solitary meditation:

> Settle thy studies, Faustus, and begin
> To sound the depth of that thou wilt profess.
> Having commenced, be a divine in show—
> Yet level at the end of every art
> And live and die in Aristotle's works.
>   [I.i.1–5][2]

Prior to any individual sin, Faustus is already an isolated subject who practices the "self-dissection" Shaftesbury later prescribes. Having received his theological degree, Faustus considers what it means to "be a divine in show." He reviews his studies: "Sweet *Analytics*, 'tis thou has ravaged me" (I.i.6). Ambition competes with the claims of

<hr>

[2]Christopher Marlowe, *Doctor Faustus*, ed. Sylvan Barnet (New York: New American Library, 1969). Numbers in text below refer to lines.

divinity, as Faustus longs for the forbidden arts that would "make men to live eternally / Or being dead raise them to life again" (I.i.22–23). He provisionally asserts that "when all is done, divinity is best" (I.i.35) and turns to Jerome's Bible. But a conjunction of passages leads Faustus to conclude that "what will be, will be! Divinity, adieu!" (I.i.45). Adversary of the divine, Mephostophilis later claims to have predetermined this outcome:

> 'Twas I, that when thou wert i' the way to heaven
> Damned up thy passage. When thou took'st the book
> To view the Scriptures, then I turned the leaves
> And led thine eye.
>   [V.ii.100–3]

Mephostophilis blocks Faustus' "passage" to heaven by misleading him through a sequence of scriptural passages. If Mephostophilis represents evil impulses within Faustus himself, then this opening scene is a confrontation between good and evil modes of reading, an encounter between the godly and demonic speech of the self. The demonic is an introjected desire that finds expression in a kabbalistic delight over magical signs:

> These metaphysics of magicians
> And negromantic books are heavenly;
> Lines, circles, letters, characters—
> Ay, these are those that Faustus most desires.
>   [I.i.47–50]

Faustus seeks "a world of profit and delight / Of power, honor, and omnipotence" (I.i.51–52), ultimately seeking to deify himself, like Adam and Eve tempted to become God's "per": "A sound magician is a demi-god! / Here tire my brains to get a deity!" (I.i.59–60).

In the scenes that follow, Faustus' solitary meditations turn into, or are figured as, choices between supernatural beings. Divinity and black magic stand in the balance. At several stages, good and evil angels enter the stage and externalize the options Faustus confronts. After he calls magicians to his aid, the angels represent the duplicity within Faustus' soul:

> *Good Angel.* O Faustus, lay that damnèd book aside
> And gaze not on it lest it tempt thy soul

> And heap God's heavy wrath upon thy head!
> Read, read the Scriptures—that is blasphemy!
> *Bad Angel.* Go forward, Faustus, in that famous art
> Wherein all nature's treasure is contained.
> Be thou on earth as Jove is in the sky,
> Lord and commander of these elements!
>
> [I.i.67–74]

At the moment of choice between books of Scripture and of black magic, the evil angel predictably tempts Faustus with the prospect of becoming God-like. His incantation, a performance rather than a prayer, figures God's name:

> Within this circle is Jehovah's name
> Forward and backward anagrammatized,
> Th' abbreviated names of holy saints,
> Figures of every adjunct to the heavens,
> And characters of signs and erring stars,
> By which the spirits are enforced to rise.
>
> [I.iii.8–9]

When Mephostophilis appears, however, he demystifies Faustus' pompous performance. "Did not my conjuring raise thee?" he asks, and Mephostophilis answers:

> That was the cause, but yet *per accidens*:
> For when we hear one rack the name of God,
> Abjure the Scriptures and his savior Christ,
> We fly in hope to get his glorious soul.
>
> [I.iii.44–48]

Faustus requests explanations of Lucifer and hell. The otherworldly meaning of Mephostophilis' answers is unsettled when Faustus asks, "How comes it then that thou are out of hell?" and Mephostophilis responds, "Why this is hell, nor am I out of it" (I.iii.75). Without losing the supernatural level of the drama, we are led to consider that the entire diabolical world may be Faustus' own projection.

Solitary, Faustus hears the voice of conscience and the voices of conflicting angels. He debates with himself: "Now, Faustus, must thou needs be damned; / Canst thou not be saved!" (II.i.1–3). A struggle between conflicting imaginations ensues when Faustus attempts to conjure away thoughts as he has conjured spirits. Faustus com-

mands: "Away with such vain fancies, and despair— / Despair in
God and trust in Belzebub!" (II.i.4–5). A first reading may suggest
that Faustus wishes to dispel both "vain fancies" and "despair." But
the noun subtly shifts toward the function of a verb, and Faustus
finds that he commands himself to despair. The following line specifies his self-deluded command, "despair in God" and "trust in Belzebub," but Faustus wavers:

> Why waver'st thou? O something soundeth in mine ear,
> "Abjure this magic, turn to God again."
> Ay, and Faustus will turn to God again.
> To God? He loves thee not;
> The god thou serv'st is thine own appetite
> Wherein is fixed the love of Belzebub!
>
> [II.i.7–12]

Faustus has tried to conjure away despair but only succeeds in bringing it on himself. Hearing internal voices that argue conflicting positions, Faustus begins to refer to himself in the third-person form.
Yet he refuses to turn back to God, because he has introjected Him:
"the god thou serv'st is thine own appetite." Within his internalized
stage, good and evil angels represent his conflict:

> *Bad Angel.* Go forward, Faustus, in that famous art.
> *Good Angel.* Sweet Faustus, leave that execrable art.
> *Faustus.* Contrition, prayer, repentance, what of these?
> *Good Angel.* O, they are means to bring thee unto heaven.
> *Bad Angel.* Rather illusions, fruits of lunacy,
> That make men foolish that do use them most.
> *Good Angel.* Sweet Faustus, think of heaven and heavenly things.
> *Bad Angel.* No Faustus, think of honor and of wealth.
>
> [II.i.15–23]

The play develops as Faustus' movement toward damnation, in connection with his series of *prises de conscience*. The angelic mechanism
again and again offers Faustus the chance to "renounce this magic
and repent." While the good angel tells Faustus to repent, for "God
will pity thee," the bad angel responds that "God cannot pity thee!"
(II.ii.12–13). For the audience, the angels are visually present, but
Faustus experiences them as voices that "buzzeth in mine ears." Faustus' externalized fantasies largely determine the world of the drama.

Though Faustus finally learns to "be silent then, for danger is in words" (V.i.27), he breaks into his most beautiful, impassioned speech at the sight of Helen:

> Was this the face that launched a thousand ships
> And burnt the topless towers of Ilium?
> Sweet Helen, make me immortal with a kiss.
> Her lips suck forth my soul. See where it flies!
> [V.i.96–99]

Faustus relinquishes his Christian soul as he imagines himself a hero of the *Iliad*:

> I will be Paris, and for love of thee
> Instead of Troy shall Wittenberg be sacked;
> And I will combat with weak Menelaus
> And wear thy colors on my plumèd crest.
> Yea, I will wound Achilles in the heel
> And then return to Helen for a kiss.
> [V.i.103–8]

Faustus is inescapably damned through his intercourse with a spirit, a kind of imaginative autoeroticism. Mephostophilis expounds the condition of "desperate lunacy" that grips Faustus; the chain of associations links fantasy, madness, and converse with the devil. Mephostophilis commands Faustus to despair, and finally even the good angel can no longer offer repentance. The dialogue of spirits employs the past tense (of Faustus' unalterable sin) and the future tense (of Faustus' unalterable punishment):

> *Good Angel.* O Faustus, if thou hadst given ear to me
> Innumerable joys had followèd thee.
> But thou did'st love the world.
> *Bad Angel.*   Gave ear to me,
> And now must taste hell's pains perpetually
> *Good Angel.* O, what will all thy riches, pleasures, pomps
> Avail thee now?
> *Bad Angel.* Nothing but vex thee more,
> To want in hell, that had on earth such store.
> [V.ii.106–12]

When the angels exit, Faustus is left with a solitude in which to reflect, but not to repent. The devils tear him apart, a logical consequence of the "self-dissection" Faustus already performs in contradictory fantasies.

Richard III recasts the Faustus story in a more naturalistically depicted political realm. Shakespeare's schemer finds himself turned away from God and toward evil. His deviation finally results in psychological disintegration. While no evil spirits enter Richard's waking world, this may be because, as Anne recognizes, he himself is a devil. The absence of supernatural beings continues as long as Richard is confident in his subjective autonomy; when he weakens, he begins to experience spiritual powers beyond himself.

Richard's opening speech combines various rhetorical devices. His use of the royal or communal "we" anticipates his later usurpation and pretends to participation in the general celebrations:

> Now is the winter of our discontent
> Made glorious summer by this sun of York;
> And all the clouds that loured upon our house
> In the deep bosom of the ocean buried.
>   [I.i.1–4][3]

The opening soliloquy serves a narrative function, raising questions about the interaction of "conventional" and "realistic" rhetoric. Yet Richard turns the generalized description into a context for his own stated divergence from norms when he finds himself excluded from the prevailing customs:

> But I, that am not shaped for sportive tricks
> Nor made to court an amorous looking glass;
> I, that am rudely stamped, and want love's majesty
> To strut before a wanton ambling nymph;
> I, that am curtailed of this fair proportion,
> Cheated of feature by dissembling Nature,
> Deformed, unfinished, sent before my time
> Into this breathing world scarce half made up,
> And that so lamely and unfashionable
> That dogs bark at me as I halt by them;
> Why, I, in this weak piping time of peace,

---

[3]William Shakespeare, *Richard III*, ed. Mark Eccles (New York: New American Library, 1964), henceforth cited by line numbers. This passage contains the first of several Faustian echoes: the "buried arms hung up for monuments" remind us of Faustus' "bills hung up as monuments" (I.i.18). A seminar that Howard Felperin held at Yale University in 1976 deeply influenced my reading of Shakespeare.

> Have no delight to pass away the time,
> Unless to spy my shadow in the sun
> And descant on mine own deformity.
> [I.i.14–27]

This single sentence, dominated by an obstinate "I," narrates the development of a monological subject. Richard maintains that nature has formed him inadequately, such that he cannot play the role of lover demanded by the times. He is like an unprepared actor "sent before my time / . . . scarce half made up." If nature has not made him the actor he wishes to be, Richard will produce his own dramatic persona. Richard's perverse delight is a self-reflective performance of himself, associated with viewing "my shadow in the sun" and decrying "mine own deformity." Deviation becomes an impetus to performance. *Richard III*, like *Doctor Faustus*, centers around the individual capacity to perform diabolical, or deviant, roles:

> And therefore, since I cannot prove a lover
> To entertain these fair well-spoken days,
> I am determinèd to prove a villain
> And hate the idle pleasures of these days.
> [I.i.28–31]

Hatred comes as a necessary concomitant of the role Richard chooses for himself. Shakespeare combines the conventionality of a traditional self-proclaiming figure of vice (determined by fate) with the realism of a specific, self-creating villain (determined by personal will). The naturalistic pretense of Richard's soliloquy is underscored when it is suddenly interrupted by his brother's entrance, and Richard exclaims, "Dive, thoughts, down to my soul" (I.i.41).

Contrary to his claim that he cannot "prove a lover," Richard begins his career as diabolical performer when he successfully courts Anne. But he is already so "determinèd to prove a villain" that he combines roles to make himself a villainous lover. Though she repeatedly calls him "devil" (I.ii.45,49,73), Anne is bewildered by his performance, and Richard exults:

> Was ever woman in this humor wooed?
> Was ever woman in this humor won?
> I'll have her, but I will not keep her long.
>   [I.ii.227–29]

Richard's only "friends to back my suit" are "the plain devil and dissembling looks" (I.ii.235–36). Consummate actor, he finds that dissembling makes him anew:

> I do mistake my person all this while.
> Upon my life, she finds, although I cannot,
> Myself to be a marv'lous proper man.
>   [I.ii.252–54]

Richard's self-presentation transforms him, for he has learned to "seem a saint when most I play the devil" (I.iii.337). Richard knows that even devilishness is an act, and the audience, aware of his performance, is implicated in his guilt.

Richard's downfall is a more realistic version of that experienced by Faustus. While spirits appear on Marlowe's stage, ambiguously literal or figurative representations of Faustus' inner conflict, the ghosts in *Richard III* occur as part of Richard's nightmare. In place of good and evil angels, then, Richard dreams of those he has murdered; all tell him to "Despair and die!" (V.iii.127–64).[4] The last of them, the ghost of Buckingham, has been more closely allied with Richard but acknowledges that "God and good angels fight on Richmond's side" (V.iii.176). These visions are naturalized, as "Richard starteth up out of a dream" and holds a devastating soliloquy that appears as a dialogue with himself:

> Soft! I did but dream.
> O coward conscience, how dost thou afflict me!
> The lights burn blue. It is now dead midnight.
> Cold fearful drops stand on my trembling flesh.
> What do I fear? Myself? There's none else by.
>   [V.iii.179–183]

The failure of Richard's military and political performances returns him to the limbo of indefinite identity:

---

[4]Compare *Doctor Faustus*, V.ii.104, in which Mephostophilis tells Faustus, " 'Tis too late, despair, farewell!"

> Richard loves Richard: that is, I am I.
> Is there a murderer here? No. Yes, I am.
> Then fly. What, from myself? Great reason why!
> Lest I revenge. What, myself upon myself?
> [V.iii.184–87]

Fragmented by his disparate performances, Richard is reproved by each tale his conscience tells:

> I am a villain. Yet I lie, I am not.
> Fool, of thyself speak well. Fool, do not flatter.
> My conscience hath a thousand several tongues,
> And every tongue brings in a several tale,
> And every tale condemns me for a villain.
> [V.iii.192–96]

Richard's fall is figured as his decline into a bad performance that even he cannot grasp, and he sees that "there is no creature loves me" (V.iii.201). To himself he has become an enigma, exactly at the moment when he sees through and hence mistrusts all his personae, and to others he is only evil. Unlike the flat repentance of Adam on the medieval stage, Richard's reflections uncover the conditions of their own performance, associating soliloquy with deviance from accepted roles. By simulating diverse characters, Richard assures the splitting of his "I"; conscience disturbs his monological schemes by bringing conflicting voices into his dreams and solitary speech.

"Alas, he's mad"

The meaning of a stylistic device, like the meaning of a word, arises as a function of its use. The meaning of dramatic monologue, then, evolves in conjunction with diverse literary frameworks. In medieval drama, soliloquy is essentially linked to the divine *Logos*, prayer, and expressions of guilt. Soliloquy, in the dramas of Faustus and Richard, reveals the workings of deviant minds that deliberately choose evil. Monologue is thus associated with deviations from God, the community, and from the good in general. But while monologue turns away from dialogue with God, its alliance with demonic (or unconscious) powers assures that no unity of the solitary voice can prevail. Shakespeare extends the conventions of soliloquy, when his plays represent psychological complexities through solitary speeches. Monologue always implies an absence, but Shakespeare shows that this lack is not merely a deficient mode of experience.

In *Macbeth*, supernatural beings partially constitute the subjective world. If the play opens as a gathering of "weird sisters," this scene is equally a representation of the confused ambitions within Macbeth: "Fair is foul, and foul is fair," the witches exclaim, and Macbeth's opening words echo theirs: "So foul and fair a day I have not seen."[5] Banquo apparently also experiences the strange creatures, yet "to me you speak not" (I.iii.57). Macbeth gives his secret fantasies away by his confused reaction. Banquo notices his confusion and asks, "Why do you start, and seem to fear / Things that do sound so fair?" (I.iii. 51–52). While Banquo is suspicious of the "instruments of darkness," Macbeth accepts their "supernatural soliciting." Macbeth's sequence of soliloquies begins in response to them, and he is oblivious while Banquo observes him: "Look, how our partner's rapt" (I.iii.143). Brought back to an awareness of the others present, Macbeth excuses himself, saying that his "dull brain was wrought / With things forgotten" (I.iii.149–50). Macbeth's excuse is partly true, for the apparitions have reminded him of "forgotten" ambitions.[6]

On the verge of murder, Macbeth's contemplative soliloquy stands between those of Richard and Hamlet. Already psychologically poisoned by his wife, Macbeth ties himself up in awkward assonances:

> If it were done when 'tis done, then 'twere well
> It were done quickly. If th' assassination
> Could trammel up the consequence, and catch,
> With his surcease, success; that but this blow
> Might be the be-all and the end-all—here,

---

[5]William Shakespeare, *Macbeth*, ed. Sylvan Barnet (New York: New American Library, 1963), I.i.10 and I.iii.38. Line numbers appear in text below.

[6]Lady Macbeth, the other central soliloquist, is reminiscent of Doctor Faustus except that she calls upon spirits to transform her. Rather than represent spirits that appear in response to her invocations, Shakespeare emphasizes the sheer act of her rhetoric: "Come, you spirits / That tend on mortal thoughts, unsex me here, / And fill me, from the crown to the toe, top-full / Of direst cruelty!" (I.v.41–44). Physical change acts as a trope for psychological hardening. Lady Macbeth desires assistance from figures of cruelty, since Macbeth is "too full o' th' milk of human kindness"; she plans to "pour my spirits in thine ear," poisoning his thought with her words.

> But here, upon this bank and shoal of time,
> We'd jump the life to come.
>
> [I.vii.1–7]

Even Macbeth's solitary speech betrays him, as if refusing to be merely an instrument of his murderous intentions: the subjunctive mode of possibility confounds his present thoughts.

When Macbeth resolves to renounce their plan, stating that "we will proceed no further in this business" (I.vii.31), Lady Macbeth again acts as his evil angel to win him over. One novelty of Shakespeare's presentation derives from the absence of any good angel to balance the evil counsel Macbeth receives. Plotting to murder Banquo, Macbeth idly imagines that he must do so for the sake of his guardian spirit, as "under him / My genius is rebuked, as it is said / Mark Antony's was by Caesar" (III.i.55–57). This "genius" has already been turned inward and perverted in accordance with Macbeth's schemes. Macbeth is so far from being able to respond to the call of conscience that his wife, or evil angel, becomes the mouthpiece for his guilt. Before several witnesses, Lady Macbeth sleepwalks and gives away their secret. The form of mad monologue begins to develop in this oblivious speaking subject. Her soliloquy echoes Macbeth's first, with the difference that dramatic conventions make Banquo unable to hear the contemplations that engross Macbeth (I.iii.127–42). Shakespeare invents a new convention in which a deviant mode of nonaddressed speech becomes accessible to other characters onstage. Consequently, the attending doctor is able to diagnose her condition:

> Foul whisp'rings are abroad. Unnatural deeds
> Do breed unnatural troubles. Infected minds
> To their deaf pillows will discharge their secrets.
> More needs she the divine than the physician.
> God, God forgive us all!
>
> [V.i.75–79]

Absent from the lives of the protagonists, divinity can be invoked only by an impassionate character who has no active part in the drama. The doctor, still supporting established theology, believes that Lady Macbeth requires the help of God. But Shakespeare's drama supersedes this wisdom, showing that theological conflicts have been transferred into the realm of psychological, solitary speech: the new problem of the monologist is not God's absence but madness.

Hamlet is Shakespeare's masterwork of monologue, so much so that the protagonist's soliloquies have virtually become canonized as independent poems. In contrast to Richard or Iago, who dominate their plays by nearly successful monological scheming, Hamlet soliloquizes in reaction to a hostile world. One might say that Hamlet turns his anger inward, transforms longed-for actions into words, and verges on madness because he cannot withstand the internal conflicts his monologue confronts.

The tradition links soliloquy and supernatural apparitions; there is also no clear separation between mad monologue and demonic intervention. When both demons and God are introjected, self-address is always also a potential demonic or divine address. The ghost of Hamlet's father reappears while Hamlet is in his mother's bedroom, and as Hamlet speaks to the apparition, the Queen comments, "Alas, he's mad" (III.iv.106).[7] Hamlet remains oblivious to her, like Macbeth before Banquo, until the ghost tells him to speak with her. She wonders,

> Alas, how is't with you
> That you do bend your eye on vacancy,
> And with th' incorporal air do hold discourse?
> . . . O gentle son,
> Upon the heat and flame of thy distemper
> Sprinkle cool patience. Whereon do you look?
> [III.iv.117–25]

To the extent that other characters do not share his experience, the monological speaker is subject to accusations of madness. Hamlet insists that he sees his father's ghost, but his mother persists in her belief that "this is the very coinage of your brain" (III.iv.138). Because Hamlet speaks of private experiences, his language is incomprehensible, semantically isolated; imagination and madness oppose communal norms. When the ghost initially reveals the murder to Hamlet, he exclaims, "O my prophetic soul!" (I.v.38). The drama does not ultimately confirm either madness or prophecy, yet Hamlet is able to speak so cogently to the Queen that his uncanny experience of ghosts comes to represent the external world in which "something is rotten."

---

[7]William Shakespeare, *Hamlet*, ed. William Farnham (Baltimore: Penguin, 1970).

As Lady Macbeth's sleepwalking reveals the suppressed cries of Macbeth's conscience, Ophelia's hysteria expresses Hamlet's imbalances. Ophelia first comments on his condition as the doctor comments on Lady Macbeth's, saying: "O heavenly powers, restore him!" (III.i.141) and "O, what a noble mind is here o'erthrown" (III.i.150). Unable to grasp his speech or to communicate with him, Ophelia can only observe Hamlet's decline. This failure of language becomes general for her, when she lapses into song and becomes incapable of addressing others. Hamlet's insulation works itself out as critical self-analysis, while Ophelia appears to be destroyed by his communicative absence.

Hamlet's monologue arises out of an experienced impotence. Rather than perform the command he thinks he receives from his father's ghost, Hamlet resorts to meditation, an effort to "unpack my heart with words" (II.ii.571). Solitary speech takes the place of action. Hamlet also understands his difficulty as an inability to perform when he responds to the feigned emotion of a traveling actor:

> O, what a rogue and peasant slave am I!
> Is it not monstrous that this player here,
> But in a fiction, in a dream of passion,
> Could force his soul so to his own conceit
> That from her working all his visage wanned,
> Tears in his eyes, distraction in his aspect,
> A broken voice, and his whole function suiting
> With forms to his conceit? And all for nothing,
> For Hecuba!
>
> [II.ii.534–42]

Hamlet wishes he were capable of such performance and attempts to stage the events that follow in a way that will improve his acting. Failing to preserve the distinction between actual and performed emotion, Hamlet imagines the player's response to his own condition:

> What would he do
> Had he the motive and the cue for passion
> That I have? He would drown the stage with tears
> And cleave the general ear with horrid speech,
> Make mad the guilty and appall the free.
>
> [II.ii. 544–48]

Hamlet dissolves the difference between life and drama by recognizing his world as a stage and blames himself for the persona that inhibits his act of revenge. To kill the usurping King would not suffice; Hamlet longs to perform the vengeful act in an appropriately dramatic way. But since Hamlet's grandest performances are *solus*, he can only stage a scene that may provoke a guilty performance from the King:

> I'll have these players
> Play something like the murder of my father
> Before mine uncle. I'll observe his looks.
> I'll tent him to the quick. If 'a do blench,
> I know my course.
>   [II.ii.580–84]

Such a performance, Hamlet judges, will be more reliable than the words of his prompting spirit:

>   The spirit that I have seen
> May be a devil, and the devil hath power
> T'assume a pleasing shape, yea, and perhaps
> Out of my weakness and my melancholy,
> As he is very potent with such spirits,
> Abuses me to damn me.
>   [II.ii.584–89]

Sensing the connection between spirits and private experience, Hamlet needs firmer grounds on which to act. But the "ground" he chooses is only a stage, for "the play's the thing / Wherein I'll catch the conscience of the king" (II.ii. 590–91).

Hamlet believes he does discover the King's guilt through the play within the play, but an equally central moment is a double soliloquy. As the King kneels in prayer, Hamlet enters the scene and soliloquizes at a distance, concluding that to murder the King would be to send his soul to heaven (III.iii.73–78). The King's posture of prayer implies a relationship to God that Hamlet lacks and declines to interrupt. But in their degraded world, the King has only discovered his inability to pray. Shakespeare presents an indirect dialogue between opposing characters.

The final scene requires that Hamlet turn performer. A fencing match sets the stage; when all are mortally wounded, Hamlet calls on Horatio to "report me and my cause aright / To the unsatisfied" (V.ii.328–29). The soliloquist longs to communicate his private thoughts:

> O God, Horatio, what a wounded name,
> Things standing thus unknown, shall live behind me!
> If thou didst ever hold me in thy heart,
> Absent thee from felicity awhile,
> And in this harsh world draw thy breath in pain,
> To tell my story.
>
> [V.ii.333–38]

Less concerned for his bodily wounds, Hamlet pleads with Horatio to tell the story that will heal his "wounded name." For a character who learns the inadequacy of solitary speech, performance is decisive. His internal narratives have been hopelessly divided; Hamlet finally commands another's narrative and its conclusion in silence.

Early English drama makes soliloquy a concomitant of sin and separation from God. As drama develops, soliloquy appears as the device by which prayer can overcome the distance between human and divine realms. Supernatural beings recurrently interact with soliloquies, as if to indicate the uncertain status of spirit, between divinity and subjectivity. The villainous world of *Richard III* becomes possible after God's absence is assumed: until his downfall, Richard unfolds his schemes without the interruption of spirits. While a spirit does enter into Hamlet's world, his isolation is so extreme that his doubts revolve around the question of the validity of the ghost's message. Supernatural beings become figures of inner turmoil; as the tensions between immanence and transcendence work themselves out in the dialectic of monological modes, the supposedly autonomous subject discovers its internal conflicts. To the extent that soliloquy is coupled with relationships to society and divine beings, it never entirely loses the connection with otherness and transcendent *Logos*. Even apparent solitude and madness show themselves as relationships to the divine. The new poetic monologue, instead of interacting with supernatural powers, turns toward contemplation on the appropriate rhetoric for imaginative expressions of the self.

6 Coleridge's Conversational Pretense

Coleridge's conversation poems extend the conventions of dramatic soliloquy to an apparently autonomous lyrical form.[1] Dramatic soliloquy and poetic monologue both generate illusions of individual speech, yet the difference in genre has decisive implications. In the dramatic context, soliloquy retains mimetic pretensions as part of a represented world, while the written conversation poem tends to draw attention to its own representational illusion. The poetic monologist is typically less concerned to describe the world than to reflect on the experiences that constitute it.

Coleridge, whose finest lyrics are representative of the Romantic monologue, writes most enthusiastically of Shakespeare's genius in connection with the great soliloquist, Hamlet. Perhaps because Coleridge identifies with Hamlet, monological forms characterize his strongest poems. Although the conversation poem does not inherently carry abnormal associations, the solitude it implies creates an opening for the aberrations of "phantom magic." Coleridge further develops the conversational mode suggested by Shakespearean so-

[1]The conversation poems also draw from traditions of songs and sonnets, but these earlier first-person forms rarely pretend to capture a particular moment and setting in time and space. John Donne's poems include notable exceptions. Shakespeare's sonnets characteristically imply a generalized, nonspecific present. Coleridge's conversational tone finds a significant echo in Wordsworth's "Tintern Abbey."

liloquy and Augustan poetry and clusters a set of related poems around supernatural phenomena. The rise and fall of Coleridge's conversational pretense may be traced as a fictional biography, from his identification with Hamlet, through "The Eolian Harp" and "Frost at Midnight," until the subversion of the conversational mode by "Kubla Khan." The multiple voices of "Kubla Khan" disrupt the scene of vision, revealing a potential threat to composition. If Coleridge's early poetry succeeds by virtue of its firm control of the conversational tone, his more radical lyrics disturb the poetic voice that had been established.

Coleridge's "Hamlet"

Coleridge's identification with Hamlet provides a key to his poetic form: while Collins, Cowper, and Young are more immediate precursors, Coleridge makes the meditative Hamlet his imaginative model. Returning year after year to the figure of Hamlet, Coleridge both characterizes him in general and attempts to grasp the secret of his soliloquies. Admiration is tempered by awareness of Hamlet's failure and deterioration; Coleridge uneasily recognizes himself in Hamlet, and fears the imbalances that accompany imaginative excess. After carefully interpreting Hamlet's soliloquies, Coleridge observes that "such a mind as Hamlet's is near akin to madness."[2] He affirms, yet fears, their kinship.

The Marginalia to the text of *Hamlet* provide an opportunity of reading, as it were, over Coleridge's shoulder. In one note dated January 7, 1819, Coleridge states Hamlet's central importance for his own career: "*Hamlet* was the play, or rather Hamlet himself was the character in the intuition and exposition of which I first made my turn for philosophical criticism, and especially for insight into the genius of Shakespeare, *noticed*" (*SC* I, 16). Coleridge notices Hamlet "especially for insight into the genius of Shakespeare," leaving ambiguous whether "genius " refers to Shakespeare's creative powers or to his mind. Hamlet is, for Coleridge, both an exemplary expression

[2]Samuel Taylor Coleridge, *Shakespearean Criticism*, 2d ed., ed. Thomas Middleton Raysor (London: J. M. Dent, 1960), vol. 2, p. 152 (henceforth cited as *SC*).

of Shakespearean dramatic method and a reflection of Shakespeare himself. In Hamlet, the style and psychology of genius come together. "I have a smack of Hamlet myself, if I may say so," Coleridge hazards to confess in the *Table Talk* of June 24, 1827.[3] He describes Hamlet's character as "the prevalence of the abstracting and generalizing habit over the practical," just as he had earlier referred to Hamlet's "predominant idealism" and "ratiocinative meditativeness" (*SC* I, 22). Coleridge admires "Shakespeare's mode of conceiving characters out of his own intellectual and moral faculties," and insistently returns to "The Character of Hamlet" (*SC* I, 34). He accepts the dramatic illusion and discerns the cause of Hamlet's excesses: the outward and the inward fail to balance.

A Lecture of 1812 asks, "What then was the point to which Shakespeare directed himself in Hamlet?" Coleridge's response elaborates the dialectics of self-presentation: "He intended to pourtray [*sic*] a person, in whose view the external world, and all its incidents and objects, were comparatively dim, and of no interest in themselves, and which began to interest only, when they were reflected in the mirror of his mind" (*SC* II, 150). Shakespeare projects himself onto Hamlet, who in turn reflects the world "in the mirror of his mind." Yet Coleridge's interest in Hamlet is similar to Hamlet's interest in the world, as a reflection of himself. Furthermore, Coleridge's account of the "mirror of the mind" hints at Richard III's impulse to view his "shadow in the sun" (*Richard III*, I.i.26; cp. I.ii.262–63), which unites psychology and performance. Coleridge does not only allude to the narcissism of perception that is reflected in an internal mirror, a displacement of the tabula rasa. He alludes to Wordsworth's "emotion recollected in tranquillity" and the final lines in the poem "I wandered lonely as a cloud" when he comments that "Hamlet beheld external things in the same way that a man of vivid imagination, who shuts his eyes, sees what has previously made an impression on his organs" (*SC* II, 150). But Coleridge's perceptual afterimage is a reflection of Shakespeare or Hamlet.

While he enthusiastically praises Hamlet, Coleridge never dissimulates the identification by which he discovers himself in Shakespeare's genius. He claims a basic affinity with Hamlet; his interpretations equally invent a Hamlet who has more than a smack

---

[3]*Table Talk of Samuel Taylor Coleridge* (London: George Routledge, 1884), 56.

of Coleridge. Reflecting on him, Coleridge finds the locus of interest in Hamlet's existence to be a "mirror of his mind," a mirror that reflects its interpreter and catches the projection of its creator. The hall of mirrors superimposes images of Shakespeare, Hamlet, and Coleridge. But by attending to the personal image of his precursor, Coleridge conceals his debt to Hamlet's characteristic form, the soliloquy, the starting point of Coleridge's poetic strength.

The Scene and Moment of Monologue

Coleridge's first literary successes, the conversation poems, are like Shakespearean soliloquies that have been freed from dramatic form. Coleridge obliquely transposes a set of conventions already centuries old. Coleridge's conversation poems are continuous with a more recent mode to the extent that they are "in the Augustan vein."[4] Yet Coleridge's conversation poems dissimulate their poetic nature—unlike the excessively "poetic" poems of Gray, Collins, and Cowper. Far closer to theatrical soliloquy, the conversation poems set a scene that takes the place of dramatic context. Coleridge's first-person speakers become the center of an implicit, unwritten drama.

"Conversation poem" is first of all an oxymoron. Conversations are not poems, nor are poems conversations. All pretense, the conversation poem creates a fictional scene in which a persona "speaks." The entire scenario is an illusion generated by poetic "voice," and Coleridge's conversation poems characteristically reveal their deception by wandering toward imaginative extremes. The fictive conversational voice returns to the initial scene only after following Hamlet's example and engaging in flights of fancy.

Coleridge's conversation poems work as invocations of presence, where the imagination acts as muse to invoke the poetic voice. "The Eolian Harp," according to one contemporary critic, "collapses in a self-surrender that augurs badly for the Imagination."[5] Yet Coleridge's early poetic monologues succeed precisely through their presentation of a poetic voice, a feigned presence that redirects the conventions

[4]Walter Jackson Bate, *Coleridge* (New York: Macmillan, 1968), 46.
[5]Harold Bloom, *The Visionary Company*, 2d ed. (Ithaca: Cornell University Press, 1971), 202.

of Shakespearean drama. Coleridge introduces novel conventions to create poems that "affect not to be poetry."

"The Eolian Harp," in *Poems on Various Subjects* (1796), was originally entitled "Effusion XXXV, Composed August 20th, 1795, at Clevedon, Somersetshire." The title links the scene of composition with that of the poetic persona, insisting that the poem be read as a kind of lived soliloquy. But the details of time and place only conceal the poem's literary pretense. The actual date and location of composition are not necessarily relevant to the imaginary scene of a monological speaker.[6]

On the surface, "The Eolian Harp" cannot be considered a monologue. The conversational voice addresses another person, as does the speaker in Shakespeare's sonnets, but within an explicit scene of discourse. What scene of dialogue does the poetic voice project? Peculiarities of the conversational pretense become obvious as soon as we attempt to specify the mode of speech it purports to represent. This is an odd scene in which apparently not a single word is spoken aloud (except perhaps those suggested by EH 52–54). By means of direct address and synecdoche, the opening lines describe and create a pose of intimacy: "My pensive Sara! thy soft cheek reclined / Thus on mine arm." The "I" addresses Sara either silently within an imaginary scene or imaginatively within a scene of writing. Coleridge activates a variety of illusions, freed from dramatic forms, such that the monologue hovers ambiguously between represented imagination (the poem's speaker is silently together with Sara) and imagined representation (the poem's author writes of himself and Sara). Verbless, indefinite in time, the words present a reciprocal contact in which there can be no final distinction between literary and real personae.

At all levels of illusion, the scene expands from the point of intimate contact to the lovers' surroundings. Spatial description combines with a hint at the recent past:

> most soothing sweet it is
> To sit beside our Cot, our Cot o'ergrown
> With white-flowered Jasmin, and the broad-leav'd Myrtle,
> (Meet emblems they of Innocence and Love!)
> And watch the clouds, that late were rich with light,

---

[6]"The Eolian Harp" (henceforth EH) is quoted from Coleridge's *Poetical Works*, ed. Ernest Hartley Coleridge (Oxford: Oxford University Press, 1912).

> Slow saddening round, and mark the star of eve
> Serenely brilliant (such should Wisdom be)
> Shine opposite!
> > [EH 2–9]

The sunset reflects the speaker's fantasy in a "soothing sweet" mood that finds sadness and serenity in nature. The following lines turn from sky to earth and from vision to smell and sound:

> > How exquisite the scents
> Snatch'd from yon bean-field! and the world *so* hushed!
> The stilly murmur of the distant Sea
> Tells us of silence.
> > [EH 9–12]

A homonymic play confuses worldly "scents" with subjective "sense," for the speaker cannot separate the language that represents objective scents from language that presents subjective sense. The demonstrative phrase, "yon bean-field," like "Thus" in line 2, signals the presupposed scene of intimacy. Exquisite scents (and sense) lead to a proclamation of "the world *so* hushed!" Paradoxically, the poetic voice refers to the "murmur of the distant Sea" that "tells us of silence." A sound, when written, bears silence. Coleridge's conversational voice is like the sea's murmur that speaks a silent communication.

The subsequent description of the Lute is a figure of poetic imagination. The wind harp stands as an emblem for the entire poem:

> > And that simplest Lute,
> Placed length-ways in the clasping casement, hark!
> How by the desultory breeze caressed,
> Like some coy maid half yielding to her lover.
> > [EH 12–15]

According to the familiar Romantic image, the poetic speaker should identify with the Lute as the muse plays upon his imagination. But images mirror each other as the harp's solo reverses the scene of the poem. In the figured reversal, Sara becomes associated with the Lute, which is "like some coy maid half yielding to her lover." Figurative development gradually detaches the speaker from his initial scene; the metaphorical relation further transforms the speaker's words into a natural breeze that caresses Sara. In a sense, the speaker takes the place of his muse.

Four moments of imaginative abstraction increasingly distance the poetic speaker from the initial scene (EH 17–25, 26–33, 34–43, 44–48) until Sara interrupts. Exclamations of pretended emotion characterize the speaker's monologue. The direction of causation is reversed, however, as an elaborate fantasy within fantasy returns the speaker to the Lute:

> And thus, my Love! as on the midway slope
> Of yonder hill I stretch my limbs at noon,
> Whilst through my half-clos'd eye-lids I behold
> The sunbeams dance, like diamonds, on the main,
> And tranquil muse upon tranquillity;
> Full many a thought uncall'd and undetain'd,
> And many idle flitting phantasies,
> Traverse my indolent and passive brain
> As wild and various as the random gales
> That swell and flutter on this subject Lute!
>
> [EH 34–43]

At first, the Lute sounds in the silence of the poetic scene; finally, the Lute reappears within an imaginative context, as a figure for the "idle flitting phantasies" that "traverse my indolent and passive brain." The poetic mind becomes an object of description, while the Lute becomes subject—to tropological modification.

Following several acceptable images, the poetic voice indulges in an excess. The fiction of the scene makes Sara's "more serious eye" the source of correction, calling the speaker back from visions of the "inward eye." The infraction is not so much that of "vain Philosophy" as of abstraction from acceptable theology. Sara's response, apparently as silent as the poetic fantasy, also calls the speaker back to her, "Meek Daughter in the family of Christ" (EH 53). The speaker learns that God is not an appropriate object of fantasy. At his most literal, then, the speaker addresses Sara by placing her in a religious tradition. He further revalues the silence that opens the poem when he discovers that "never guiltless may I speak of him / The Incomprehensible" (EH 58–59). Multiple pretenses allow a fictional present to be infused by intimations of diverse absences; monologue as a poetic device suggests a scene of imaginary address.

The imagery of "Frost at Midnight," in contrast to the spatial im-

agery of the poem that purports to have been "Composed at Clevedon, Somersetshire," works through temporal fantasies toward the
strengthened illusion of monological presence. The midnight speaker
weaves together past reminiscences, the present moment, and future
anticipations. Invoked presences intersect at midnight, a meeting of
yesterday, today, tomorrow. "Frost at Midnight" also creates the
illusion of a solitude more radical than that of "The Eolian Harp,"
for the speaker only addresses his sleeping child.[7] Neither speaker
appears entirely alone, but as the speaker of "Frost at Midnight"
observes,

> The inmates of my cottage, all at rest,
> Have left me to that solitude, which suits
> Abstruser musings.
>
> [FM 4–6]

"Frost at Midnight" is comparable to a Shakespearean soliloquy
without theatrical context. The drama of internal turmoil or "abstruser
musing" animates Colderidge's conversation poems, as when a mysterious natural scenario opens the midnight monologue:

> The Frost performs its secret ministry
> Unhelped by any wind. The owlet's cry
> Came loud—and hark, again! loud as before.
>
> [FM 1–3]

The "secret ministry" of frost eludes perception, apparently creating
ex nihilo. At this troubled moment, no imaginative wind activates
poetic creation, whether figured as eolian melodies or as ice crystals.
By projection or identification, frost at midnight is also the poet at
midnight; the poem works through the speaker's effort to achieve
reassurance through figuration. Whereas the speaker of "The Eolian
Harp" is inspired by his surroundings, the speaker of "Frost at Midnight" experiences difficulties that equally derive from his
environment:

> 'Tis calm indeed! so calm, that it disturbs
> And vexes meditation with its strange

[7] I shall cite "Frost at Midnight" (henceforth FM) from Coleridge's *Poetical Works*, ed.
Ernest Hartley Coleridge.

> And extreme silentness. Sea, hill, and wood,
> This populous village! Sea, and hill, and wood,
> With all the numberless goings-on of life,
> Inaudible as dreams!
>
> [FM 8–13]

Solitude at first "suits / Abstruser musings," but excessive calm "disturbs / And vexes meditation." Starting from the mysterious rite of
natural creation, the poetic voice presents the corresponding human
form of imaginative creation, linked to nature by the relation of father
and son. The speaker is unsettled by an uncanny presence: " 'Tis
calm indeed! so calm, that it disturbs / And vexes meditation." An
indefinite "it" eludes comprehension, and the speaker falls into baf-
fled repetition of "sea, and hill, and wood." Negative description of
the "numberless" and "inaudible" surroundings press the speaker
toward paralysis until he invents a presence, like the Lute, that initiates further poetic development.

The speaker, who like Coleridge's Hamlet seeks reflections of his
own mind, makes an ash in his fireplace into a "companionable form":

> the thin blue flame
> Lies on my low-burnt fire, and quivers not;
> Only that film, which fluttered on the grate,
> Still flutters there, the sole unquiet thing.
> Methinks, its motion in this hush of nature
> Gives it dim sympathies with me who live,
> Making it a companionable form,
> Whose puny flaps and freaks the idling Spirit
> By its own moods interprets, every where
> Echo or mirror seeking of itself,
> And makes a toy of Thought.
>
> [FM 13–23]

Coleridge is aware that the "idling Spirit" has a propensity to interpret
as an "Echo or mirror seeking of itself." Poetic creation is also, for
such a speaker, the activity of a voice that seeks realization through
poetry.

If "The Eolian Harp" operates by figurative abstraction to fantastic
imagery, "Frost at Midnight" works backward and forward in time
to establish the continuity between father and son. Like the opening
of "The Eolian Harp," stanza 3 addresses another:

> Dear Babe, that sleepest cradled by my side,
> Whose gentle breathings, heard in this deep calm,
> Fill up the interspersèd vacancies
> And momentary pauses of the thought!
>
> [FM 43–47]

The child's breathing, unlike Sara's reproving glance, is a sheer rhetorical bridge between "the interspersèd vacancies / And momentary pauses of the thought." The speaker identifies with the film on the grate; then, recognizing the arbitrariness of this figurative identification, he establishes a more "natural" trope, in which his son acts to fuse past, present, and future. No interruption curtails the processes of fantasy:

>   it thrills my heart
> With tender gladness, thus to look at thee,
> And think that thou shalt learn far other lore,
> And in far other scenes! For I was reared
> In the great city, pent 'mid cloisters dim,
> And saw nought lovely but the sky and stars.
> But *thou*, my babe! shalt wander like a breeze
> By lakes and sandy shores, beneath the crags
> Of ancient mountain.
>
> [FM 48–56]

The speaker of "The Eolian Harp" loses sight of Sara, but the speaker of "Frost at Midnight" makes the "Dear Babe" central to his imaginative affirmation. In a sense, the child becomes the speaker's inspiring "breeze." The final stanza projects further into the future, at the same time that a rhetorical device completes the circle, returning to the first line and present of the poem:

> Therefore all seasons shall be sweet to thee,
>   . . . whether the eave-drops fall
> Heard only in the trances of the blast,
> Or if the secret ministry of frost
> Shall hang them up in silent icicles,
> Quietly shining to the quiet Moon.
>
> [FM 65–74]

The troubling "secret ministry" is redefined in service to a poetic trance that dominates the naturalistic imagery. The midnight scene becomes a place of creation, with icicle poems created in the light of the moon.

Coleridge writes soliloquies that continue, and yet finally abscond from, the dramatic tradition. The conversation poem feigns representational space and time in order to present a situated, lyrical monologue. Ultimately, the written form of conversational poetry only feigns to be voice, but the imaginative representation of presences can create a compelling illusion of the speaking subject. If the conversation poem pretends not to be poetry, it aims at the pretense of a speaking subject whose imagination transposes private experience into an accessible poetic form.

Voices of Decay

"Kubla Khan," the culmination of Coleridge's conversation poems, both employs and destroys the conversational mode. Replete with exclamations that indicate a presumed immediacy of feeling, Coleridge's strongest short poem no longer begins with a corresponding, intimate scene. Rather than present a scene of intimacy as the point of departure for imaginative wanderings, "Kubla Khan" opens with a fantastic landscape of Xanadu. The speaker's present is initially an absence from the poem, a lack that Coleridge's preface counters by describing the conditions of composition. But Coleridge presents a most peculiar scene of composition, in which the words of the poem purportedly accompany private imagery of a dream. On one level, the conversation poems strive to represent commonplace domestic situations, while "Kubla Khan" breaks off its elaborate fantasy in conjunction with a threat of madness.

The prose preface operates as do the opening lines of "The Eolian Harp" and "Frost at Midnight," delineating a place and time of creative activity. Whereas the conversation poems only implicitly represent the moment of writing in their scenes of monologue, the preface explicitly discusses the genealogy of "Kubla Khan." Narrating a scene of interruption, the preface fosters the conception of "Kubla Khan" as "a vision in a dream" that has been only partially recovered by waking memory.

Although prefaces are conventionally more literal than poems, critics have doubted the accuracy of Coleridge's autobiographical data.

A naive reading wishes to accept the preface as an accurate description of the scene of composition,[8] while a more sober reading concludes that it is unreliable.[9] If we recognize preface and poem as equal literary fictions, however, neither half of Coleridge's double text merits special status. Both preface and poem voice a pseudoautobiographical "I," a parallel that unsettles the facile dichotomy between prose and verse as literal (or referential) and figurative (or fictional). Preface and poem unsettle the conventional notions of representational correspondence in different genres. Too marvelous for strict autobiography, but not too literal for fiction, the preface need not depend on a pretension to autobiographical truth.

The preface, "Of the Fragment of Kubla Khan," insistently refers to "the following fragment," emphasizing a part-whole relationship between present words and some unspecified totality. Coleridge denies independent status to the poem "Kubla Khan," perhaps because it breaks the familiar pattern of the conversation poems. The synecdoche is accompanied by a perspectivizing allusion to "a poet of great and deserved celebrity," whose estimation of the poem contrasts the author's. Is the fragment great or small, heavy or light? "Fragments" also "vaulted like rebounding hail" in line 21 of the poem, before compared with "chaffy grain beneath the thresher's flail." The *ground* of this literary fragment shows itself to be as unsteady as are the fragments in "that deep romantic chasm" and will not support weightier pretensions. The fragment is published, "as far as the Author's own opinions are concerned, rather as a psychological curiosity, than on the ground of any supposed *poetic* merits" (Pr. 1).[10] The request of Lord Byron, whose fame appears secure, provides ground for publication, even if not on the basis of "*poetic* merits."

If "Kubla Khan" is a "psychological curiosity," the preface further insists on the authenticity of its narrative by citing purportedly real chronology and geography (Pr. 2). Yet Coleridge discusses the poem's "Author" at a distance suggested by the third-person form. The language of cause and effect, illness and cure, add to an impression of

[8]See John Livingston Lowes, *The Road to Xanadu: A Study in the Ways of Imagination* (New York: Houghton Mifflin, 1927).
[9]See Elisabeth Schneider, *Coleridge, Opium, and Kubla Khan* (New York: Octagon, 1966).
[10]I cite the preface ("Pr.") by sentence number and the poem ("KK") by line number as they appear in Coleridge's *Poetical Works*, ed. Ernest Hartley Coleridge.

necessity in the narrated events: "In consequence of a slight indis-
position, an anodyne had been prescribed, from the effects of which
he fell asleep in his chair at the moment that he was reading the
following sentence, or words of the same substance, in 'Purchas's
Pilgrimage': 'Here the Khan Kubla commanded a palace to be built,
and a stately garden thereunto. And thus ten miles of fertile ground
were inclosed with a wall' " (Pr. 3–4). The author reads Kubla's command at the moment when a drug induces sleep, allowing him to
evade the problems of conscious borrowing. The poem's allusions are
thus casually ascribed to the influence of a virtually unconscious reading rather than to a controlled act of writing. Purchas' words appear
to ground Coleridge's fragment more firmly than do "*poetic* merits."
Sleep further frees the author from responsibilities associated with
deliberate action: "The Author continued for about three hours in a
profound sleep, at least of the external senses" (Pr. 5). If Coleridge
as dreamer does not consciously control the act of composition, an
external-internal opposition gives his creativity the appearance of self-
generation.

By describing a three-stage procedure, Coleridge effectively traces
"Kubla Khan" to a creative act based on unconscious processes.

Step 1, *dream composition*, is also not composition, because the author "could not have composed less than from two to three hundred
lines; if that indeed can be called composition in which all the images
rose up before him as *things*, with a parallel production of the correspondent expressions, without any sensation or consciousness of
effort" (Pr. 5). Can that be called composition "in which all the images
rose up before him as *things*"? The previous images of "substance,"
"ground," and "fragment" suggest an affinity between physical and
textual realities; here the extraordinarily substantial images may be
either visual or poetic. The visionary moment is itself presumably
extralinguistic, because Coleridge writes of a "parallel production of
the correspondent expressions." Simultaneous with but not equivalent to the images, the correspondent expressions appear as if naturally or necessarily linked to what they express. Although words
suggest themselves in parallel, the narrator indicates that the unu-
sually concrete images are his primary impression. In contrast to this
claim, the underlying *poetic* meaning of "images" keeps his "vision"
in literary bounds from the start. The ambiguous "image" begins to

undo the primary claim of an effortless vision that naturally gives rise to correspondent expressions.

Step 2, *transcription* of the dream composition, follows immediately, when the author "appeared to himself to have a distinct recollection of the whole, and taking his pen, ink and paper, instantly and eagerly wrote down the lines that are here preserved" (Pr. 6). The instantaneous impulse to write implies that the poetic lines precisely reproduce the dreamed expressions. Unlike the prolonged dream period of "about three hours," the secondary scene of writing condenses into an instant. There is no need to judge whether the fifty-four crafted lines of "Kubla Khan" could actually be instantly or automatically composed: Coleridge's claim to a later, synchronic "recollection of the whole" is an aspect of his double text. The alleged instantaneous scene of writing strives to unify the diachronic process during which "all the images rose up before him as *things*." This moment captures the dream sequence as a simultaneous order, admitting no break until the author completes "the lines that are here preserved."[11]

Step 3, *interruption*, occurs as suddenly as does the transcription. The "moment" of reading already appears in sentence 3 when the author "fell asleep in his chair at the moment that he was reading the following sentence." The necessity of a secondary act of reading, or dream interpretation, shows itself with the event of interruption. The published preface eludes any intimation of deliberate craft, however, by reducing the time interval to a moment: "At this moment he was unfortunately called out by a person on business from Porlock,

---

[11] A manuscript note unpublished until 1934 calls into question the claim to a genetic unity of "Kubla Khan." It similarly raises questions about the conscious intentions of a drugged subject but makes steps 1 and 2 appear to form part of the same process, for "a sort of Reverie" is contemporaneous with the act of composition: "This fragment with a good deal more, not recoverable, composed in a sort of Reverie brought on by two grains of Opium, taken to check a dysentery, at a Farm House between Porlock & Linton, a quarter of a mile from Culbone Church, in the fall of the year, 1797." Probably written long before the Preface of 1816, this note is cited by Schneider, *Coleridge, Opium, and Kubla Khan*, 24–25. In discussing the double text of "Kubla Khan" as published, rather than the "facts" of its composition, we do not need to take the manuscript note into consideration. But the earlier, less extravagant version interestingly contrasts the dualistic account of a dream followed by recollection; steps 1 and 2 appear to take place simultaneously. The preface narrator emphasizes an immediate "vision" that is directly accompanied by a corresponding voice; "This fragment . . . composed in a sort of Reverie" only grammatically omits the speaker ("I") from his act of composition and leaves the possibility of deliberate creation.

and detained by him above an hour" (Pr. 7). The dream and period of detainment both have measurable durations, but the transcription seems to break off in the midst of its lightning-fast burst. The preface subsequently refers to "the vision" retrospectively; on returning to his room, the author "found, to his no small surprise and mortification, that though he still retained some vague and dim recollection of the general purport of the vision, yet, with the exception of some eight or ten scattered lines and images, all the rest had passed away like images on the surface of a stream into which a stone has been cast, but, alas! without the after restoration of the latter!" (Pr. 7). The mention of dissolving images affirms the independent, picturelike quality of an initial vision. But the speaker's subsequent "mortification" establishes a gloomier connection between the fading vision and loss of life: *mortificare* is to cause to die. The interruption of the processes of writing is a symbolic death, especially for the older Coleridge, who knows that he has lost his poetic genius.

As if to revise the preceding simile and derive new assurance, the preface cites ten lines from Coleridge's poem "The Picture." This allusion is part of the effort to ground "Kubla Khan" visually. A "poor youth" suffers a loss like that of the narrator, and "then all the charm / Is broken—all that phantom-world so fair / Vanishes" (Pr. 8). But for the youth of "The Picture," in a narcissistic fantasy, natural events restitute what has been lost:

> The stream will soon renew its smoothness, soon
> The visions will return! . . .
> And soon the fragments dim of lovely forms
> Come trembling back, unite, and now once more
> The pool becomes a mirror.
> [Pr. 9–10]

Coleridge's conversation poems and reading of Hamlet similarly revolve around this quest after a mirror of the self. For the preface narrator, however, the metaphor fails: although he retains "some vague and dim recollection" of the vision, his fragments do not unite. In the narrative that describes the author's dream and transcription, the disruption is nonreversible and does not end in restoration. Falling short of the author's "phantom-world," the preface only mirrors another text.

The final paragraph of the preface contrasts the author's deliberate intentions and his spontaneous creation: "from the still surviving recollections in his mind, the Author has frequently purposed to finish for himself what had been originally, as it were, given to him" (Pr. 11). The author's sleep writing takes on the aura of an inspired moment, "given" by unexplainable forces and inaccessible to conscious intentions. The preface thus claims that "Kubla Khan" is an inspired fragment never resumed after its abrupt interruption. The closing sentence projects a hypothetical future and readership by citing Theocritus' words, "I'll sing to you a sweeter song another day" (later emended to "I'll sing to you a sweeter song tomorrow"). Like the final lines of the poem, this final proleptic awareness combines positive anticipation with a negative moment: "but the to-morrow is yet to come."

The last stanza of "Kubla Khan" does not appear to derive from the same effortless, unreflective impulse that allegedly produces "the lines that are here preserved." Thus critics have been as skeptical of the poem's formal unity as doubtful of its genetic unity. Several interpreters consider the poem to be divided into two disparate parts, before and after the shift to first person in the third stanza.[12] According to the critical cliché, an impersonal voice describes Kubla's pleasure dome and grounds, after which a first-person speaker recalls a past vision, loosely associated with Xanadu. Based on the shift in "vision" that occurs in the last stanza, this received idea ignores the complications of the middle stanza, yet a two-part structure of the poem is commonly admitted.

In the closing lines of the poem, a first-person voice presents an alternative version of origins. Like the preface, these lines interpret the mysteries of vision: "A damsel with a dulcimer / In a vision once I saw" (KK 37–38). Discontinuous with previous descriptions by the first stanza, these words implicate the speaker in his visionary experience and locate the vision at a distinct, past time. The dream is over. No longer speaking as if the forests were "here" and the gardens "there," the nostalgic voice recollects something that is no longer

---

[12]Schneider, *Coleridge, Opium, and Kubla Khan*, 242–47; Walter Jackson Bate, *Coleridge* (New York: Macmillan, 1968), 78; George Watson, *Coleridge the Poet* (London: Routledge and Kegan Paul, 1966), 124. One exception is an article by Alan Purves, "Formal Structure in 'Kubla Khan,' " *Studies in Romanticism*, 1 (1962), 187–91. On the basis of formal analysis, Purves concludes that the poem is finished and unified and that any further continuation would destroy its symmetrical precision.

immediately present, even to imagination. The first appearance of Kubla's world emphasizes the visual, but the damsel vision attends to sound:

> It was an Abyssinian maid,
> And on her dulcimer she played,
> Singing of Mount Abora.
> [KK 39–41]

A new set of proper names displaces Xanadu, Kubla, and Alph.[13] The modified proper names, like the damsel's song, introduce additional words into the vision. As his earlier imaginative scene is superseded, the speaker loses his referential assurance, breaks off his representational pretense, and tries to recall the song of his imaginary figure: the Abyssinian Maid sings of a place, in a referential mode. Rather than strive to regain his attempted correspondence to immediate vision, the speaker gives up his own song in order to seek hers:

> Could I revive within me
> Her symphony and song,
> To such a deep delight 'twould win me,
> That with music loud and long,
> I would build that dome in air,
> That sunny dome! those caves of ice!
> [KK 42–47]

An imagined recollection of the damsel's music replaces the visions of Xanadu. But the relationship between damsel and dome is mysterious: what does the new vision have in common with the old? If the visions are linked, why is the damsel absent from Kubla's domain? The speaker's imagined damsel, playing her "sweet" instrument, contrasts the "woman wailing" he projects into Kubla's turbulent pleasure grounds. The speaker implicitly acknowledges the instability of poetic constructs when he anticipates building "that dome in air."

As he longs to regain his lost vision, the speaker echoes intentions stated by the preface: "from the still surviving recollections in his mind, the Author has frequently purposed to finish for himself what

---

[13]Could this "Alph" be the first letter of the Hebrew (or Greek) alphabet, making the sacred river a sacred language that flows "through caverns measureless to man"?

had been originally, as it were, given to him." As in the citation from Theocritus (Pr. 12), completion depends on the existence of an imagined audience: "And all who heard should see them there." The audience retraces the sequence of the author's creative process: his vision gives him a voice, and their hearing produces a visionary sight. Could the author speak his vision, the private would become public, establishing a previously isolated vision as a common referent. At the same time, the speaker would be perceived as mad and banished to a circle for the purposes of exorcism.

This hypothetical communication would be incomprehensible, and provoke excommunication, because the audience could only respond with fear: "all should cry, Beware! Beware! / His flashing eyes, his floating hair!" (KK 48–49). The speaker is inscribed in the prosopopoeia that presents others' imaginary discourse, and hearers try to remedy the inspired state he now has them represent and invoke. The previous occurrence of things visionary makes relevant a warning to "weave a circle round him thrice, / And close your eyes with holy dread." Suddenly the auditor-speakers are like Kubla: they seek to enclose the threatening poet, as Kubla's decrees try to secure his pleasure grounds. A reversal takes place: whereas the speaker earlier identifies with Kubla and the poetic effort to stabilize a dome of pleasure, now he and his vision specifically endanger customary boundaries. Once the speaker renounces efforts to build on ground, instead seeking to "build that dome in air," he is associated with the destabilizing forces that undo Kubla's pleasure. Deviation from the conversational mode unleashes dangerous forces. The radicalized mode of monologue, a self-referential innovation that pretends to present the language of a dream, threatens to overturn the entire monological reference.

Similar to the second half of the preface, the final stanza of "Kubla Khan" recognizes that the vision has faded. The preface explicitly narrates the scene of interruption and accepts the poem as a fragment. The poem, however, only implies and does not directly acknowledge the disappearance of vision. Without thematizing this loss, the speaker attempts to recuperate what has gone or rather considers the possible consequences of such a recuperation. The imagined speech of auditors at first affirms the preceding visionary stanzas, yet their response also works against affirmation. Because "I cannot" is implied by the conditional statement that begins, "Could I," the first two stanzas are undermined.[14] If the poet cannot "build that dome in air," then the speaker himself judges his rendering of Xanadu unsuccessful. At the moment the voice reads and speaks its own failure to represent, the fictional pretense is undone and the poem ends. Though the poem ultimately strives for assurance, its final prosopopoeia narrates as complete a deterioration as the preface, only figuratively. While the preface unifies the poem by linking it to a single scene of writing, the final stanza of the poem shifts scenes as it projects voices and intensifies the speaker's retrospective confession of dissolution. The preface recalls a visionary writing that is abruptly disrupted; the poem (p)refigures this external interruption as an internalized self-undoing.

Coleridge's conversational poems and "Kubla Khan" exemplify one stage in the shifting traditions of literary monologue. Expressing a particular moment in time and treating "Kubla Khan" as a psychological curiosity, Coleridge presents a text that purports to transcribe mental processes. Romantic and post-Romantic monologues combine lyrical voice and dramatic scene to create a moment of feigned discourse, on the boundary between writing and representation.

Coleridge's conversation poems turn against their origins in Shakespearean soliloquy. Because the fictive speaker does not form part of a dramatic scenario, this persona is haunted by an absence that inheres in its pretense. "Kubla Khan" brings an end to the naive conversational mode, which it interrupts through the final acknowledgment: the dream is over. Whereas the conversation poems affirm the solitary voice, "Kubla Khan" shows its inadequacy, as it succumbs to a combination of external and internal pressures. The monologist, compelled to follow the peculiar constraints of written conversation, tends to lose touch with mimetic conventions. Pointing the way beyond Hamlet and toward poetic monologues by Shelley and Browning, "Kubla Khan" uncovers the affinity between monologue and

---

[14]Humphry House, *Coleridge: The Clark Lectures, 1951–52* (London: Rupert Hart-Davis, 1967), 115, and Marshall Suther, *Visions of Xanadu* (New York: Columbia University Press, 1967), 275, interpret "Could I" as "I can." Carl R. Woodring, "Coleridge and the Khan," in *Essays in Criticism*, 9 (1959), 362, opposes House and interprets "Could I" as signifying "I cannot." This ambiguity adds to the differential scar that sets the poem in contrast to the prose statement of incompletion. Can a text appropriate the story its tropes tell, by thematizing substitution, negation, interruption, or decay?

madness.[15] As developed by nineteenth-century authors, the conventions of poetic monologue both create and disrupt the illusion of
a speaking subject. Monologue as a rhetorical swerve joins with monologue as a fiction of solitude. Mad monologues gradually displace
the eolian monologue of meditation and move toward a new literary
type that finds further expression in first-person narratives.

[15]See, for example, Shelley's "Julian and Maddalo" and Browning's "Madhouse
Cells."

7 Poe's Narrative Monologues

Edgar Allan Poe's narrative monologues border on madness and disrupt the normally associated conventions of voice. Monologue is solitary speech, whether physically isolated, morally deviant, or semantically opaque; Poe's strongest narrators are not only solitary human beings, for as a fictive consequence of the criminal acts they narrate, they often speak from solitary confinement. But while his narrators appear isolated and deviant, Poe's narratives themselves swerve away from norms. An initial problem is to distinguish between the narrative conventions Poe borrows, transforms, and creates, because the superficially popular genre of his fiction conceals the relationship to English literary tradition. By emphasizing the intensity of reader experience above all else, Poe himself neglects literary history, yet even the most emotionally charged reception of a text is made possible by literary context. Although Poe does respond to conventions of the Gothic novel, his revision of epistolary narrative and conversational poetry is more decisive.

Poe's most compelling fictions succeed as representations of diverse and often pathological characters.[1] Yet if we suspect that consciousness, in literature, is "a fictive appearance generated by language,

[1]Compare David Halliburton's *Edgar Allan Poe: A Phenomenological View* (Princeton: Princeton University Press, 1973), 27, 246–47.

rather than something language describes or reflects,"[2] then we must attend to the devices by which fiction creates the illusion of representing a consciousness. Such devices depend on intertextual relations in literary history. The "I" emerges at various stages and in all genres of English literature, including dramatic soliloquy, conversational poetry, and first-person narrative. Whereas the dramatic frame clarifies what it means for a character to say "I," the poetic and narrative "I" raises problems that derive from the disparity between the actual form of writing and the imaginary scene of speaking. Poe revises the conversational mode to present dreams, fantasies, passions, obsessions.[3]

The meaning of first-person narrative in stories by Poe becomes clearer in the context of his eighteenth-century precursors. The earliest epistolary fiction of Samuel Richardson brings the narrator into a peculiar condition of identity with the narrated world. If the surest truth of experience is "I think," the most irrefutable literary assertion is "I write." Yet who is the "I" of such a statement? The fictional "I" creates itself and, simultaneously, its frame. Especially where the letters of only one character constitute a fictional world, there is no clear separation between the narrating persona and the world narrated. After Richardson, then, the scene of writing is an accepted component of the English novel. This scene influences the later development of self-conscious prose and particularly modern internal monologue that pretends to reproduce a scene of unwritten thoughts.

Prior narrative traditions are tame, however, when compared with those introduced by Poe's first-person tales. In a sense, Poe transfers the intensely present "I" of Romantic verse to an analogous "I" of narrative. But his first-person accounts do not merely transpose the conversation poem into a narrative form: Poe's narrated monologues unsettle the representational conventions on which they initially depend. At the same time that a first-person voice reveals exalted states

---

[2]J. Hillis Miller, *The Disappearance of God*, 2d ed. (Cambridge: Harvard University Press, 1975), ix.
[3]Poe's "The Raven" may be viewed as a post-Romantic conversation poem. Taking the colloquial first-person voice for granted, Poe characteristically infuses formal devices of assonance, rhythm, and rhyme. The tensions already present in Coleridge's works are therefore intensified when Poe opposes the mental imbalance of his speaker to the formal precision of his verses.

of consciousness, Poe subverts the realistic pretense by focusing attention on the act of writing. The scene of Poe's greatest originality is the point at which he disrupts the conversational tradition by tampering with the unexamined illusion of narrative voice.

"I write in the present tense"

Apart from the obvious, yet superficial, influence of Gothic novels, Poe is most significantly influenced by the first-person form of epistolary fiction. A first-person "voice" is clearly essential to the genre based on personal letters and diary entries.

Samuel Richardson innovates in a monological vein by producing the epistolary novel *Pamela* (1740). Twentieth-century literary norms make the novelty of Richardson's narrative devices difficult to appreciate: Richardson introduces a genre of self-reflective writing while planting the seeds of its undoing. Early in *Pamela*, for example, the heroine represents her past thoughts in a letter to her parents: "O Pamela, said I to myself, why art thou so foolish and fearful? Thou hast done no harm! What, if thou fearest an unjust judge, when thou are innocent, would'st thou do before a just one, if thou wert guilty? Have courage, Pamela, thou knowest the worst! . . . So I cheered myself; but yet my poor heart sunk, and my spirits were quite broken."[4] Recalling her thoughts in the form of a pseudodialogue at a specific moment, Pamela apparently practices what Shaftesbury calls the "Home-*Dialect* of *Soliloquy*." As Shaftesbury's analysis predicts, the soliloquist becomes "two distinct *Persons*" when Pamela reasons with herself.[5] At the height of perplexity she contemplates suicide and thinks: "Pause here a little, Pamela, on what thou art about, before thou takest the dreadful leap; and consider whether there be no way yet left, no hope, if not to escape from this wicked house, yet from the mischiefs threatened thee in it" (*Pam.* 180). On one level, this passage works as psychological realism that represents a process of thought. At the same time, the pause in Pamela's thoughts is a pause in her narrative of events, like the dramatic monologue Diderot describes as "a moment of repose for the action, and of turmoil for the

---

[4] Samuel Richardson, *Pamela* (New York: W. W. Norton, 1958), 28 (henceforth cited as *Pam.*).
[5] *Char.* I, 170 and 158.

character.'"[6] While these passages represent past thoughts, the narrative form appears to correspond to the represented moment.

Richardson's Pamela also shows a self-conscious awareness of the process of writing. She accounts for her possession of writing materials (*Pam.* 100, 154) and at several points notes her time of composition to the hour. Pamela's activity of writing is, in addition, occasionally interrupted by the world she describes. Amid contemplations, Pamela writes, "But I must break off; here's somebody coming" (*Pam.* 75). Even more vividly, she writes of her feeling of dread and its influence on writing: "Though I dread to see him, yet do I wonder I have not. . . . I can hardly write; yet, as I can do nothing else, I know not how to forbear!—Yet I cannot hold my pen—How crooked and trembling the lines!—I must leave off, till I can get quieter fingers!— "(*Pam.* 191). After Pamela describes her inability to write, the narrative breaks. As the fictional Pamela exists only by virtue of her writing, she literally "can do nothing else." Her peculiar self-awareness only slightly disturbs the representational illusion with the recognition that "Pamela" exists only as a fictive writer. We experience Pamela primarily as a writer, but she remains a realistic character within the fiction.

Richardson's novel explicitly narrates Mr. B's approach to Pamela, and it tells a parallel tale of the reader's approach to her texts. Mr. B must fight to obtain Pamela's writings, a struggle which identifies him with the reader, who now holds the texts that are also objects within the fictional world. Like a sympathetic reader, Mr. B understands and loves Pamela all the more for the words she pens (*Pam.* 242–44); in fact, he only begins to acknowledge the depth of her character through her writing, just as the reader discovers her.

"I write, therefore I am" is the principle of first-person narration. Even for Mr. B, Pamela is most truly herself in her writings. Yet as Mr. B. kidnaps and isolates her, she is pushed toward a mode of writing that is not intended to be read. Pamela cherishes the notion that she can be identical with what she writes and defends herself against charges of insincerity: "I know I write my heart; and that is not deceitful" (*Pam.* 240). The purity of her manuscripts at first depends on their remaining untouched by Mr. B; when he demands to see all she writes, he undermines the very possibility of writing (*Pam.*

[6]Denis Diderot, *De la poésie dramatique* (Paris: Librairie Larousse, 1970), 91.

251). Pamela imagines that she will no longer be able to write "with any face"—or heart?—if she must write without monological isolation, in the expectation of Mr. B's readership. In a sense, then, the novel ought to end as soon as she and Mr. B are united; Pamela writes, of necessity, for only as long as they are separated and she contemplates matters that she must hide from him. The scene of writing is linked to the developments that overcome Pamela's solitude by bringing her closer to the reader and to Mr. B.

Henry Fielding proves to be a genuine critic when he subsequently lambastes the new epistolary fiction in his *Shamela* (1741), revealing the essence of Richardson's narrative monologues by means of comic distortions. *Shamela* does not merely parody *Pamela*'s more obvious quirks, such as the ambiguous character of the heroine. Fielding's caricature pokes fun at the improbable narrative device by which Pamela continues to write during the most heated moments of action, and in so doing, Fielding reveals the nature of Richardson's epistolary form.

One of Shamela's most humorous diary entries, purportedly written "Thursday Night, Twelve o'Clock," may serve as an introduction to Poe's revision of narrative conventions. In a style that obliquely prepares the way for Molly Bloom's internal monologue, Shamela describes events as they occur:

> Mrs. Jervis and I are just in bed, and the door unlocked; if my master should come—Odsbobs! I hear him just coming in at the door. You see I write in the present tense, as Parson Williams says. Well, he is in bed between us, we both shamming a sleep; he steals his hand into my bosom, which I, as if in my sleep, press close to me with mine, and then pretend to awake.—I no sooner see him, but I scream out to Mrs. Jervis, she feigns likewise but just to come to herself; we both begin, she to becall, and I to bescratch very liberally. After having made a pretty free use of my fingers, without any great regard to the parts I attacked, I counterfeit a swoon.[7]

Shamela is a counterfeiter both in bed and in her narrative pretense that suggests simultaneity with narrated action. She can as easily feign an impossible narrative stance as she can "counterfeit a swoon." Thus the parody of Pamela's character combines with a comic exaggeration

---

[7]Henry Fielding, *"Joseph Andrews" and "Shamela,"* ed. Martin C. Battestin (Boston: Houghton Mifflin, 1961), 313. The parallel scene in *Pam.*, Letter 25, does not actually employ the present tense. For comic effect Fielding combines this outrageous scene with the most radical of Richardson's stylistic innovations.

of her manner of writing: Fielding exposes the possibly bizarre consequences of Richardson's innovation. First-person, present-tense writing results in a variety of difficulties, such as the paradoxical illusion that Shamela can simultaneously write her diary and engage in a battle with Mr. B. Nothing in *Pamela* reaches such self-contradictory extremes, of course, yet Fielding aptly captures the potential turns of perversity made possible by Richardson's representations of thought and of moments of writing. One hundred years later, E. A. Poe develops a kindred genre in which diabolical monologists appear menacingly present.

"Why *will* you say that I am mad?"

In one sense, then, Poe's first-person narrators stand firmly in the tradition of epistolary fiction as initiated by Richardson and parodied by Fielding. But when Poe situates his work in relation to tradition, he refers almost exclusively to poetic models. In "The Poetic Principle," Poe establishes both an aesthetic theory and a canon of "English and American poems which best suit my taste."[8] While Poe argues strongly that he has discerned *the* poetic principle, he describes something that he himself invents, in connection with his own poetic preferences. Poe favors short poems of high intensity, on the basis of a "peculiar principle" of psychology:

> a poem deserves its title only inasmuch as it excites, by elevating the soul. The value of the poem is in the ration of this elevating excitement. But all excitements are, through a psychal necessity, transient. That degree of excitement which would entitle a poem to be so called at all, cannot be sustained throughout a composition of any great length. After the lapse of half an hour, at the very utmost, it flags—fails—a revulsion ensues—and then the poem is, in effect, and in fact, no longer such. [*CPS* II, 1021]

On the surface, Poe's principle of literary taste is a "psychal necessity," the human inability to sustain a state of excitement for longer than half an hour. Imposing a half-hour limit that is not literally

[8]E. A. Poe, *The Complete Poems and Stories of Edgar Allan Poe*, ed. Arthur Hobson Quinn and Edward H. O'Neill (New York: Alfred A. Knopf, 1946), vol. 2, p. 1021 (henceforth cited as *CPS*).

necessary, Poe imagines a faintly sexual scene, derived from figurative demands of a literary scene in which the excitement "flags—fails—a revulsion ensues," and the poem loses its status as poem. An emotional coupling between poem and reader takes place. But does the poetic principle really derive from "psychal necessity," or does poetry control psychology? Only superficially do Poe's poetics depend on exclusively psychological principles. If Poe admires verses that produce an exalted state in the mind of the reader, he seeks poetic personae that create illusions of similarly exalted conditions.

The poetic principle of elevating excitement produces a present scene analogous to that of Coleridge's conversational poetry. A moment in the speaker's experience corresponds to the reader's exalted experience. One mode of Poe's writing is, then, a radicalization of the poetic genre Coleridge begins with "The Eolian Harp." In his "Letter to B——," he admires Coleridge's "towering intellect" and "gigantic power" yet adds that "in reading that man's poetry, I tremble like one who stands upon a volcano, conscious from the very darkness bursting from the crater, of the fire and the light that are weltering below" (CPS II, 860). Whereas Coleridge "imprisoned his own conceptions," Poe—for the sake of an exalted half hour—strives to free the bound forces, as in "Tamerlane," the dream poems, "The Raven," "The Sleeper," and "Annabel Lee." Poe's tales present even more powerful first-person presences. Often enough, Poe's narrators are themselves imprisoned, yet in some way liberated by the scene of narration. The liberation of bound forces and representation of an exalted consciousness are initial premises for Poe's fiction. Poe gives free expression to *thanatos*, an impulse toward death or destruction; beyond their scenes of murder, Poe's narrators perform their own self-destruction in dramas linked to "the imp of the perverse."

The deviant narrators of "The Tell-Tale Heart," "The Black Cat," and "The Imp of the Perverse" in some ways extend into short fiction the epistolary and conversational modes developed by Richardson, Coleridge, and their followers. Yet Poe's narrators often confront the representational illusion at the same time that they dispute the superficial claim that they are insane. In Poe's texts, the scene of madness combines with a controlled scene of writing; at exactly this point, Poe destabilizes the genre he assumes: rhetorical forms both constitute and question a conversational pretense.

On one level, Poe's mad monologues may be read as expressions of psychological realism. "The Tell-Tale Heart," for example, presents itself as the spontaneous narrative of a murderer: "True!—nervous—very, very dreadfully nervous I had been and am! but why *will* you say that I am mad? The disease had sharpened my senses—not destroyed—not dulled them. Above all was the sense of hearing acute. I heard all things in the heaven and in the earth. I heard many things in hell. How, then, am I mad? Hearken! and observe how healthily—how calmly I can tell you the whole story" (*CPS* I, 445). As the scene of discourse, we may imagine ourselves in conversation with a confined lunatic. His denial of madness only intensifies the effect of his bizarre claim to have "heard all things in the heaven and in the earth." The opening words imply that we have provoked the speaker by asserting what he denies: far from being insane, he says, "the disease had sharpened my senses," and if we choose to listen, we will share his exalted mood for a few minutes. As soon as we begin to read, then, we find ourselves written into a drama in which we have accused the speaker of being nervous or mad. The narrative opens with a paradox, however, which unsettles the representational illusion. The speaker combines mad assertions with narrative lucidity and presents a disconcerting contradiction between his representing and represented personae. The discrepancy between sane narrator and madman perhaps shows the error of assuming that linguistic normalcy implies psychological normalcy. The narrator is mad, or at least abnormal, according to his own account, because he kills an old man for no reason. He is doubly mad when he imagines he hears the pounding of the dead man's heart and gives away the crime he had concealed. Yet the narrator tells a coherent tale, as if to demonstrate out of spite that he is sane, refuting the ordinary belief that he must be mad. This contradiction overturns mimetic conventions: a literal reading of the mad narrator shows itself to be naive, because only Poe's textual pretense creates the illusion of disparity between madman and sane narrator.

"The Black Cat" follows similar patterns, without the exclamatory wildness of the tell-tale narration. The contradiction is even sharper in "the most wild yet most homely narrative which I am about to pen," for the scene of writing is explicit. Condemned to death, the narrator explains: "To-morrow I die, and to-day I would unburthen my soul. My immediate purpose is to place before the world, plainly, succinctly, and without comment, a series of mere household events.

In their consequences, these events have terrified—have tortured—have destroyed me. Yet I will not attempt to expound them" (*CPS* I, 476). Again Poe invents a situation of radical conflict, in which lurid and lucid details compete. Renouncing all value judgments, the narrator resolves to tell his tale in the most indifferent tones. He explains his peculiar behavior only by reference to a philosophical principle. The speaker has been prone to mysterious states, as when "the fury of a demon instantly possessed me"; the narrator attributes his ultimate downfall to perversity:

> Of this spirit philosophy takes no account. Yet I am not more sure that my soul lives, than I am that perverseness is one of the primitive impulses of the human heart—one of the indivisible primary faculties, or sentiments, which give direction to the character of Man. Who has not, a hundred times, found himself committing a vile or a silly action, for no other reason than because he knows he should *not*? Have we not a perpetual inclination, in the teeth of our best judgment, to violate that which is *Law*, merely because we understand it to be such? [*CPS* I, 478]

Similar to an evil genius, the "spirit of perverseness" appears as a reversal of the *daimonion* that turns Socrates away from evil. The spirit of perverseness inverts, turns upside down, subverts: "It was this unfathomable longing of the soul to *vex itself*—to offer violence to its own nature—to do wrong for the wrong's sake only—that urged me to continue and finally to consummate the injury I had inflicted upon the unoffending brute" (ibid.). Rather than speak of some psychological drive that leads men to evil, the narrator points to an abstract, counterrational impulse to violate whatever is—nature or law. The impulse to perverseness, governed by the rhetorical figure of chiasmus, is a kind of hidden nature in man. The mad narrator undoes himself both through his perverse actions and in his submerged story of textual subversion, a tribute to "the power of words" (*CPS* II, 637). The spirit of perverseness is an anti*daimonion* that turns the speaker against himself; the overt instigator, a black cat, bears the name of Pluto, god of the underworld.

"The Imp of the Perverse" reveals more explicitly the perverse power of words. Half treatise and half tale, the text opens in the tone of philosophical inquiry: "In the consideration of the faculties and impulses—of the *prima mobilia* of the human soul, the phrenologists have failed to make room for a propensity which, although obviously existing as a radical, primitive, irreducible sentiment, has been equally overlooked by all the moralists who have preceded them. In the pure arrogance of the reason, we have all overlooked it." The neglected primum mobile resists the efforts of reason, of perception, of human purpose. Speaking in the tones of rationality, Poe's narrator points to the limits of reason, beyond which our senses must be guided by belief. Experiencing vertigo on the edge of an abyss, we encounter "a shape, far more terrible than any genius or any demon of a tale." A thought takes form: "Because our reason violently deters us from the brink, *therefore* do we the most impetuously approach it" (*CPS* II, 639–40). Rather than call us away from evil, the perverted "genius" presses us toward the abyss. The perverse further opposes reason and systems of good and evil because it can at least appear to "operate in furtherance of good."

The narrator condenses the paradoxical perverseness into a definition: "It is, in fact, a *mobile* without motive, a motive not *motivirt* [*sic*]" (*CPS* II, 638). Displacing comfortable theological beliefs according to which God is the primum mobile, this alternative, an introjected "mobile without motive," upsets all order. The perverse suggests that there can be motion without any rational ground, and even the apparent motive can be without motivation.

By a perverse logic, the entire analytical discourse is transformed when the speaker describes his present situation. Not only does the apparently unmotivated take on motive; perversely, we become visitors to a prison rather than readers of a philosophical discourse:

> I have said thus much, that in some measure I may answer your question, that I may explain to you why I am here, that I may assign to you something that shall have at last the faint aspect of a cause for my wearing these fetters, and for my tenanting this cell of the condemned. Had I not been thus prolix, you might either have misunderstood me altogether; or, with the rabble, have fancied me mad. As it is, you will easily perceive that I am one of the many uncounted victims of the Imp of the Perverse. [*CPS* II, 640]

The speaker denies his madness by calling himself a victim of the principle he has outlined. Yet his language hovers between calculation and illogic. The narrator explains "why I am here . . . wearing these fetters" by reference to a cause that is only a perverse absence of cause. From the standpoint of realistic representation, the perverse narrator betrays his deviance through linguistic peculiarities. He begins his tale: "It is impossible that any deed could have been wrought with a more thorough deliberation. For weeks, for months, I pondered upon the means of the murder" (ibid.). Like the narrator of "The Tell-Tale Heart" who comments that "it is impossible to say how first the idea entered my brain" (*CPS* I, 445), he assumes an understanding of what he has not yet explained. Both fictional speakers break accepted conventions by employing the definite article, where "*the* idea" and "*the* murder" have not been previously explicated. If we read these narrators as mimetic characters, their linguistic deviations may be signs of defective mental processes. From another perspective, however, ill-formed syntax is a contradiction embedded in the narrative by Poe, to enhance the contradictions in the narrator's account.

The narrator undoes himself in a scene of internalized self-address, after the words "I am safe" have become his standard refrain: "One day, whilst sauntering along the streets, I arrested myself in the act of murmuring, half aloud, these customary syllables. In a fit of petulance, I remodelled them thus; 'I am safe—I am safe—yes—if I be not fool enough to make open confession!' " (*CPS* II, 641). Language overthrows him, for as soon as he asserts one thing, the perverse drives him to subvert this rational thesis:

> No sooner had I spoken these words, than I felt an icy chill creep to my heart. I had had some experience in these fits of perversity, (whose nature I have been at some trouble to explain), and I remembered well, that in no instance, I had successfully resisted their attacks. And now my own casual self-suggestion that I might possibly be fool enough to confess the murder of which I had been guilty, confronted me, as if the very ghost of him whom I had murdered—and beckoned me on to death. [*CPS* II, 641]

A rhetorical moment takes the place of all ghosts, when "the imp of the perverse" drives the speaker to confess. "The rabble" would understand his behavior as a symptom of madness, but his perversity turns out to be a reflex inherent in words.

"Ms. Found in a Bottle"

Poe's radical revision of the conversational pretense derives, then, not from the poetic principle of psychological exaltation, but from a rhetorical application of the spirit of perverseness. The mad monologues achieve powerful effects of psychological realism and can be read as the conversations of deranged speakers. Beyond the operation of perverseness in self-destructive behavior, however, Poe's narrators show that language may undermine its own theses. As soon as a murderer tells himself, "I am safe—yes—if I be not fool enough to make open confession" (*CPS* II, 641), he already assures that he will pronounce his doom. In the tradition of the epistolary and confessional novel, several of Poe's short fictions more radically disrupt the conversational mode by recognizing themselves as writing, and the realistic pretense fades.

"Ms. Found in a Bottle" initially confronts the reader with an uncertainty: Is *this* the manuscript found, or will it describe a recovery of some other document in a bottle? The manuscript we read is not, in any obvious sense, found in a bottle. Apparently, the story may be *about* a "Ms. Found in a Bottle," or it may actually *be* this manuscript. The story generates the odd illusion that it exists within itself. A perplexing ambiguity makes impossible any clear distinction between the text that represents and the text that is represented. Midway through the narrative, we are informed: "It was no long while ago that I ventured into the captain's own private cabin, and took thence the materials with which I write, and have written. I shall from time to time continue this journal. It is true that I may not find an opportunity of transmitting it to the world, but I will not fail to make the endeavor. At the last moment I will enclose the MS. in a bottle, and cast it within the sea" (*CPS* I, 133). The bottle is a familiar figure of textuality, of the metonymic relation between form and content, literary container and the thing contained. But the expected configuration is inverted: whereas the container is a bottle within the textual world, what is contained is the text itself. This illusion is also destroyed, however, because the bottle only exists by virtue of the text "inside" that describes its existence. Perversely, the text of "Ms. Found in a Bottle" usurps the world it describes by showing that it is identical with that world. The mimetic convention slips away when the text discloses itself merely as a text; the bottle and the wine merge, the container and the contained become inseparable.

Yet the representational level remains: "At the last moment I will enclose the MS. in a bottle, and cast it within the sea." The text masquerades as an object in the world it represents; Poe, by titling the story, pretends to verify this pretense. Poe also "adds" an epigraph that accords a special status to the words of the desperate writer: "Qui n'a plus qu'un moment à vivre / N'a plus rien à dissimuler" ("One who has only a moment to live / Has nothing more to conceal")." According to this proverb, then, no dissimulation can occur if the writer is on the verge of death. In the final lines of the story, "amid a roaring, and bellowing, and thundering of ocean and tempest," the narrator writes that "the ship is quivering—oh God! and— going down!" At this moment, presumably, the text is enclosed in the bottle, just as the ship is swallowed up by the sea. But the representational illusion is also engulfed as the moment of writing becomes the moment of death: we can never remove the text from its alleged bottle, for text and bottle are identical. According to the rhetorical figure, the inside of the bottle should represent its contained meanings, but the fullest meaning of Poe's story is that this text is identical with its inside, the entire text is its meaning, so that in some sense the bottle can never be uncorked.[9]

The writer or speaker in "The Cask of Amontillado" never reveals his present place, yet he embeds figurative clues within the tale he narrates. In connection with the story of ruthless murder, a first level of allegory makes the unfortunate Fortunato a stand-in for the reader. As readers, our mistake is to think we can confidently, safely uncork a text and savor its wine. Within the representational illusion, Fortunato shows the same *faiblesse*: "He had a weak point—this Fortunato—although in other regards he was a man to be respected and even feared. He prided himself on his connoisseurship in wine" (*CPS* II, 667). The narrator rightly claims that "I did not differ from him materially"—because, of course, both are textual fictions—"and bought largely whenever I could." Yet they do differ: Fortunato prides himself on an ability at wine tasting; the narrator represents himself primarily as a buyer of wines. Fortunato is like a presumptuous literary critic, while Montressor is a writer who stores his textual bottles in endless vaults. While staging Fortunato's death, the narrator figures himself as a writer within the story. Fortunato makes the mistake of wishing to outdo Luchresi, who is reputed to have a fine "critical turn" (ibid.).

As he walks unknowingly toward his tomb, Fortunato laughs and "threw the bottle upward with a gesticulation I did not understand."

[9]Intertextual relations between Poe's "Ms. Found in a Bottle" and Defoe's *Robinson Crusoe* constitute another extramimetic level of meaning, analysis of which is beyond the scope of the present discussion.

This is a potentially troubling moment for the narrator, whose reader has taken the text, or the act of signifying, into his own hands:

> I looked at him in surprise. He repeated the movement—a grotesque one.
> "You do not comprehend?" he said.
> "Not I," I replied.
> "Then you are not of the brotherhood."
> "How?"
> "You are not of the masons." [*CPS* II, 669]

The speaker is troubled by his victim's continued independence. How can the author of a text or scheme respond to such a rebellion? At this provocation, which is like that of an elusive reader, the narrator turns the situation around:

> "You are not of the masons."
> "Yes, yes," I said; "yes, yes."
> "You? Impossible! A mason?"
> "A mason," I replied.
> "A sign," he said.
> "It is this," I answered, producing a trowel from beneath the folds of my *roquelaire*.
> "You jest," he exclaimed, recoiling a few paces. [Ibid.]

At first, "mason" refers to the secret order of Masons, an order that separates itself by means of arcane signs. Yet the narrator quells his reader's rebellion by demonstrating that his signs escape him; we now understand the opening line of the story: "The thousand injuries of Fortunato I had borne as I best could, but when he ventured upon insult, I vowed revenge" (*CPS* II, 666). Poe's persona takes revenge on his critics, showing their inability to understand what they say by literalizing their figures of speech and demonstrating that their error entombs them. Fortunato believes that the Masonic order controls its secret language, but he learns that its language can control him. The pun on "mason" turns a trowel into an ominously literal sign of the Mason's demise, and Fortunato can only lean heavily on the narrator's arm as he walks toward his death.

"The Cask of Amontillado" suppresses the rebellious reader by writing him into the text and by entombing him in a subterranean vault. The trowel, a figure for the stylus, walls up unfortunate Fortunato, who tries to dismiss Montressor's action as a joke. But the act of writing is utterly serious: as "I forced the last stone into its position; I plastered it up" (*CPS* II, 671), and the story ends. The Mason, unable to control his trope, finds himself victimized by the perverse action of masonry. The narrator becomes confused with what is narrated, the container with the contained, as if urging us to disbelieve the mimetic conventions that pretend to present the voice of a speaking subject. The reader, too, should be unable to savor his wine, confronted by a double who has become like wine decomposing within a bottle, the corpse within a textual tomb.

Poe takes up the first-person form only to transgress its usual limitations. The "I" no longer rests with a stable representational function, for behind the mask are only contours of the mask. Where the fictionally speaking voice becomes inextricably bound up with the events it speaks, the more solid ground of mimetic fiction crumbles. There remains an enhanced sensitivity to the dynamics of textual illusion.

First-person narratives, from Richardson to Poe, enact the unification of narrator and narrated, narration and event, creator and created. When the mimetic framework is questioned by internal contradictions, self-narrative unsettles the barrier between signifying and referential functions of language. To represent a self, narration reflects itself.

The literary life of self perhaps corresponds to an equally fictional worldly self that depends on performance for its existence. The monos of monologue can no longer stand as a subject or monad and is rather a textual swerve. For monologue is not the *logos* of subjectivity but only the linguistic embodiment of isolation and deviance that reveals perverse origins of the fictive subject.

8 The Genius of Internal Monologue

"Internal monologue" and stream-of-consciousness techniques purport to represent, or even to transcribe, fictional characters' internal speech.[1] But how is it possible for written words to stand for unspoken language? The conventions of internal monologue appear most justified by the notion of thought as "speech minus sound." If talking to oneself is no different from talking aloud, then the inwardness of a subject might as well be represented in the familiar language of dialogue. While some authors do employ internal monologue as if to transcribe internal speech, the more radical twentieth-century novels break literary conventions by representing internal speech in ways that deviate from ordinary language. Opposing the psychologists who maintain that subjectivity can be transcribed, writers of stream-of-consciousness technique strive to create the illusion of an inwardness that eludes transcription.

According to a deceptively simple commonplace of literary history, modern literature strives to represent the "inner life" of subjects. This inwardness is, however, never as autonomous as it superficially appears to be. The innovative works by Edouard Dujardin, Arthur Schnitzler, and James Joyce demonstrate that the language of selfhood depends on otherness for its existence, because monologue always

---

[1] Throughout this chapter the reader should place the (perhaps unavoidable) misnomer "internal monologue" in imaginary quotation marks.

incorporates elements of dialogue. The context of vocalized speech is a sub-text of internal dialogue, and the context of writing is formed by the pre-texts of literary history.

Late nineteenth-century psychology suggests a distinction between "internal speech" and "stream of consciousness." While internal speech is the essentially linguistic process of thought, "stream of consciousness" refers to an extralinguistic level. Victor Egger opens his systematic discussion in *La parole intérieure* (1881) by stating, "At every instant, the soul speaks its thought internally."[2] Egger suggests that internal and external speech are substantially alike. But Henri Bergson's *Essai sur les données immédiates de la conscience* (1888) and William James's *Principles of Psychology* (1890) emphasize the nonverbal character of the "stream of thought." Stream of consciousness is conceived as a nebulous experiential process to which language is foreign, while internal speech occurs in our language of everyday communication.

Literary developments evidently parallel changes in psychological theory when they affirm these conceptions of thought. Internal monologue purports to represent internal speech directly, while stream-of-consciousness technique creates the illusion of representing a pre-linguistic realm. Literary critics for the most part agree on this distinction.[3]

One central tension within modern fiction derives from the contradictory claims of internal monologue and stream-of-consciousness techniques. Before the rise of the novel, Shaftesbury prepares a way for psychological fiction by discussing soliloquy at great length. In the eighteenth and nineteenth centuries, then, characters' thoughts are often introduced as a kind of coherent talking to oneself. Such rationalistic conceptions begin to collapse with the rise of modern psychology and symbolist writing. Edouard Dujardin is among the first wave of writers whose fictions attempt to capture the extrarational workings of the mind; Arthur Schnitzler's coherent narratives of internal speech return to a more rationalistic form. James Joyce presses

[2]Victor Egger, *La parole intérieure: Essai de psychologie descriptive* (Paris: Germer Baillière, 1881), 1.
[3]See Lawrence Edward Bowling, "What Is the Stream of Consciousness Technique?" in *PMLA*, 65 (June 1950), 345; Francis Scarfe, *The Art of Paul Valéry* (Melbourne: William Heinemann, 1954), 111; and Robert Scholes and Robert Kellogg, *The Nature of Narrative* (London: Oxford University Press, 1966), 177. But compare Melvin Freedman, *Stream of Consciousness: A Study in Literary Method* (London: Oxford University Press, 1955).

further into the textual unconscious that is inaccessible to ordinary language but that finds a possible expression in diverse forms of stream-of-consciousness technique. In no case can there be a direct correspondence of a literary passage to a represented process of thought: the relationship always depends on elaborate conventions of mimesis. The problem is not to evaluate these conventions, then, but to discern a competition between different formal devices and their structural differences in relation to thought.

The history of literary monologue is a story of the rhetorical processes that transform codes, literary devices that purport to correspond to phenomena of internal speech. The relationship between lived internal speech and literary internal monologue is, like the relationship Nietzsche describes between object and subject, "an indicative carry-over, a stammering translation into a completely foreign language."[4]

The Consciousness of Internal Monologue

According to Edouard Dujardin, one of the central goals of literary internal monologue is to eliminate the apparent discrepancy between represented thought and the technique of representation. In his own terms, internal monologue suppresses the appearance of narrative intrusions: "The first object of internal monologue is, remaining within the conditions and the framework of the novel, to suppress the intervention, at least the apparent intervention, of the author, and to permit the character to express himself directly, as does the traditional monologue at the theatre."[5] The monologue aims to "express thoughts" and achieve the unmediated illusion by allowing a fictional character "to express himself directly" (*MI* 215). According to Dujardin, there are essential differences between monologue in drama and in the novel, since narrative monologue can accompany continued action, whereas the action of a play stops when a monologue begins. In fact, the essential difference between internal monologue and first-person narration is that the internal monologue can follow a character in the

---

[4]Friedrich Nietzsche, "Über Wahrheit und Lüge im aussermoralischen Sinne."
[5]Edouard Dujardin, "*Les lauriers sont coupés*" and "*Le monologue intérieur*," ed. Carmen Licari (Rome: Bulzoni, 1977), 214. I shall henceforth cite the former as *LC* and the latter as *MI*.

172 LITERATURE OF MONOLOGUE

present tense while he moves through a fictional world, but as Fielding's *Shamela* demonstrates, first-person narrative easily becomes ri-
diculous when it describes a present action other than the scene of
writing.

Internal monologue in fiction is supposed to correspond to a scene
and moment of thought. Simultaneity is essential, as Valéry Larbaud
observes when he writes that internal monologue seizes thought "close
to its conception."[6] If we conceive internal speech as a linguistic phenomenon that can be transcribed, then internal monologue is a pretended record of the linguistic stream of thought. But if internal speech
is already a kind of writing in code,[7] then the relationship between
internal speech and internal monologue is closer to a translation from
one code to another. The different types of internal monologue technique imply different conceptions of internal speech and of its rhetorical accessibility to narrative. The thoughts of a fictional character
do not first exist in order to be secondarily represented, however, so
that only the primary illusion is of a correspondence between writing
and the scene of internal speech.[8]

Les lauriers sont coupés (1887) opens impersonally, with a description
that contains no trace of personal pronoun or verb: "An evening of
setting sun, of distant air, of profound skies; and of confused crowds;
of noises, of shadows, of multitudes; spaces infinitely extended; a
vague evening."[9] This disjointed sentence produces a double effect
of mystery. The evening is modified by a sequence of genitive con-
structions; the twilight scene is replete with ambiguous distances in
the air, sky, and space. To whom does the scene belong? "Of" confuses subjective and objective genitive to suggest that the evening
belongs to the sun, air, confused crowds. Or is the scene only a

---

[6]In his preface to the second edition of *LC* (Paris: Albert Messein, 1924), 6.
[7]See L. S. Wygotski, *Denken und Sprechen*, trans. Gerhard Sewekov (Stuttgart: S.
Fischer, 1969), chap. 7.
[8]Internal monologue clearly differs from Coleridge's conversational pretense to the
extent that internal speech is not conscious of itself as a writing. Naturalistic internal
monologue contrasts with Shakespearean dramatic soliloquy, because internal speech
does not obviously occur in the eloquent diction of Shakespeare's verse. Internal monologue further differs from Poe's first-person narrations in which a character appears
to address the reader, because a character's internal speech is addressed to himself or
is addressed only imaginatively to another individual. Yet internal monologue shares,
with all other forms of monologue, complex conventions that create illusions of
subjectivity.
[9]*LC* 93. In English, see Edouard Dujardin, *We'll to the Woods No More*, trans. Stuart
Gilbert (New York: New Directions, 1938).

mysterious "infinitely extended" literary space? After the sequence of modifications, the only progress is from "an evening" to "a vague evening" until the continuation produces "a clear evening." The text revels in an invocation of elusive objects.

The second sentence-paragraph suggests the language of causal explanation when it introduces the narrative "I": "For under the chaos of appearances, among the durations and sites, in the illusion of things that engender and beget themselves, one among the others, one like the others, one the same and one more, of the infinitude of possible existences, I arise; and observe how time and place become precise; it is the today; it is the here; the hour that tolls; and, around me, life; the hour, the place, an evening in April, Paris, a clear evening of setting sun" (*LC* 93). The apparently unmotivated "For" (*Car*) points toward a new presence, the first-person consciousness. An "illusion of things that engender and beget themselves," the temporal and spatial chaos, is also a narrative illusion. The initial two sentences confront each other as two distinct narrative pretenses: impersonal and personal voice. Things only appear to "engender themselves" to the extent that the consciousness of the "I" is concealed. The text narrates a discovery of its own voice of internal monologue. Despite the fragmentary character of descriptive clauses, however, this voice sounds less like a transcription than like a written transformation of internal speech.

The evening remains "vague" until the "I" specifies, in Hegelian fashion, its particular moment and place: "it is the today; it is the here." The moment becomes "sweeter" by being reflected in a consciousness. The narrative takes pleasure in this turn, observing "a joy of being someone, of walking." Previously bound to impersonal description, the voice admits to a pleasure at becoming "someone," a center of consciousness and a body within the fictive world.

Echoing the opening section, chapter 8 speaks from the now established voice. Daniel Prince rides through Paris in a carriage with Lea: "In the streets the car in motion . . . .One in the crowd of unlimited existences, thus I henceforth take my course, one definitively among the others; thus the today and the here, the hour, life are created in me" (*LC* 163; ellipses in original). The "I" creates itself by representing the moment in itself. The "I" is an illusory point source, an "internal" generator of language that invents its place as the physical companion of Lea and as the narrative companion of the reader.

At the start of the novel, Daniel Prince is lost in a crowd; now he reaches the height of self-attainment, as his narrative vehicle carries him and Lea together: "It is a feminine dream, the today; it is a touched feminine flesh, my here; my hour; it is a woman whom I approach; and observe the dream towards which my life goes, this girl on this night" (ibid.). The evening has been redefined by the "I" that invokes and desires a feminine presence. "Observe the dream": fusing with the text, the voice is and tells its dream. The world of the fiction is "in me," where the "I" is both Daniel Prince's inner text and the text itself as origin of the illusion. Ultimately, there is no inner/outer dichotomy within the language of the narrative. No apparent intervention separates narrator from narrated because the narrative unifies this double illusion of the personal and impersonal.

One moment of internal language is especially riddled by paradox. Daniel Prince hears a slow waltz, and the narrative reproduces several measures of musical notation (*LC* 148).[10] What rhetorical device produces this effect? There is an obvious discrepancy between written notation and inner experience. How can a musical language be part of internal monologue? On first consideration, one might believe that the musical staff stands for the experience of hearing the transcribed sounds. Or one might say that Daniel Prince imagines the notes, hums them to himself, perhaps even visualizes their notation. But these approaches take the mimetic pretense for granted. Musical notation is a written code that, by virtue of unstated conventions, forms part of a feigned presentation of the code of internal speech. According to the pretense, literary internal monologue stands in a relation to speech as musical notation to musical sound. Elaborate conventions make possible the fictive correspondences between writing and internal speech (or between musical notation and musical experience).

Although Dujardin names his stylistic device "monologue intérieur," his narrative rarely appears to transcribe coherent inner thought. Instead, along the lines of what is now called stream-of-consciousness technique, Dujardin represents disjointed associations and inchoate fantasies. The distinctly modern character of his project lies in its close linkage of narration with silent consciousness.

---

[10]Compare Arthur Schnitzler's more extensive use of musical notation in the closing pages of *Fräulein Else*, and that of James Joyce in *Ulysses*.

Interiority Turns Outward

The fiction of Arthur Schnitzler, a Viennese physician working in psychiatry, introduces new conventions in the representation of thought. Unlike Dujardin's narrative, Schnitzler's *Leutnant Gustl* (1901) and *Fräulein Else* (1924) often appear as transcriptions of internal speech. Despite the borderline states of consciousness they express, these characters' internal monologues give an overriding impression of rational contemplation. This does not necessarily imply, however, that the represented internal speech is as coherent as the internal monologue that represents it; the problem is that we cannot confidently establish the difference.

Schnitzler acknowledges his formal debt to Dujardin in a letter to Georg Brandes: "I am pleased that the novella of Lieutenant Gustl amused you. A novella of Dostoyevsky, Krotkaya, which I do not know, is supposed to exhibit the same technique of thought-monologue. But the first inducement to the *form* was given to me by a story of Dujardin, entitled les lauriers sont coupés. Only that this author did not know how to find the right material for his form."[11] While *Les lauriers sont coupés* crucially influences the form of *Leutnant Gustl*, several differences are immediately obvious. Dujardin anticipates the later stream-of-consciousness technique by hinting at a representation of Daniel Prince's incoherent, vaguely formulated impressions; Schnitzler writes an internal monologue that appears to transcribe only the rational processes of Lieutenant Gustl's thoughts. Dujardin implies that his narrative captures the prelinguistic stream of consciousness, but Schnitzler restricts himself to the fictive internal speech.

Leutnant Gustl is, in fact, one of the earliest works of fiction to be entirely structured around the represented internal speech of a protagonist. Apart from modifying the meaning of internal monologue, Schnitzler chooses a peculiar, though in some ways typical, center of consciousness. In contrast to Daniel Prince, who flows with his aestheticized world, Lieutenant Gustl bristles with animosity. Schnit-

---

[11]Dated June 11, 1901, this letter appears in *Georg Brandes und Arthur Schnitzler: Ein Briefwechsel*, ed. Kurt Bergel (Bern: A. Francke, 1956), 87–88. Compare the letter to Marie Reinhard, dated October 3, 1898: "Read . . . a very peculiar story (novel) of Dujardin, 'les lauriers sont coupés' " (in Arthur Schnitzler's *Briefe, 1875–1912*, ed. Therese Nickl and Heinrich Schnitzler [Frankfurt am Main: S. Fischer, 1981], 354).

zler's character strives to follow the military code in every respect, yet he constantly confronts "situations where inwardly he is not at one with the demands of his social *persona*."[12] The contradictions within him serve as the starting point for Schnitzler's attack on the military order Gustl represents. Whereas Daniel Prince is at worst a naive and affected aesthete, Lieutenant Gustl is a despicable type. We may uneasily recognize aspects of ourselves in him, but we can hardly identify with Gustl. A dialogue of conflicting values is thus written into Schnitzler's story.

Dialogue is explicit even in the language of Gustl's internal speech. Imagining conversations with the doctor he has challenged to a duel, he thinks: "Just wait, Herr Doktor, you will lose the habit of making such remarks!"[13] Later, when he contemplates suicide, he holds an imaginary dialogue: "Yes, you'll never see me again, Klara—finished! What, little sister, when you accompanied me to the train on New Year's, you didn't think that you would never see me again?"(*LG* 23). Dialogical tensions also characterize a sequence of Gustl's addresses to himself.[14] Resolved momentarily to commit suicide in consequence of a baker's insult, Gustl thinks: "All right, you've heard, Gustl: finished, finished, your life is over!" (*LG* 17). Gustl appears to contain the critical author or reader in himself when he exclaims, "No, it won't be made so easy for you, Herr Lieutenant" (*LG* 21). At one moment, Gustl tries to gain rational control of his thoughts: "Look, Gustl, you've come here specially . . . , in the middle of the night, where not a soul disturbs you—now you can calmly think over everything for yourself" (*LG* 25). But control is elusive, morbid ideas unsettle him, and he desperately seeks to calm himself: "Gustl, be good: as it is, things are bad enough" (*LG* 35).

The narrative, as if situated inside Gustl's mind, nevertheless implies an ironic distance. We ultimately feel "closer" to Daniel Prince although bored by him. Schnitzler's use of internal monologue produces a powerful effect; Gustl stands for the established military code and at the same time undoes this code by discovering inconsistencies

---

[12]Martin Swales, *Arthur Schnitzler: A Critical Study* (Oxford: Clarendon Press, 1971), 103–4.
[13]Arthur Schnitzler, *Leutnant Gustl* (Berlin: S. Fischer, 1967), 4 (henceforth cited as *LG*).
[14]See also William H. Rey, *Arthur Schnitzler: Die späte Prosa als Gipfel seines Schaffens* (Berlin: Erich Schmidt, 1968), 73–74.

within himself. Gustl falls asleep in the park, too irresolute to decide on suicide, and awakens in the despairing fashion of Richard III: "What is it then?—Hey, Johann, bring me a glass of fresh water... What is it?...Where...Yes, am I dreaming?...My skull...o blast it....I can't open my eyes!" (*LG* 26–27; ellipses in original). Like Richard, Gustl finds that "no creature loves me": "It really is sad to have absolutely no one" (*LG* 28). If they do not approach madness, the characteristic form of literary monologists often leads them to be loners and extreme individualists.

While internal monologue purports to represent internal speech with complete accuracy, this apparent proximity can be riddled with ironic distances. At the moment of solitary crisis on the night before his duel, Gustl achieves no convincing individuality but only reveals the inability of a social type to escape or master its governing clichés. Schnitzler thus reveals that internal speech may constitute only an illusory form of autonomy: dominated by military codes of honor, Lieutenant Gustl finds himself incapable of independent thinking. In his irresolute decision to die, Gustl merely responds to a petty insult, and his continued life is an equally arbitrary result of the baker's sudden death. Lieutenant Gustl is a puppet of the society that authors him, or of the author who, within the fiction, pretends to let him speak for himself.

Fräulein Else, Schnitzler's major work of fiction based on internal monologue, also demonstrates that despite appearances of autonomy, internal speech is controlled by outside forces. This demonstration operates on both the mimetic and narrative levels. Manipulated by her parents, Else is also the puppet of the narrative; suicide is her individual response to this double bind.

An economic model governs the plot. Else's parents have sent her to an expensive resort, on vacation with her aunt and cousin. Else realizes that their money buys extreme solitude: "How alone I am here!"[15] But an urgent letter intrudes. Her mother asks her to request a loan from another vacationer, which forces her into a system of exchange. Throughout, Else is identified with her reflective internal speech; according to the convention, she exists for us only by virtue of the fictional words that she purportedly speaks inwardly. But her

---

[15]Arthur Schnitzler, *Fräulein Else*, in *Erzählungen* (Frankfurt am Main: Suhrkamp, 1968), 159 (henceforth cited as *FE*). In English, see Arthur Schnitzler, *Fräulein Else*, trans. Robert A. Simon (New York: Simon and Schuster, 1925).

father's debt and mother's plea demand that she enter into a new mode of language, a request. Monologue, a Marxist critic might say, is a luxury—or a delusion—of the rich.[16] As soon as Else must pay for her dependence on others, she also loses her linguistic freedom. Language and flesh become the media of exchange. To the extent that human existence is based on interdependence, of course, the use of language is characterized by a threatened fall from freedom; the conflicting tendencies of the internal monologue impose this threat that can never be evaded unless a speaker gives up all efforts to assert individual identity.

Dorsday, a wealthy art dealer, agrees to satisfy the financial need that has been transferred from Else's father to Else, on the condition that she reveal herself to him naked. As a specialist in buying and selling beautiful objects, Dorsday wishes to buy Else's denuded image. Because she is essentially a character of inwardness, the situation of mercenary exchange destroys her: for Else to expose her nudity is like giving up the privacy of her thoughts. In a sense—and this is one of the paradoxes of the story—she always does give up her internal speech, to the reader.

Else's predicament parallels a literary dilemma. The internal monologist appears to present herself, yet she is obviously manipulated by the author, her father. The language of the internal monologist is supposedly private and yet exposed to the reader, Dorsday. If Schnitzler is Else's true father, the reader is her insidious seducer, a patron who buys her text as Dorsday buys a glimpse of her nudity. When the narrative ends, we have all finished with her, and she dies. Within her predicament, Else is painfully self-conscious: not only aware that men manipulate her, she understands that she has been asked to sell herself (*FE* 157, 185). Furthermore, she recognizes that she is being asked to perform; at the same time her internal monologue is the totality of her performance.

Else has in fact always wanted to become an actress, but her family will hear nothing of this disreputable trade. As the story opens, she has just stopped playing tennis, and her cousin asks: "You really don't want to play any more, Else?" (*FE* 145). The story both opens and closes with an impulse to break off the performance, in conformity

---

[16]See Mikhail Bakhtin, *Problems of Dostoevsky's Poetics*, trans. and ed. Caryl Emerson (Minneapolis: University of Minnesota, 1984), 288.

with Else's strong urge to keep her expressions private. Formally, the speech of other characters, printed in italics, disrupts the flow of Else's internal speech. As a result of her father's addiction to financial gambling, a *Spielleidenschaft* (FE 180), Else must also become a passionate player, or a player of passions. When Else has prepared herself for self-exposure, she thinks: "The show can begin" (*Die Vorstellung kann beginnen*) (FE 200). Despite her parents' wish that she avoid an improper profession, then, Else makes her debut in what she ironically calls a "grand performance" (FE 202). She observes the justice of this return of the repressed: because stage acting has been made impossible, her peculiar performance will "serve them right, all of them," who "only raised me up in order to sell myself, one way or another" (FE 185). Else longs for a theatrical role, but she gives herself up in a live drama instead. Like all who sell themselves in love or marriage, Else may also stand for mercenary inclinations of the writer.

After uncovering her body and poisoning herself, Else falls inward and becomes all internal speech, all internal monologue, completely isolated from the world that exploits her. Escape is perhaps impossible. Psychologically, she has already determined that she must isolate herself: "I don't want to see anyone more" (ibid.). Despite the system of exchange that controls her, Else realizes that no one has been truly concerned for her inwardness. While we read what passes through her mind, Else condemns us along with those who think they know her: "But what goes on in me, what churns in me and agonizes me, have you ever been concerned for that?" (FE 186).

Like Dorsday, we pay to see Else naked; what do we really care what agitates her? We want to possess her private world, as does her cousin when he complains, "You are somewhere else with your thoughts" (FE 164). Absorbed in hidden language, Else is "secretive, daemonic, seductive" (ibid.). Her consciousness has been appropriated by the narrative, captured in or made identical with the text, so that suicide becomes her only option. For a moment she views her own image in a mirror, and enjoys a narcissistic fantasy: "Ah, come nearer, you beautiful girl. I want to kiss your blood-red lips. I want to press your breasts against mine. What a shame that the glass is between us, the cold glass. How well we would get along with each other. Isn't it so? We would need no one else" (FE 198). Else's existence hovers between the incompatible poles of autonomy and dependence, autoeroticism and rape, private and public language. When

her consciousness fades out with the fiction, she disappears behind
the text. In a somewhat incestuous fantasy, Else imagines joining
hands with her father, her author. Ultimately, no one can call her
back to the represented world:

> *"Else! Else!"*
> They call from so far away! What do you want, anyway? Don't wake
> me. I'm sleeping so well. Tomorrow morning. I'm dreaming and flying.
> I'm flying... flying... flying... sleep and dream... and fly... don't
> wake... tomorrow morning...
> *"El..."*
> I'm flying... I'm dreaming... I'm sleeping... I dre... dre—I'm fly
> ...... [FE 219; ellipses in original]

The death of consciousness corresponds to textual closure.
Dujardin's and Schnitzler's monologues bring a narrative paradox
into sharp focus. From a formal standpoint, Lieutenant Gustl and
Fräulein Else appear to speak more autonomously than does Daniel
Prince; yet their internal speech only reveals an inability to control
their lives. Internal speech is threatened by diverse absences.

The Genius of Modern Narrative

"Penelope," the final chapter of *Ulysses*, is the culmination of the
literary tradition of internal monologue begun by Dujardin. Joyce was
familiar with *Les lauriers sont coupés* and suggested that Valéry Larbaud
read this novel in which "the reader finds himself installed, from the
first lines, in the thought of the principal character."[17] Although Joyce
is often said to write stream-of-consciousness technique, "Penelope"
appears more as a representation of internal speech than of preverbal
consciousness. We may thus refer to this section as Molly's internal
monologue, which has, for various reasons, dominated the general
reception of Joyce's work.[18] In eight paragraphs without punctuation,
Joyce closes his novel as if striving to complete Western literary history
since Homer.

---

[17]As attested by Valéry Larbaud in his preface to the second, 1924 edition of *LC* (p.
7).
    [18]Compare Therese Fischer-Seidel's essay in her critical anthology, *James Joyces "Ulys-
ses": Neuere deutsche Aufsätze* (Frankfurt am Main: Suhrkamp, 1977), 309.

After Molly's Odysseus returns home, they exchange questions and (somewhat deceptive) answers. On another level, the narrator has returned to Athena, the guardian spirit, or muse. If the penultimate chapter is "the ceremonious exchange between narrator and Muse," then the final pages constitute a language of "Muse without narrator."[19] From the standpoint of mystical genius, the language of Molly's internal monologue appears to "show us how the Muse behaves without Homer"; in terms of authorial genius, the final chapter is "the voice of the pure composing faculty" (ibid., pp. 98–99). Bloom's return is simultaneously the return of narrator to listener and of author to muse and the awakening of narrative to inner potentials.

One of Joyce's letters supports the view that the concluding chapter is "the clou [sic] of the book."[20] Joyce describes "Penelope" as if it were based on a kind of linguistic, erotic kabbala: "It begins and ends with the female word, yes. It turns like the huge earth ball slowly surely and evenly round and round spinning, its four cardinal points being the female breasts, arse, womb and . . . expressed by the words because, bottom (in all senses bottom button, bottom of the class, bottom of the sea, bottom of his heart), woman, yes" (ibid.). This image draws attention to the merging of mimetic illusion with sheer linguistic play. If the entire section turns "like the huge earth ball" around "female breasts, arse, womb and . . . ," this world finds bizarre expression in the unlikely words, "because, bottom, woman, yes." While the arse-bottom and womb-woman connections seem natural enough, Joyce pushes beyond the simple identification by expositing "bottom" associatively as "in all senses bottom button, bottom of the class, bottom of the sea, bottom of his heart"; the pairing of "womb" and "woman" is only motivated by Joyce's choice of this synecdoche and homonymic play. Between "breasts" and "because", "yes" and " . . . " there is no obvious relationship of even a conventional kind. Joyce generates a linguistic mythology that creates a set of unexpected parallels.

Joyce's letter continues beyond the linguistic mythology, suggesting a comic revision of Goethe: "Though probably more obscene than any preceding episode," Joyce adds, "it seems to me to be perfectly

[19]Hugh Kenner, *Joyce's Voices* (Berkeley: University of California Press, 1978), 98.
[20]*Letters of James Joyce*, vol. 1, ed. Stuart Gilbert (New York: Viking, 1966), 170. In the following quotation, the ellipsis is introduced by Gilbert. Compare Shakespeare's *The Comedy of Errors*, Act 2, Scene 2: "She is spherical, like a globe. I could find out countries in her."

sane full amoral fertilisable untrustworthy engaging shrewd limited prudent indifferent *Weib*. *Ich bin der* [*sic*] *Fleisch der stets bejaht* [. . . Woman. I am the flesh that constantly affirms]" (ibid.). Molly Bloom is the womb-woman who says Yes and the flesh that constantly affirms. Placing himself once again in the position of writing Molly's words for her, Joyce has Molly speak her essence by reversing Mephistopheles' lines: "I am the spirit that constantly denies" (*Ich bin der Geist, der stets verneint*).[21] Instead of being the spirit that negates, Molly is the body that affirms. Supernatural agency is once again introjected. Paradoxically, however, Molly is no body but only a text that refers endlessly to other texts; on the most profound level, Molly can exist only as a reversal of Mephistopheles. By negation of a negator, she affirms. This produces, in the "depths" of Molly's consciousness, a language of affirmation, an acceptance of her textual past as individual, muse, genius.[22] Because Stuart Gilbert's edition of Joyce's letters omits the word that corresponds to "yes," the censored signifier remains an absence through which all human life is affirmed and sustained. Molly is all Woman, carrying on the life of humanity by saying Yes to the flesh. She also says Yes to a textual past, as she refigures Penelope, Athena, Mephistopheles, Daniel Prince, and Lieutenant Gustl. Like her successor Fräulein Else, Molly concludes with sleep, a textual death.

Echoing an entire personal and impersonal past, Molly's internal monologue eludes commentary as it eludes punctuation. But Joyce offers a means of access by mentioning her "four cardinal points." Joyce's image is literally overdetermined, however, because a sphere spins on an axis that is sufficiently defined by two points. One reading would define these two points as the opening and closing words, "Yes . . . Yes."[23] But an early passage links "yes" and "sex": "Mr Bloom reached Essex bridge. Yes, Mr Bloom crossed bridge of Yessex."[24] "Yessex" is the axis around which Molly's thoughts turn.

[21]Johann Wolfgang von Goethe, *Faust*, ed. Erich Trunz (Munich: C. H. Beck, 1972), l. 1338.
[22]In *The Stream of Consciousness and Beyond in Ulysses* (Pittsburgh: University of Pittsburgh Press, 1973), Erwin R. Steinberg unconvincingly disputes Joyce's interpretation of Molly as an affirmer.
[23]Compare the final monologue of Faulkner's Darl, in *As I Lay Dying*, where the repeated "yes" works as an affirmation, not of life, but of madness, an inability to make sense. Perhaps there is a connection.
[24]James Joyce, *Ulysses* (New York: Random House, 1961), 261 (page numbers appear in text below). The association of "yes" with Eros is especially clear in the light of the

In the final chapter of *Ulysses*, Molly Bloom's internal monologue is not obviously controlled by outside forces. At two points a train whistle blows, but otherwise her language appears to follow from the train of her uninterrupted associations. Daniel Prince, Lieutenant Gustl, and Fräulein Else all live through experiences during their internal monologues, but no simultaneous events impinge on Molly. The distinction between external and internal events breaks down, finally, to the extent that Molly's internal monologue is its own performance, a union of narrative process with narrated world.

An interaction of narrative modes is evident in the uses of the word "yes." On one level, "yes" appears to transcribe Molly's inner speech; but on another level, "yes" is a sheer connective that stands for an elusive, prelinguistic moment. The section opens with a transition from the dialogue Bloom and Molly have shared: "Yes because he never did a thing like that before as ask to get his breakfast in bed with a couple of eggs since the *City Arms* hotel when he used to be pretending to be laid up with a sick voice doing his highness to make himself interesting" (p. 738). Apparently without regard for what would be a logical starting point, the narrative slips into a stream of language. Bloom's request to have breakfast in bed takes Molly back to a past time, but neither "yes" nor "because" follows any obvious antecedent. Rather than form part of a worldly logic, Molly's words are connectives in the verbal stream.[25] Schnitzler employs ellipses and dashes to indicate what Coleridge calls "the interspersèd vacancies / And momentary pauses of the thought."[26] Molly's "yes because" works in much the same way (pp. 738, 739, 744), as a textual pause, no longer standing for an unvoiced *phōnē*. In part, then, the words

---

new *Ulysses: A Critical and Synoptic Edition*, 3 vols., ed. Hans Walter Gabler, Wolfhard Steppe, and Claus Melchior (New York: Garland, 1984), I, 418–19 (henceforth cited as *CSE*). In the corrected "Scylla and Charybdis" episode, Stephen thinks: "Do you know what you are talking about? Love, yes."

[25]In at least one passage, "yes because" does function as a logical connective. This phrase is an affirmation of both sexuality and the narrative itself, assenting to a human coupling while carrying the text further in its stream: "Of course some men can be dreadfully aggravating drive you mad and always the worst word in the world what do they ask us to marry them for if were so bad as all that comes to yes because they cant get on without us" (p. 744). Men speak "the worst word," a "no" of criticism, and yet always ask women to say, "yes." Like Molly's stream of words, men cannot get along without the female "yes."

[26]"Frost at Midnight," ll. 46–47.

of internal monologue relinquish the pretense of transcribing internal speech or stream of consciousness.

As Molly falls asleep and her internal monologue draws to its close, "yes because" turns toward the single "yes." In the early days of their relationship, Bloom "pestered me to say yes" (p. 746).[27] The "yes" to sexuality always joins with a narrative "yes": "I had to say Im a fright yes but he was a real old gent" (p. 747). "Yes" remains profoundly sexual: "theyre all mad to get in there where they come out of youd think they could never get far enough up and then theyre done with you in a way till the next time yes because theres a wonderful feeling there all the time so tender how did we finish it off yes O yes I pulled him off into my handkerchief" (p. 760). The muse says "yes" to the poet, to the narrative. For Bloom, like Odysseus, is a great "Deceiver" (p. 746). On occasion, where she does not stand opposite her own kind, she must say "no": "I hate an unlucky man and if I knew what it meant of course I had to say no for form sake dont understand you" (p. 747).

Molly's affirmation reaches a climax in the final pages. She recalls the day "I gave him all the pleasure I could leading him on till he asked me to say yes." In this primal scene of election, "yes" flows between the languages of past and present: "The day I got him to propose to me yes first I gave him the bit of seedcake out of my mouth and it was leapyear like now yes 16 years ago my God after that long kiss I near lost my breath yes he said I was a flower of the mountain yes so we are flowers all a womans body yes" (p. 782). Molly the muse passes her breath to Bloom the poet, who then voices the most clichéd of images. No matter, he is right; yes, by synecdoche a woman's body is like a flower. The poet speaks an image that convinces the muse that he knows her: "yes that was why I liked him because I saw he understood or felt what a woman is."

The "yes" of Molly's internal monologue builds toward the "yes" by which she affirms his selection of her, and they are to be wedded for life. Molly does not answer Bloom's question but interrupts their dialogue as she looks "out over the sea and the sky I was thinking of so many things he didnt know of." How can the muse limit herself to one poet? After an imaginative flight around "all the ends of Eu-

---

[27]This "yes" can also function within the recalled scenes or reasoning logic: "does that suit me yes take that" (p. 752); "didnt I cry yes I believe I did" (p. 756).

rope," Molly returns to their scene through the connective agency of a "yes," when "I thought well as well him as another" (p. 783). Aware of this arbitrariness, the muse comically undermines the poetic myth of a fated choice. Bloom wants to claim Molly as his own, but even Athena spreads her favors among several heroes. The narrative strives to appropriate her language, but language is always common property. Again, "yes" hovers between meaningful affirmation and meaningless connective, rising to a crescendo: "then I asked him with my eyes to ask again yes and then he asked me would I yes to say yes my mountain flower and first I put my arms around him yes and drew him down to me so he could feel my breasts all perfume yes and his heart was going like mad" (p. 783). Grammatical structures compete. The implied phrase, "he asked me . . . to say yes" is disrupted by a "would I yes." She must both say and perform "yes." The "would I yes" is Molly's connective, almost a verb of affirmation. Molly says and does "yes" by embracing Bloom, "and yes I said yes I will Yes." Where is punctuation implied, and what are the words of Molly's response? At first we may read her answer as being, "Yes, yes I will, Yes." But according to another reading Molly reports, "I said. . . . I will," punctuated by a thrice-repeated "yes" of narration that affirms the narrative of affirmation. In fact, a previous draft of the final words reads, "I said I will yes."[28] Superimposed in the published edition, several possibilities stand together, as

"Yes," I said, "Yes, I will. Yes"

and

(Yes) I said, (yes) "I will" (yes).

The affirmation of poetic desire corresponds to an affirmation of the process of language that creates *Ulysses*. In the final monologue, or Mollylogue, key words function both symbolically and by contiguity, metaphorically and metonymically.

[28]*CSE* III, 1726. This edition substantially illuminates the processes of Joyce's verbal art. While the recurrent, sexually charged "yes" in the original edition of *Ulysses* (p. 760) is present at an early stage (see *CSE* III, 1680), Joyce inserts many of the connective instances later (*CSE* III, 1724–26); "yes because" already acts as a connective in the earlier versions. Particularly in the closing lines of the book, successive drafts multiply the rhythmic "yes," building toward the climax of the final "Yes," as Joyce holds a dialogue with Molly and encourages her yes to merge with the stream of textual affirmation.

"Monologue" names several types of solitary speech that deviate from dialogical norms. By a sequence of innovations, the literary tradition corresponds to human solitude through the forms of syntactic and semantic solitude. First-person monologues draw attention to the present of the monological act of speech, whether represented by staged soliloquy, conversational poetry, narrative, or internal monologue. As the psychological novel cedes to more radical writing as monologue, the moment of thought becomes inseparable from the act of writing. Internal monologue is, finally, not a representation of internal speech but its enactment; internal speech is already a kind of code. European literature does not develop exclusively toward dramatized scenes of writing, but this movement in the direction of internal monologue does parallel the transformations of genius.

Internal monologue and stream-of-consciousness techniques, when they question psychological assumptions and accept themselves as writing, hold a privileged place in modern literature. One critic refers to the breakdown of mimetic monologue, ascertaining that in the internal monologue "there is in general no authentic speaking, but rather there whispers [es raunt] a sequence of associations."[29] An unspoken "whispering" moves away from representation of consciousness, toward hints at "a differentiation in the illusion." At first, the narrator appears to enter the monologist's thought, but their proximity actually dissolves the distinction between narrator and narrated and enhances a self-reflective awareness of the narrative illusion. Other literary critics have, while according a privileged place to internal monologue, sought more exact terminology. Taking the final chapter of Ulysses as "the most famous and the most perfectly executed specimen of its species," one critic discusses the genre of "autonomous monologue."[30] Analyses of Schnitzler and Joyce show, however, that monologists are incapable of attaining the autonomy they superficially seek.

In his Critique et vérité, Roland Barthes opposes classical criticism, with its naive belief in the "fullness" of the subject. In contrast, Barthes' criticism holds that "the subject is not an individual plenitude . . . , but on the contrary an emptiness around which the writer weaves

---

[29]Gerhard Storz, "Über den 'Monologue intérieur' oder die 'Erlebte Rede,' " in Der Deutschunterricht, vol. 7, no. 1 (1955), 50.
[30]Dorrit Cohn, Transparent Minds: Narrative Modes for Presenting Consciousness in Fiction (Princeton: Princeton University Press, 1978), 217.

an infinitely transformed speech (inserted into a chain of transformation), such that every writing *which does not lie* designates, not the
internal attributes of the subject, but its absence."[31] The absence of
the traditional subject turns out to mean that, from another standpoint, language is itself the subject.

Gérard Genette, in a parallel discussion, refers to Paul Valéry, Maurice Blanchot, and Albert Thibaudet. Valéry suggests that the author
"is positively no one—or better, that one of the functions of language,
and of literature as language, is to destroy its interlocutor and to
designate it as absent."[32] As cited by Genette, Blanchot proposes that
the writer "belongs to a language which no one speaks, which is
addressed to no one, which has no center, which reveals nothing."
Genette closes his discussion of the abolition of the subject by reference to Thibaudet and the figure of the *génie*. Genette paraphrases:
"Genius . . . is at once the superlative of the individual and the breakup
[*l'éclatement*] of individuality" (*Fig*. 13). Thibaudet further explains that
"genius" can refer to an individual, a genre, an epoch, or a religion.[33]
The secret of genius reminds us of the power of language to designate
the absence of the subject at the same time that it brings this subject
into apparent existence. Like the language of modern literature that
collapses the narrat*ing* with the narrat*ed*, genius points to the stream
of invention beyond the flow of invented objects and subjects. Proust
discovered his *génie*, Genette comments, "at the moment when he
found in his work the place of language where his individuality would
be able to break up and dissolve itself in the Idea" (*Fig*. 14).

The final "Yes" of *Ulysses* circles back to Greek myth, slips away
from its cognitive function, and unites with a narrative stream that
re-presents the stream of consciousness. By affirming itself as language, even as language that corresponds to an absence of coherent
language, the emerging literature of internal monologue discovers

[31]Roland Barthes, *Critique et vérité* (Paris: Editions du Seuil, 1966), 70. Compare Paul
Ricoeur, "The Question of the Subject: The Challenge of Semiology," in *The Conflict
of Interpretations*, ed. Don Ihde (Evanston: Northwestern University Press, 1974), 236–
66.
[32]Gérard Genette, *Figures II* (Paris: Editions du Seuil, 1969), 13 (henceforth cited as
Fig.).
[33]Albert Thibaudet, *Physiologie de la Critique* (Paris: Nouvelle Revue Critique, 1930),
125. In his own words, genius is "la plus haute figure de l'individu, le superlatif de
l'individuel, et cependent le secret du génie c'est de faire éclater l'individualité, d'être
Idée, de représenter, par-delà l'invention, le courant d'invention" (pp. 139–40).

limits of the philosophical monad. The monological genius is neither object nor subject, neither an externally conceived Socratic *daimonion*, nor a psychologically conceived Romantic genius, but the figure that disrupts this opposition in the peculiar literary modes that dissolve individuality, efface personae by taking the part of the muse, and become identified with the guardian genius, an intertextual force, a stream of literary work in progress, riverrun. . . .

Conclusions

I

An exploration of philosophic genius and literary monologue retraces shifting intertextual pathways, for as meaning is in general
created through differential relations, "criticism is the art of knowing
the hidden roads that go from poem to poem."[1] A master trope in
the development of "genius" and "monologue" at first appears to be
introjection: myths of external divinity are internalized and transformed into the spirit of an individual. Rhetorical awareness unsettles
the assumed inner-outer distinction, however, for it demonstrates
that these categories depend on types of figuration; genius and monologue accumulate and transform meanings within linguistic systems,
and the disjunction between ancient and modern beliefs finds expression in rhetorical differences. Theological and philosophical expressions of genius are replaced by the literary forms of monologue in a
movement that is not accessible to traditional intellectual history.

In the context of polytheistic Greek *daimones*, Homer and Plato move
toward more abstract theological language. Alongside *theos*, the Homeric *daimōn* is a mysterious term that suggests divinity; Plato refers
to the Socratic *daimonion*, an even more radical synecdoche that re-

---

[1]Harold Bloom, *A Map of Misreading* (New York: Oxford University Press, 1975), 96.

places the Olympian gods by "something divine" only negatively experienced by Socrates. Against the background of monotheistic Hebrew YHWH, Philo and rabbinic commentators drift toward esoteric teachings of multiple divine presences, represented by angels. The daemonic gradually takes on evil connotations, as legends of *satan* multiply.

Modern aesthetics displaces or introjects the divinity associated with creativity. To the extent that eighteenth-century genius retains a theological dimension, it becomes "that god within," linked to conscience. Shaftesbury writes of soliloquy as the force of subjective genius, while Kant unsuccessfully strives to purge genius of its mystical associations. Kant's transcendental philosophy and Husserl's phenomenology attempt to secure the island of pure reason or immanent sphere of consciousness, but Heidegger turns their tropes inside out, transforms the philosophic monad into a literary nomad by redirecting Dasein to metaphysical transcendence, and affirms that "language speaks" beyond the deliberate intentions controlled by speakers.

"Monologue," as a collective term for counternormative swerves, might be viewed as a master trope of intertextuality. While solitary speech is not necessarily deviant, individual speech turns away from unified systems of language. In one sense, then, monologue names the most general phenomenon of literary revisionism. Yet monologue has both formal and material, tropological and topological manifestations. The intertextual development of monologue is a process of revisionary swerves and re-presentations of solitary speech.

From medieval drama to modern narrative, the potential for soliloquy expands in the space cleared by distance from God's revelation. Only demonic spirits remain when Shakespeare's villains find themselves at the mercy of dark powers that appear to emanate from their own hallucinations and dreams. Coleridge carries the conversational mode further, yet his potentially controlled poetic personae repeatedly drift toward "phantom magic" or madness and encounter the monological subversion of norms. Poe makes narrative monologue the focal point of disorienting perspectival illusions. One text swallows itself, another turns itself inside out, and as mad narrators tell cogent tales, the representational pretense erodes. Modernist internal monologue responds to the genius of language, as when Joyce's stream of consciousness becomes a stream of textuality. Antiquity returns in modern colors when Molly, a literary reincarnation of Athena and Penelope, speaks alone as muse in a language of divine affirmation.

II

Lev Vygotsky writes *Thought and Language* soon after James Joyce and Arthur Schnitzler publish their major works of internal monologue, and he responds explicitly to Jean Piaget's *Le langage et la pensée chez l'enfant* (1923).[2] According to Piaget, the earliest autistic thinking becomes childhood egocentric thinking, which in turn gives way to mature rational thinking. Vygotsky questions Piaget's assumptions by showing that egocentric language is more fundamentally linked to adult internal speech than to autistic inarticulateness; and where Piaget conceives child development as a process of socialization, Vygotsky conceives it as a process of individuation. Vygotsky in some ways reverses the movement Piaget traces from autism to social language and from fantasy to logic. Rather than being reduced to a deficient mode, internal speech that creates anew by turning inward and away from the social becomes the epitome of linguistic development.

Vygotsky increasingly rejects the established external forms of language as he probes deeper into "the inner side of language." Against the unquestioned supremacy of socialization, he posits different linguistic functions such as internal speech, which (unlike external speech) receives its character as language for the speaker alone. In contrast to Piaget, Vygotsky conceives linguistic development as one of gradual individuation, in which the death of egocentric language corresponds to the birth of internal speech. Vygotsky's discussion of internal speech as a special linguistic function includes literary examples. Not only does his analysis touch on phenomena of madness, deviance, and the unconscious, which dominate the expressions of monologue in literature; Vygotsky shows an unexpected link between internal speech and writing.[3]

[2]L. S. Wygotski, *Denken und Sprechen*, trans. Gerhard Sewekow (Stuttgart: S. Fischer, 1969). The author's name is transliterated "Vygotsky" on the title page of the English edition, *Thought and Language*, trans. and ed. Eugenia Hanfmann and Gertrude Vakar (Cambridge: MIT Press, 1962), which abridges the Russian text. I cite the German edition; all translations from the German are my own.
[3]Vygotsky believes that neither writing nor internal speech conforms to ordinary

Whereas psychology has tended to view human development as a process of bondage to social norms, Vygotsky focuses on a possible liberation. Not intended for voiced communication, internal speech is closely allied with subjectivity and may give rise to a kind of inner dialect. Vygotsky writes that "in our language there is always a hidden thought," the abbreviated internal speech, analogous to writing in code. Vygotsky's *Thought and Language* was suppressed during the Soviet purges of 1936, only two years after publication, for it set out on an unpopular path toward theories of individuality in language.

III

Mikhail Bakhtin is the sharpest critic of monologue, which he interprets primarily as the striving for single-voiced philosophical argumentation or literary representation. The monological novel is, according to Bakhtin, dominated by a univocal ideology or worldview that fails to interact with conflicting voices. Although Bakhtin attacks monological forms, his *Problems of Dostoevsky's Poetics* shares with Vygotsky's *Thought and Language* a special interest in the subjectivity of fictional characters and shows that self-consciousness does not exist as autonomous introspection. Observing that "faith in the self-sufficiency of a single consciousness" characterizes post-Enlightenment literature, Bakhtin argues that this faith is illusory.[4] The forces of "internal" signification are actually external to the subject.[5]

Bakhtin's approach to dialogue thus makes possible the discovery of an inwardness that is inseparable from relations with others. Echoing Hegel's conception of self-consciousness, Bakhtin points to internal dialogues "in which the other's discourse has seized control" (*PDP* 219). Bakhtin's manuscript notes reconfirm that the supposedly

---

social speech (*Denken und Sprechen*, 224); his description of internal speech reflects its essential constitution as a kind of writing. Like the language of dreams, according to Freud's analyses, the internal language is characterized by condensation (*Verdichtung*). The two poles of Vygotsky's opposition, abbreviated internal speech and highly developed written language, come together if internal speech is structured like a form of writing in code.

[4]Mikhail Bakhtin, *Problems of Dostoevsky's Poetics*, trans. and ed. Caryl Emerson (Minneapolis: University of Minnesota, 1984), 74, 88, henceforth cited as *PDP*.

[5]Mikhail Bakhtine, *Le Marxisme et la philosophie du langage*, trans. Marina Yaguello (Paris: Editions de Minuit, 1977), 122–23.

monological "I" depends on dialogical interactions. Bakhtin values Dostoevsky's novels, not because they invent a dialogical type of language, but because they uncover the dissimulated dialogical element that inheres in the word; Dostoevsky represents the individual consciousness dialogically. Had he written on English literature, Bakhtin might have demonstrated that in European traditions from pre-Shakespearean soliloquy to twentieth-century internal monologue, solitary speech depends on a concealed relation to otherness.

Like Hegelian sense certainty, monologue discovers that it mistakes itself to be something that is in fact unattainable. If monologue is a misconception of thought and language, however, it is a delusion that has determined the progress of Western existence and literary art. Commitment to monologue is linked to the "death of God," after which man asserts the legitimacy of monological reason. Bakhtin's work contains an implicit metaphysical impetus, a theology of dialogue: "the very being of man (both external and internal) is the deepest *communion*" (*PDP* 287). After encountering the most extreme forms of solitary consciousness, we are impelled to recognize the failure of our monological exertions. The division or decentering of the subject is already implicit in Hegel's master-slave dialectic, the Freudian unconscious, and Heidegger's ec-static Dasein—prophetic voices of a new transcendence.

IV

The intertextual pathways from genius to monologue pass through theological, philosophical, psychological, and literary domains. Classical traditions emphasize the place of divine guidance that becomes unacceptable to enlightened rationalism. In the eighteenth century theology and psychology confront each other, and art chooses the genius of soliloquy as its muse. Yet even the imagination of Kant's "genius" tends to deviate, to wander beyond its innate capacity for exemplary originality. For twentieth-century thought, psychological genius becomes as questionable as was theological genius in the eighteenth century. When contemporary critics demonstrate the inescapable difference from oneself within monologue, deviation becomes a new, errant genius.

From Greek *monos* + *logos*, "monologue" derives the meaning of solitary speech. But the physical solitude of internal speech is phil-osophically the least significant form of linguistic isolation. When "monologue" is linked to modes of language that swerve from or-dinary dialogical speech, the new deviant monologue makes its ap-pearance. Linguistic deviance turns away from norms of speech as genius turns away from norms of artistic creation.[6] But deviation from convention always threatens meaning, for how can an individual invent new forms and still be understood? By asserting an individual style or deviant form of expression, monologue borders on meaning-lessness. Literary monologues provide the basis for inquiry into se-mantic solitude, associated with idiolects that strive to preserve their autonomy while reaching for an elusive otherness.

Introjection makes genius into monologue, and projection reclaims monologue as transcendent genius of language. There is no way to transcend human language and attain the language of God, because "divine speech" is always a trope. Turn away, Moses, and inscribe for yourself two tablets of stone. The ineffable *daimonion* and YHWH do not permit direct revelation: to see God is to transcend human experience, to die. But to exclude all languages of transcendence, if this were possible, would only be to imprison ourselves in a repetitive world without even the creative sublime of rhetorical play.

Genius and Monologue, to the extent that it reads the palimpsests of genius and monologue, necessarily superimposes several layers of textuality. On the surface, then, this book resembles a mosaic of citations. The originality myth has died, and only a prospect of endless swerves remains. We cling to a mythological *Logos* that justifies belief in poetry as the site of authenticity, but we know that all writing grafts itself onto preexisting textuality. If the divine *Logos* is an in-accessible source of inspiration, we can only lose ourselves by error, deviation from the mazes of overtrodden paths.

The new transcendence is a transference, a *metapherein* that sur-passes the present, transforms past figures through imaginative ob-sessions, and constitutes the self in endless dialogues.

—Everything is always different.

—We repeat.

[6]Compare *PDP* 138, where dialogism is linked to experiences of a person who "has deviated from the general norm" and stands "on the *threshold* of insanity." As in Hegel's interpretation of Socrates' *daimonion,* a theological moment is bound up with aberrant psychology.

Selected Bibliography

Introduction

Bickerton, Derek. "Modes of Interior Monologue: A Formal Definition." *Modern Language Quarterly*, 28 (1967), 229–39.

Bowling, Lawrence Edward. "What Is the Stream of Consciousness Technique?" *PMLA*, 65 (June 1950), 333–45.

de Man, Paul. *Allegories of Reading: Figural Language in Rousseau, Nietzsche, Rilke, and Proust*. New Haven: Yale University Press, 1979.

Egger, Victor. *La parole intérieure: Essai de psychologie descriptive*. Paris: Germer Baillière, 1881.

Erlich, Victor. "Notes on the Uses of Monologue in Artistic Prose." *International Journal of Slavic Linguistics and Poetics* 1/2 (1959), 223–31.

———."Some Uses of Monologue in Prose Fiction: Narrative Manner and World-View." In *Stil- und Formprobleme in der Literatur*. Ed. Paul Böckmann. Heidelberg: Carl Winter, 1959.

Friedman, Melvin. *Stream of Consciousness: A Study in Literary Method*. London: Oxford University Press, 1955.

Godel, Robert. *Les sources manuscrites du "Cours de linguistique générale."* Geneva: E. Droz, 1957.

Hédelin d'Aubignac. *La pratique du théatre*. Amsterdam: Jean Frederic Bernard, 1715.

Hjelmslev, Louis. "Langue et parole." *Cahiers Ferdinand de Saussure*, 2 (1942), 29–44.

Humphrey, Robert. *Stream of Consciousness in the Modern Novel*. Berkeley: University of California Press, 1954.

———.'' 'Stream of Consciousness': Technique or Genre?'' *Philological Quarterly*, 30 (1951), 434–36.

Jespersen, Otto. *Mankind, Nation, and Individual from a Linguistic Point of View*. Oslo: H. Aschehoug, 1925.

Leo, Friedrich. ''Der Monolog im Drama: Ein Beitrag zur griechisch-römische Poetik.'' In *Abhandlungen der königlichen Gesellschaft der Wissenschaften zu Göttingen, Philologisch-Historische Klasse*, n.s., vol. 10, no. 5. Berlin: Weidmann, 1908.

Roessler, Erwin W. *The Soliloquy in German Drama*. New York: Columbia University Press, 1915.

Saussure, F. de. *Cours de linguistique générale*. Ed. C. Bally, A. Sechehaye, and T. de Mauro. Paris: Payot, 1972.

Schadewaldt, Wolfgang. *Monolog und Selbstgespräch: Untersuchungen zur Formgeschichte der griechischen Tragödie*. Berlin: Weidmann, 1926.

Schwartz, William Leonard. '' 'Monologue Intérieur' in 1845.'' *MLN*, 63 (June 1948), 409–10.

Sechehaye, Albert. ''Les trois linguistiques saussuriennes.'' *Vox Romanica*, 5 (1940), 1–48.

Spence, N. C. W. ''A Hardy Perennial: The Problem of *la langue* and *la parole*.'' *Archivum Linguisticum*, 9 (1957), 1–27.

Storz, Gerhard. ''Über den 'Monologue intérieur' oder die 'erlebte Rede.' '' *Der Deutschunterricht*, vol. 7, no. 1 (1955), 41–53.

Struve, Gleb. ''Monologue Intérieur: The Origins of the Formula and the First Statement of Its Possibilities.'' *PMLA*, 69 (1954), 1101–11.

Urbach, Otto. ''Zur Ehrenrettung des Monologs.'' *Die Literatur*, 39 (1937), 531–32.

Wittgenstein, Ludwig. *Philosophische Untersuchungen*. Frankfurt am Main: Suhrkamp, 1971.

1. Greek Gods, *daimōn*, and Socrates' *daimonion*

ANCIENT TEXTS: EDITIONS AND TRANSLATIONS

Apuleius Madaurensis. ''Du Dieu de Socrate.'' In *Opuscules philosophiques*. Latin with French trans. by Jean Beaujeu. Paris: Société d'Edition ''Les Belles Lettres,'' 1973.

Diels, Hermann, and Walther Kranz. *Die Fragmente der Vorsokratiker*. 3 vols. Berlin: Weidmann, 1954.

Hesiod. *The Homeric Hymns and Homerica*. Greek with English trans. by Hugh G. Evelyn-White. Loeb Classical Library. Cambridge: Harvard University Press, 1914.

———.*The Works and Days, Theogony, The Shield of Herakles*. Trans. Richmond Lattimore. Ann Arbor: University of Michigan Press, 1959.

Homer. *The Iliad*. Trans. Robert Fitzgerald. New York: Doubleday, 1974.

———.*The Iliad*. Trans. Richmond Lattimore. Chicago: University of Chicago Press, 1951.

———.*The Odyssey*. Trans. Robert Fitzgerald. New York: Doubleday, 1961.

———.*Opera*. Vols. 1–4. Ed. David B. Monro and Thomas W. Allen. 3d ed. Oxford: Clarendon, 1917–20.

Plato. *The Collected Dialogues*. Ed. Edith Hamilton and Huntington Cairns. Bollingen Series. Princeton: Princeton University Press, 1961.

———.*Opera*. Vols. 1–5. Ed. John Burnet. Oxford: Clarendon Press, 1900–7.

———.*Werke*. 2d ed. Trans. F. Schleiermacher. Pt. 1. Vol. 2. Berlin: Realschulbuchhandlung, 1818/1804.

Plutarch. "On the Sign of Socrates." In *Moralia*, vol. 7, Greek with English trans. by Phillip H. Lacy and Benedict Einarson. Loeb Classical Library. Cambridge: Harvard University Press, 1959.

Xenophon. *Memorabilia*. In *Socratic Discourses*, trans. J. S. Watson. New York: E. P. Dutton, 1910.

———.*Opera*. Vol. 2. 2d ed. Oxford: Clarendon Press, 1921.

MODERN TEXTS

Brunius-Nilsson, Elisabeth. *DAIMONIE: An Inquiry into a Mode of Apostrophe in Old Greek Literature*. Uppsala: Almquist and Wiksell, 1955.

Camarero, Antonio. *Socrates y las creencias demónicas griegas*. Bahia Blanca: Cuadernos del Sur, 1968.

Chantraine, Pierre. "Le divin et les dieux chez Homère." In *La notion du divin depuis Homère jusqu'à Platon: Sept exposés et discussions* by H. J. Rose et al. Geneva: Vandoeuvres, 1952.

Detienne, M. *La notion de daimôn dans le pythagorisme ancien*. Paris: Société d'Edition "Les Belles Lettres," 1963.

Ehnmark, Erland. *The Idea of God in Homer*. Uppsala: Almquist and Wiksell, 1935.

Else, Gerald F. "God and Gods in Early Greek Thought." *Proceedings of the American Philosophical Association*, 80 (1949), 24–36.

François, Gilbert. *Le polythéisme et l'emploi au singulier des mots "theos," "daïmôn," dans la littérature grecque d'Homère à Platon*. Paris: Société d'Edition "Les Belles Lettres," 1957.

Friedländer, Paul. *Platon*. 2d ed. Vol. 1. Berlin: Walter de Gruyter, 1954.

Gerhard, Eduard. "Über Wesen, Verwandtschaft, und Ursprung der Dämonen und Genien." In *Abhandlungen der Königlichen Akademie der Wissenschaften*. Berlin: Besser, 1852.

Gundert, Hermann. "Platon und das Daimonion des Sokrates." *Gymnasium: Zeitschrift für Kultur der Antike und Humanistische Bildung*, 61 (1954), 513–31.

Hamann, Johann Georg. *Sokratische Denkwürdigkeiten*. In *Hamanns Schriften*, vol. 2, ed. Friedrich Roth. Berlin: Reimer, 1821.

Hedén, Erik. *Homerische Götterstudien*. Uppsala: K. W. Appelberg, 1912.

Hegel, G. W. F. *Vorlesungen über die Geschichte der Philosophie*. In *Werke in zwanzig Bänden*, vols. 18–20. Frankfurt am Main: Suhrkamp, 1974.

Heinze, Richard. *Xenokrates: Darstellung der Lehre und Sammlung der Fragmente*. Leipzig: B. G. Teubner, 1892.

Jörgensen, Ove. "Das Auftreten der Götter in den Büchern i–m der Odyssee." *Hermes*, 39 (1904), 357–82.

Kierkegaard, Søren. *The Concept of Irony with Constant Reference to Socrates*. Trans. Lee M. Capel. Bloomington: Indiana University Press, 1968.

Kunkel, Hille. *Der Römische Genius: Mitteilungen des deutschen archaeologischen Instituts, Römische Abteilung*. Supp. vol. 20. Heidelberg: F. H. Kerle, 1974.

Lélut, L. F. *Du démon de Socrate: Spécimen d'une application de la science psychologique à celle de l'histoire*. 2d ed. Paris: J. B. Ballière, 1856.

Mühl, Max. "Die Traditionsgeschichtlichen Grundlagen in Platons Lehre von den Dämonen." In *Archiv für Begriffsgeschichte: Bausteine zu einem historischen Wörterbuch der Philosophie*. Vol. 10. Ed. Erich Rothacker. Bonn: Bouvier, 1966.

Nares, Robert. *An Essay on the Demon or Divination of Socrates*. London: T. Payne, 1782.

Nilsson, Martin P. *A History of the Greek Religion*. 2d ed. Trans. F. J. Fielden. Oxford: Clarendon Press, 1949.

Nitzsche, Jane Chance. *The Genius Figure in Antiquity and the Middle Ages*. New York: Columbia University Press, 1975.

Nowak, Herbert. *Zur Entwicklungsgeschichte des Begriffs Daimon*. Bonn: Reinische Friedrich-Wilhelms-Universität, 1960.

Soury, Guy. *La démonologie de Plutarque*. Paris: Société d'Edition "Les Belles Lettres," 1942.

Stanley, Thomas. "Socrates: Of His Daemon." In *The History of Philosophy*, 3d ed., London, 1701.

Taylor, A. E. "The Impiety of Socrates." In *Varia Socratica*. Oxford: James Parker, 1911.

Ukert, Friedrich August. "Über Dämonen, Heroen, and Genien." In *Abhandlungen der Königlichen Sächsischen Gesellschaft der Wissenschaften*, 2, *Philologische-Historische Klasse*, 1. Leipzig, 1850.

Usener, Hermann. *Götternamen: Versuch einer Lehre von der religiösen Begriffsbildung*. Bonn: Friedrich Cohen, 1896.

Wissowa, Georg et al. "Daimon." In *Paulys Realencyclopädie der Classischen Altertumswissenschaft*. Supp. vol. 3. Stuttgart: Alfred Druckenmüller, 1918.

Zilsel, Edgar. *Die Entstehung des Geniebegriffs*. Tübingen: J. C. B. Mohr, 1926.

2. Hebrew Angels, *satan*, and Philo's *logoi*

ANCIENT TEXTS: TRANSLATIONS

The Apocrypha and Pseudepigrapha of the Old Testament. Vols. 1–2. Ed. R. H. Charles. Oxford: Clarendon Press, 1913.

Bet ha-Midrasch: Sammlung kleiner Midraschim. Pt. 1. 3d ed. Ed. Adolph Jellinek. Jerusalem: Wahrmann, 1967.

The Book of Jubilees; or, The Little Genesis. Trans. R. H. Charles. New York: Macmillan, 1917.

The Dead Sea Scriptures. Trans. Theodor H. Gaster. New York: Doubleday, 1956.

Genesis Rabbah. In *The Midrash Rabbah*, trans. H. Freedman and Maurice Simon, vol. 1. London: Soncino, 1939.

Philo. Vols. 1–10. Greek with English trans. by F. H. Colson and G. H. Whitaker. Loeb Classical Library. London: William Heinemann, 1929–43.

Sanhedrin. In *The Babylonian Talmud, Seder Nezikin*, vol. 3, trans. H. Freedman, ed. I. Epstein. London: Soncino, 1961.

MODERN TEXTS

Auerbach, Erich. *Mimesis: The Representation of Reality in Western Literature*. Trans. Willard Trask. Princeton: Princeton University Press, 1953.

Bamberger, Bernard J. *Fallen Angels*. Philadelphia: Jewish Publication Society, 1952.

Boman, Thorleif. *Hebrew Thought Compared with Greek*. Trans. Jules L. Moreau. New York: Norton, 1960.

Bréhier, Emile. *Les idées philosophiques et religieuses de Philon d'Alexandrie*. Paris: Vrin, 1925.

Bucher, Jordan. *Philonische Studien*. Tübingen: Zu-Guttenberg, 1848.

Buschmann, Joseph. *Die Persönlichkeit des philonischen Logos*. Aachen: M. Ulrichs Sohn, 1873.

Dupont-Sommer, A. *Les écrits esséniens découvertes près de la Mer Morte*. Paris: Payot, 1957.

Frey, J.–B. "L'angelologie juive au temps de Jésus-Christ." *Revue des sciences philosophiques et théologiques*, 5 (1911), 75–110.

Gfrörer, August. *Philo und die alexandrinische Theosophie*. Stuttgart: Schweizerbart, 1831.

Heidt, William George. *Angelology of the Old Testament.* Washington: Catholic University Press of America, 1949.

Heinze, Max. *Die Lehre vom Logos in der griechischen Philosophie.* Oldenburg: Ferdinand Schmidt, 1872.

Keferstein, Friedrich. *Philo's Lehre von den göttlichen Mittelwesen.* Leipzig: Wilhelm Juranz, 1846.

Kelber, Wilhelm. *Die Logoslehre von Heraklit bis Origenes.* Stuttgart: Urachhaus, 1958.

Kluger, Rivkah Schärf. *Satan in the Old Testament.* Trans. Hildegard Nagel. Evanston: Northwestern University Press, 1967.

Langton, Edward. *Essentials of Demonology.* London: Epworth, 1949.

Porter, Frank Chamberlin. *The Yeçer Hara: A Study in the Jewish Doctrine of Sin.* Biblical and Semitic Studies. New York: Scribner, 1901.

Schäfer, Peter. *Rivalität zwischen Engeln und Menschen.* Berlin: Walter de Gruyter, 1975.

———.*Studien zur Geschichte und Theologie des rabbinischen Judentums.* Leiden: E. J. Brill, 1978.

———.*Die Vorstellung vom Heiligen Geist in der rabbinischen Literatur.* Munich: Kösel, 1972.

Segal, Alan F. *Two Powers in Heaven: Early Rabbinic Reports about Christianity and Gnosticism.* Leiden: E. J. Brill, 1977.

Soulier, Henry. *La doctrine du Logos chez Philon d'Alexandrie.* Turin: Vincent Bona, 1876.

Spiegel, Shalom. *The Last Trial.* Trans. Judah Goldin. New York: Pantheon Books, 1967.

Stier, Fridolin. *Gott und sein Engel im alten Testament.* Münster: Aschendorff, 1934.

Tur-Sinai, N. H. (H. Torczyner). *The Book of Job: A New Commentary.* Jerusalem: Kiryath Sepher, 1957.

Weber, Ferdinand. *Jüdische Theologie auf Grund des Talmud und verwandter Schriften gemeinfasslich dargestellt.* Ed. Franz Delitzsch and Georg Schnedermann. Hildesheim: Georg Olms, 1975.

Wolff, M. *Die philonische Philosophie in ihren Hauptmomenten dargestellt.* Gothenburg: D. F. Bonnier, 1858.

Wolfson, Harry Austryn. *Philo.* Vols. 1–2. Cambridge: Harvard University Press, 1947.

3. The Eighteenth-Century Introjection of Genius

Addison, Joseph. *Selected Essays from "The Tatler," "The Spectator," and "The Guardian."* Ed. Daniel Mcdonald. New York: Bobbs-Merrill, 1973.

Bate, W. Jackson. *The Burden of the Past and the English Poet*. Cambridge: Harvard University Press, 1970.

Diderot, Denis (?). "Génie." *Encyclopédie*. Paris, 1751.

Duff, William. *An Essay on Original Genius and Its Various Modes of Exertion in Philosophy and the Fine Arts, particularly in Poetry*. London: Edward and Charles Dilly, 1767.

Gerard, Alexander. *An Essay on Genius*. London: W. Strahan, 1774.

———.*An Essay on Taste* (1759). 3d ed. London: T. Cadell, 1780.

Hartman, Geoffrey H. "False Themes and Gentle Minds." *Philological Quarterly*, 48 (January 1968), 55–68.

Hildebrandt, R. "Genie." In *Deutsches Wörterbuch*, ed. Jakob Grimm and Wilhelm Grimm. Leipzig, 1854.

Johnson, Samuel. "Genius." In *Dictionary*. London, 1755.

Kant, Immanuel. *Werke in sechs Bänden*. Ed. Wilhelm Weischedel. Frankfurt am Main: Insel, 1956–64.

Lewis, C. S. "Genius and Genius." In *Studies in Medieval and Renaissance Literature*. Cambridge: Cambridge University Press, 1966.

Nahm, Milton C. *The Artist as Creator: An Essay of Human Freedom*. Baltimore: Johns Hopkins University Press, 1956.

Rosenthal, B. *Der Geniebegriff des Aufklärungszeitalters*. Berlin: Emil Ebering, 1933.

Schlapp, Otto. *Kants Lehre vom Genie*. Göttingen: Vandenhoeck & Ruprecht, 1901.

Schmidt-Dengler, Wendelin. *Genius: Zur Wirkungsgeschichte antiker Mythologeme in der Goethezeit*. Munich: C. H. Beck, 1978.

Shaftesbury, Anthony. *Characteristicks of Men, Manners, Opinions, and Times*. Vols. 1–3. London, 1711.

Sharpe, William. *Dissertation on Genius* (London, 1755).

Witkowski, Georg. *Miniaturen*. Leipzig: E. A. Seemann, 1922.

Young, Edward. *Conjectures on Original Composition* (1759). In *The Works of Edward Young*, vol. 6. Edinburgh: C. Elliot, 1774.

4. The Transcendence of Monologue

Declève, Henri. *Heidegger et Kant*. The Hague: Martinus Nijhoff, 1970.

Derrida, Jacques. *De la grammatologie*. Paris: Editions de Minuit, 1967.

———.*Of Grammatology*. Trans. Gayatri Chakravorty Spivak. Baltimore: Johns Hopkins University Press, 1976.

———.*Speech and Phenomenon and Other Essays on Husserl's Theory of Signs*. Trans. David Allison. Evanston: Northwestern University Press, 1973.

——.*La voix et le phénomène*. Paris: Presses Universitaires de France, 1967.

Heidegger, Martin. *Being and Time*. Trans. John Macquarrie and Edward Robinson. New York: Harper and Row, 1962.

——.*Early Greek Thinking*. Trans. David Farrell Krell and Frank A. Capuzzi. New York: Harper and Row, 1975.

——.*Erläuterungen zu Hölderlins Dichtung*. Frankfurt am Main: Vittorio Klostermann, 1971.

——.*Heraklit* [1943]. In the *Gesamtausgabe*, vol. 55, ed. Manfred S. Frings. Frankfurt am Main: Vittorio Klostermann, 1979.

——.*Kant and the Problem of Metaphysics*. Trans. James S. Churchill. Bloomington: Indiana University Press, 1962.

——.*Kant und das Problem der Metaphysik*. 4th ed. Frankfurt am Main: Vittorio Klostermann, 1973.

——.*"Logos (Heraklit, Fragment 50)."* In *Vorträge und Aufsätze*. Pfullingen: Neske, 1954.

——.*Metaphysische Anfangsgründe der Logik im Ausgang von Leibniz*. In the *Gesamtausgabe*, vol. 26, ed. Klaus Held. Frankfurt am Main: Vittorio Klostermann, 1978.

——.*On the Way to Language*. Trans. Peter D. Hertz. New York: Harper and Row, 1971.

——.*Poetry, Language, Thought*. Trans. Albert Hofstadter. New York: Harper and Row, 1971.

——.*Sein und Zeit*. 4th ed. Tübingen: Max Niemeyer, 1977.

——.*Unterwegs zur Sprache*. Pfullingen: Neske, 1959.

——.*"Vom Wesen des Grundes."* In *Wegmarken*. 2d ed. Frankfurt am Main: Vittorio Klostermann, 1978.

——.*"Was ist Metaphysik?"* In *Wegmarken*. 2d ed. Frankfurt am Main: Vittorio Klostermann, 1978.

Husserl, Edmund. *Cartesian Meditations: An Introduction to Phenomenology*. Trans. Dorion Cairns. The Hague: Martinus Nijhoff, 1960.

——.*Cartesianische Meditationen und Pariser Vorträge*. In *Husserliana*, vol. 1, ed. S. Strasser. The Hague: Martinus Nijhoff, 1973.

——.*Erste Philosophie, 1923–24*. In *Husserliana*, vol. 7, ed. Rudolf Boehm. The Hague: Martinus Nijhoff, 1956.

——.*Ideas Pertaining to a Pure Phenomenology and to a Phenomenological Philosophy*. Vols. 1–2. Trans. F. Kersten. The Hague: Martinus Nijhoff, 1976.

——.*Ideen zu einer reinen Phänomenologie und phänomenologische Philosophie*. In *Husserliana*, vol. 3, ed. Karl Schuhmann. The Hague: Martinus Nijhoff, 1976.

——.*Logical Investigations*. Vols. 1–2. Trans. J. N. Findlay. New York: Humanities Press, 1970.

——.*Logische Untersuchungen.* 2d ed. Vols. 1–2. Tübingen: Max Niemeyer, 1913.

Kant, Immanuel. *Kritik der reinen Vernunft.* Ed. Raymund Schmidt. Hamburg: Felix Meiner, 1956.

——.*Kritik der Urteilskraft.* Ed. Karl Vorländer. Hamburg: Felix Meiner, 1924.

Kern, Iso. *Husserl und Kant.* The Hague: Martinus Nijhoff, 1964.

Novalis. *Werke, Tagebücher, und Briefe Friedrich von Hardenbergs.* Ed. Hans-Joachim Mähl and Richard Samuel. Munich: Carl Hanser, 1978.

Rousseau, Jean-Jacques. *Les confessions.* Vols. 1–2. Paris: Garnier-Flammarion, 1968.

Sartre, J.-P. "Une idée fondamentale de la phénoménologie de Husserl: L'intentionalité." In *Situations*, vol. 1. Paris: Editions Gallimard, 1947.

Tugendhat, Ernst. *Selbstbewusstsein und Selbstbestimmung: Sprachanalytische Interpretationen.* Frankfurt am Main: Suhrkamp, 1979.

5. Pre-Shakespearean and Shakespearean Soliloquies

Bevington, David. *Medieval Drama.* Boston: Houghton Mifflin, 1975.

Lott, Bernhard. *Der Monolog im englischen Drama vor Shakespeare.* Greifswald: Julius Abel, 1909.

Marlowe, Christopher. *Doctor Faustus.* Ed. Sylvan Barnet. New York: New American Library, 1969.

Poepperling, Hermann. *Studien über den Monolog in den Dramen Shakespeares.* Darmstadt: K. F. Bender, 1912.

Shakespeare, William. *Hamlet.* Ed. Willard Farnham. Baltimore: Penguin, 1970.

——.*Macbeth.* Ed. Sylvan Barnet. New York: New American Library, 1963.

——.*Richard III.* Ed. Mark Eccles. New York: New American Library, 1964.

Vollmann, Elisabeth. *Ursprung und Entwicklung des Monologs bis zu seiner Entfaltung bei Shakespeare.* Bonn: Peter Hanstein, 1934.

6. Coleridge's Conversational Pretense

Bate, Walter Jackson. *Coleridge.* New York: Macmillan, 1968.

Bloom, Harold. *The Visionary Company.* 2d ed. Ithaca: Cornell University Press, 1971.

Coleridge, Samuel Taylor. *Biographia Literaria.* Vols. 1–3. Ed. J. Shawcross. Oxford: Oxford University Press, 1954.

——.*The Notebooks of Samuel Taylor Coleridge.* Ed. Kathleen Coburn. Bollingen Series. Princeton: Princeton University Press, 1957–.

——. *Poetical Works*. Ed. Ernest Hartley Coleridge. Oxford: Oxford University Press, 1912.

——. *Shakespearean Criticism*. Vols. 1–2. 2d ed. Ed. Thomas Middleton Raysor. London: J. M. Dent, 1960.

House, Humphry. *Coleridge: The Clark Lectures, 1951–52*. London: Rupert Hart-Davis, 1967.

Langbaum, Robert. *The Poetry of Experience*. New York: W. W. Norton, 1957.

Lowes, John Livingston. *The Road to Xanadu: A Study in the Ways of the Imagination*. New York: Houghton Mifflin, 1927.

McFarland, Thomas. *Coleridge and the Pantheist Tradition*. Oxford: Clarendon Press, 1969.

Purves, Alan C. "Formal Structure in 'Kubla Khan.' " *Studies in Romanticism*, 1 (1962), 187–91.

Schneider, Elisabeth. *Coleridge, Opium, and Kubla Khan*. New York: Octagon Books, 1966.

Suther, Marshall. *Visions of Xanadu*. New York: Columbia University Press, 1965.

Watson, George. *Coleridge the Poet*. London: Routledge and Kegan Paul, 1966.

Woodring, Carl R. "Coleridge and the Khan." *Essays in Criticism*, 9 (1959), 361–68.

7. Poe's Narrative Monologue

Defoe, Daniel. *Robinson Crusoe*. Ed. Michael Shinagel. New York: W. W. Norton, 1975.

Diderot, Denis. *Discours de la poésie dramatique*. Ed. Jean-Pol Caput. Paris: Librairie Larousse, 1970.

Fielding, Henry. *"Joseph Andrews" and "Shamela."* Ed. Martin C. Battestin. Boston: Houghton Mifflin, 1961.

Poe, E. A. *The Complete Poems and Stories of Edgar Allan Poe*. Ed. Arthur Hobson Quinn and Edward H. O'Neill. New York: Alfred A. Knopf, 1946.

Richardson, Samuel. *Pamela*. Ed. William M. Sale. New York: W. W. Norton, 1958.

Rowe, John Carlos. "Writing and Truth in Poe's 'The Narrative of Arthur Gordon Pym.' " *Glyph: Johns Hopkins Textual Studies*, 2 (1977), 102–121.

8. The Genius of Internal Monologue

Barthes, Roland. *Critique et vérité*. Paris: Editions du Seuil, 1966.

Bordaz, Robert. "Edouard Dujardin et le monologue intérieur." *La Revue des Deux Mondes* (December 1970), 591–94.

Cohn, Dorrit. "Narrated Monologue: Definition of a Fictional Style." *Comparative Literature*, 18 (1966), 97–112.

———. *Transparent Minds: Narrative Modes for Presenting Consciousness in Fiction*. Princeton: Princeton University Press, 1978.

Dujardin, Edouard. *"Les lauriers sont coupés" and "Le monologue intérieur."* Rome: Bulzoni, 1977.

Ellmann, Richard. *Ulysses on the Liffey*. New York: Oxford University Press, 1972.

Joyce, James. *Ulysses*. New York: Random House, 1961.

———. *Ulysses: A Critical and Synoptic Edition*. Ed. Hans Walter Gabler, Wolfhard Steppe, and Claus Melchior. New York: Garland, 1984.

Kenner, Hugh. *Joyce's Voices*. Berkeley: University of California Press, 1978.

———. *Ulysses*. London: George Allen and Unwin, 1980.

King, C. D. "Edouard Dujardin and the Genesis of the Inner Monologue." *French Studies*, 9 (April 1955), 101–15.

Lillyman, W. J. "The Interior Monologue in James Joyce and Otto Ludwig." *Comparative Literature*, 23 (1971), 45–54.

Neuse, Werner. " 'Erlebte Rede' und 'innerer Monolog' in den erzählenden Schriften Arthur Schnitzlers." *PMLA*, 49 (1934), 327–55.

Plant, Richard. "Notes on Arthur Schnitzler's Literary Technique." *Germanic Review*, 25 (150), 13–25.

Rey, William H. *Arthur Schnitzler: Die späte Prosa als Gipfel seines Schaffens*. Berlin: Erich Schmidt, 1968.

Riquelme, John Paul. *Teller and Tale in Joyce's Fiction*. Baltimore: Johns Hopkins University Press, 1983.

Schnitzler, Arthur. *Fräulein Else*. In *Erzählungen*. Frankfurt am Main: S. Fischer, 1961.

———.*Leutnant Gustl*. Berlin: S. Fischer, 1967.

Swales, Martin. *Arthur Schnitzler: A Critical Study*. Oxford: Clarendon, 1971.

Zenke, Jürgen. *Die deutsche Monologerzählung im 20. Jahrhundert*. Cologne: Böhlav, 1976.

Conclusions

Bakhtin, Mikhail. *Problems of Dostoevsky's Poetics*. Trans. and ed. Caryl Emerson. Minneapolis: University of Minnesota, 1984.

Bakhtine, Mikhail. *Le Marxisme et la philosophie du langage*. Trans. Marina Yaguello. Paris: Editions de Minuit, 1977.

Bloom, Harold. *A Map of Misreading*. New York: Oxford University Press, 1975.

Piaget, Jean. *Le langage et la pensée chez l'enfant*. 3d ed. Paris: Delachaux et Niestlé, 1948.

Vygotsky, Lev. *Thought and Language*. Trans. and ed. Eugenia Hanfmann and Gertrude Vakar. Cambridge: MIT Press, 1962.

Wygotski, L. S. *Denken und Sprechen*. Trans. Gerhard Sewekow. Stuttgart: S. Fischer, 1969.

Index

Addison, Joseph, 8, 16, 66–74, 80–83
Aeschylus, 34
Akedah, 16, 47, 48–49, 59–64
Allegory: in eighteenth-century discussions, 65n, 68–69; in Philo's works, 56–57; in Poe's fiction, 166–68; of Socrates' life, 29–32, 47
Angeloi, 49–51, 57
Angelos, 49, 53–54, 57–58
Angels, 8, 16, 32, 60, 126, 129, 190; in the Bible, 48–53; in *Doctor Faustus*, 119–23; in Midrashic literature, 63–65; in Philo's works, 54, 56–58. *See also Angelos; Malachim*
Apocrypha, 48, 52, 60–61
Apuleius, 34, 38–39
Asceticism, 57–59, 64–65
Associationism: and genius, 71–72, 81, 83
Auerbach, Erich, 59n
Authenticity, 17, 63, 145, 194; Heideggerian, 16, 85, 104–108
Autoaffection, 84–85, 91–95, 179
Autonomy, 7, 17, 134, 192, 194; of Shakespearean soliloquists, 124, 133; of twentieth-century internal monologists, 169, 177, 179–80, 186

Bakhtin, Mikhail, 91n, 178, 192–94
Barthes, Roland, 21n, 186–87

Being-in-the-world, 97–102
Benveniste, Emile, 91n
Bergson, Henri, 170
Bible, Hebrew: Exodus, Book of, 50–51; Genesis, Book of, 48, 49–52, 59–64; Job, Book of, 47, 48, 51–52, 61–62; Numbers, Book of, 51; Psalms, Book of, 62
Blake, William, 59
Blanchot, Maurice, 187
Bloom, Harold, 137, 189. *See also* Intertextuality; Swerve
Browning, Robert, 152–53
Bucher, Jordan: *Philonische Studien*, 54–56
Burke, Kenneth, 23

Chiasmus, 162–64
Coleridge, Samuel Taylor, 8, 18, 160. Works: "The Eolian Harp," 135, 138–44; "Frost at Midnight," 140–44, 183; "Kubla Khan," 144–52; *Shakespearean Criticism*, 135–37; *Table Talk*, 136
Conscience, 111–12, 118–19, 121, 190; in Shakespearean drama, 126–27, 129, 131–32; and Socrates' *daimonion*, 32–33, 41, 46, 54, 79
Conversational poetry, 18, 134–35, 137–44, 152, 154–55, 160, 186
Corpus Christi Cycle: Wakefield, 115–18; Brome, 118

207

Daemons, 68, 80, 83
Daimōn, 15, 28, 33–38, 47, 67, 82, 189; as
    divinity or fate, 36; as a "floating sig-
    nifier," 35; as a *génie*, 37–38
Daimones: compared to Hebraic traditions,
    50, 52–53, 56–57; in the tradition of He-
    siod, 15, 29, 33–35, 42, 46–47, 104, 189
Daimonia, 28, 34, 39–40, 43, 47
Daimonion, 8, 15–16, 27–34, 37, 38–47, 54,
    56, 65, 79, 162, 188, 189, 194; absence
    of, 45; active power of, 28; divinity of,
    31–33, 42, 44; as genius, 32, 39; gram-
    matical form of, 42, 46–47; not a guard-
    ian spirit, 32–33; opposed to the *dēmos*,
    44, 46; pathology of, 30–32, 41, 46; as
    preventing false steps, 40–41, 45;
    prophetic powers of, 30–31, 40–41; as
    Socrates' "divine sign," 8, 15; as
    "something divine," 27, 38–46 passim;
    as something unconscious, 30–31, 33,
    44; turns Socrates inward, 31, 46; as a
    voice, 41, 44
Dasein, 96–104, 107, 190
de Man, Paul, 23
Demons, 16, 53, 63, 113, 116, 163
Dēmos, 30n, 44, 46
Derrida, Jacques, 8, 17. Works: *De la gram-
    matologie*, 84, 93–95; *La voix et le phén-
    omène*, 84, 89–93
Deviance, 20, 160, 164, 168
Deviant discourse, 17–18, 20–21, 111, 129,
    154, 169, 186, 190, 194
Deviation: caused by *satan*, 51, 65, 114; of
    genius, 76–77, 79, 83, 193; in the history
    of monologue, 19, 112, 151, 194; of
    Shakespearean soliloquists, 124–25, 127.
    See also Swerve
Devil: in pre-Shakespearean and Shakes-
    pearean drama, 112–15, 117–18, 123–
    26, 132
Dialogue: with devils, 113; divine, 16, 63–
    64, 112, 114–15, 118–19; human, 117,
    138, 184; internal, 16–18, 56, 68, 109,
    111, 120–23, 126–27, 156, 176–80; in
    monologue, 93, 109, 169–70, 176, 192–
    94
Diderot, Denis, 19, 69n, 109, 156–57
Différance, 91–93, 95
Difference, 18, 84, 91–92, 189, 194; onto-
    logical, 96n, 97, 99–100, 107
Dreams, 126–27, 142, 144, 146–49, 151–52,

155, 160, 174, 177, 180, 190
Duff, William, 16, 67; *Essay on Original Ge-
    nius*, 73, 76–79
Dujardin, Edouard, 169–71. Works: *Les
    lauriers sont coupés*, 171–76, 180; *Le mon-
    ologue intérieur*, 171

Egger, Victor, 170
Empedocles, 34
Essenes, 52–53, 57, 64–65
Essentialism, 22–23, 35–36, 42
Euripides, 34

Fielding, Henry, 67, 71–72, 158–59, 172
Figuration, 59, 95, 167, 189; in Coleridge's
    poetry, 139–42, 145, 152; in discussions
    of genius, 74–75, 78–80; in pre-Shake-
    spearean and Shakespearean drama,
    112–13, 115, 117, 120, 126
Freud, Sigmund, 21, 192n, 193
Functionalism, 22–23, 37, 42, 127

Geist, 29, 82; and genius, 66–67
Genesis, Book of. *See* Bible, Hebrew
Genette, Gérard, 187
Génie, 28, 37, 69–70, 81, 187
Genii, 71
Genius, 8, 15, 20, 28, 37, 52n, 67–69, 79–
    82, 188; in the eighteenth century, 15,
    65n, 66–83 passim, 190; as exemplary
    originality, 82; as "that god within," 16,
    66, 79, 83, 190 (*see also Logos endiathetos*);
    greatness of, 70–72; introjection of, 23,
    66, 83, 189; Johnson's definition of, 73;
    landscapes of, 68–69, 73–83; and na-
    ture, 70–71, 73, 75–77, 79, 81; theolog-
    ical dimension of, 15–16, 66, 79–83
Gerard, Alexander, 16; *An Essay on Taste*,
    72–73, 81
Goethe, Johann Wolfgang von, 181–82
Grimm, Jakob and Wilhelm, 28n
Guardian genius, 39, 52n, 69, 81, 188
Guardian spirits, 129, 181; and eight-
    eenth-century genius, 68–69, 79, 81; and
    Socrates' *daimonion*, 29, 32–33, 34–35,
    38–39
Guilt, 30n, 43; of dramatic soliloquists, 111,
    113, 117–19, 126–27, 129, 131–32

Hamann, Johann Georg, 39
Hédelin d'Aubignac, 19

Hegel, Georg Wilhelm Friedrich, 28–33, 41, 46, 173, 192–93, 194n
Heidegger, Martin, 8, 16–17, 56n, 57n, 84, 95–108, 193; "Language speaks," 8, 104–108, 190. Works: "Hölderlin und das Wesen der Dichtung," 104; *Kant und das Problem der Metaphysik*, 92, 95–96; *Metaphysische Anfangsgründe der Logik*, 101–103; *Sein und Zeit*, 95–99, 103–104; *Unterwegs zur Sprache*, 104–107, *Der Ursprung des Kunstwerkes*, 104–105; "Vom Wesen des Grundes," 99–101
Heraklitus, 31n, 34, 107–108
Hesiod, 15, 29, 33–34, 38, 42, 52. See also *Daimones*
Homer, 70, 76 , 180; *daimōn* in, 15, 29, 33–38, 47, 189; *Iliad*, 123
Horace, 69
Husserl, Edmund, 8, 16, 99–100, 102–103. Works: *Cartesianische Meditationen*, 88–89; *Ideen*, 86–88; *Logische Untersuchungen*, 84, 89–93

Idiolect, 17, 44, 46, 194
Imagery, 58–59, 78, 80–81, 143, 146–48
Immanence: and transcendence, 16, 18, 84–89, 101, 190
Individuality, 7, 15, 111 (*see also* Deviant discourse; Originality; Subjectivity); of internal monologists, 177, 187 (*see also* Autonomy); in language, 17–18, 20–21, 192; of Socrates, 44, 46
Ingenium, 69, 81–82
Innovation, 17, 21, 69, 79, 159, 186; in religion, 28, 30, 33, 39–40, 42–43
Inspiration, 7, 16, 20, 23, 79, 81–82, 194
Intellectual history, 7, 22–23, 67, 189
Intentionality, 97–100, 102
Internal monologue, 19–20, 22, 158, 169–86 passim; differentiated from stream-of-consciousness technique, 19–20, 170–71
Internal speech, 17–19, 55–56, 169–80; differentiated from stream of consciousness, 170; as writing in code, 172, 186, 191–92
Intertextuality, 8, 15, 18, 22, 23, 48, 60, 154–55, 166, 175, 188, 189–90, 193
Introjection, 16, 20, 23, 28, 129–30, 163, 182, 188, 189, 194; in *Doctor Faustus*, 120, 122; of eighteenth-century genius,
66, 69, 79, 83, 90
Inwardness, 7, 17, 98, 169, 178–79, 192
Irony, 41, 42n, 176, 179

James, William, 170
Job, Book of. See Bible, Hebrew
Johnson, Samuel, 73
Joyce, James, 8, 18, 169–71, 174n. Works: *Finnegans Wake*, 188; *Ulysses*, 158, 180–85, 187–88
Jubilees, Book of, 60–61

Kaina daimonia, 28, 34, 38–39, 47
Kant, Immanuel, 8, 67, 81–82, 84–86, 95–96, 190, 193
Key word, 22–23, 28–29, 91, 96n–97n, 185
Kierkegaard, Søren, 32n, 42

Langton, Edward, 51–52
Larbaud, Valéry, 172, 180
Logoi, 16, 48–49, 50–51, 53–59
Logos, 17, 53–59, 65, 93, 103, 107–108, 168; divine, 16, 49, 53–54, 56–59, 107–108, 114–16, 119, 127, 133, 194; interpreted by Heidegger, 103–108; in Philo's works, 53–59, 65
Logos endiathetos, 49, 54–57, 59, 65
Logos prophorikos, 49, 54–57
Lovejoy, Arthur, 22–23
Lucifer, 111, 116, 119

Madness, 7–8, 18–19, 177, 182n; of dramatic soliloquists, 111–15, 119, 123, 127–31, 133, 135; of Poe's narrators, 154–55, 159–65; of poetic monologues, 144, 151–53, 190; of Socrates, 32n
Malachim, 16, 48–65 passim, 104. *See also* Angels
Malach YHWH, 49–50, 63–64
Mandelkern, Solomon, 49n
Manual of Discipline, 52–53
Marlowe, Christopher, 18; *Doctor Faustus*, 119–24
Masks, 7, 23, 80, 168
Masteen, 63
Mastema, Prince of, 60–61
Master tropes, 22–23, 189
Maximus of Tyre, 34, 38–39
Mephistopheles (or Mephostophilis), 120–21, 123, 182

Metaphor, 49, 97–98, 100–103, 107n, 115, 139, 148, 185, 194
Metonymy, 103, 165–66, 168, 185
Midrash, 48–49, 53, 59–65
Mirrors, 136–37, 142, 148
Monologue: and dialogue, 18, 68, 91, 93, 126, 176, 192–93; as dialogue with oneself, 68, 126, 176, 192–93; failure of, 193; after the Fall, 114, 119; immanent, 17, 84 (see also Autonomy; Subject; Subjectivity); impossibility of, 89–95; of God, 18, 111, 115–16; as luxury of the rich, 178; and sin, 18, 111–19, 123, 133; as solitary speech, 17, 20, 154, 186, 193–94 (see also Internal speech; Soliloquy); as swerve, 17–18, 20–21; and transcendence, 85, 105–108
Monotheism, 29, 38, 47, 48, 64–65
Muse, 181–82, 184–85, 188, 190–91, 193

Nares, Robert, 39
Nietzsche, Friedrich, 6, 89, 171
Norms, 17n, 70, 156, 161, 192; Athenian, 28, 30; divergence from, 18, 20, 124, 130, 154, 186, 190, 194
Novalis (Friedrich von Hardenberg), 104–106; "Monolog," 105n

Ordo Repraesentationis Adae (Jeu d'Adam), 112–15
Originality, 20, 71, 73–83, 106–107, 156, 193–94. See also Deviation; Individuality
Oxymoron, 137

Palimpsest, 82, 106, 194
Personification, 54, 58
Perversity, 52, 125; in Poe's fiction, 18, 160, 162–65, 168
Philo of Alexandria, 16, 48–51, 53–59, 190
Piaget, Jean, 191
Plato, 15–16, 27, 38, 189. Works: Apology, 28–29, 31–32, 39–40, 42–45, 47; Euthydemus, 40; Euthyphro, 40, 42; Phaedrus, 41; Sophist, 56; Symposium, 31, 53, 57; Theaetetus, 40
Plutarch, 34, 38–39
Poe, Edgar Allan, 8, 18, 154–68, 190. Works: "The Black Cat," 161–62; "The Cask of Amontillado," 166–68; "The Imp of the Perverse," 162–64; "Ms. Found in a Bottle," 164–66; "The Poetic Prin-ciple," 159–60; "The Tell-Tale Heart," 160–61, 164
Polytheism, 27, 29, 34, 38, 42, 47, 48–49; and dualistic tendencies, 52–53, 63–65
Prayer, 6, 16; in dramatic soliloquies, 18, 111–12, 116–19, 121, 127, 132–33
Projection, 95, 121, 194; in the work of Coleridge, 136–38, 141, 143, 150, 152
Prosopopoeia, 23, 151–52
Pseudepigrapha. See Jubilees, Book of

Qumran documents, 52–53

Reader, 74, 157–58, 173, 178–80; in Poe's works, 154, 159–61, 163, 166–68
Rhetoric, 84, 91, 93, 128n, 133. See also Figuration; Tropes
Rhetorical criticism, 7–8, 22–23, 35–39, 54, 189
Rhetorical devices, 124, 143, 160, 162. See also Figuration; Tropes
Richardson, Samuel, 74, 155–60
Rousseau, Jean-Jacques: Les confessions, 84–85, 93–95

Samael, 62n
Sanhedrin, Tractate, 60–62
Sartre, Jean-Paul, 87n
Satan, 8, 16, 18, 113–15; in the Bible, 51–53; in Midrashic literature, 48–49, 59–65, 190. See also Devil; Lucifer; Masteen; Mephistopheles; Samael
Saussure, Ferdinand de, 20–21
Schleiermacher, Friedrich, 32, 39
Schnitzler, Arthur, 18, 169–80. Works: Fräulein Else, 174n, 177–80; Leutnant Gustl, 175–77
Shaftesbury, Anthony, 8, 16, 119, 170, 190; "Soliloquy," 66–68, 80n, 82, 156
Shakespeare, William, 8, 18, 73, 111, 124–33, 141, 152, 190; genius of, 70, 134–36. Works: The Comedy of Errors, 181n; Hamlet, 111, 130–33, 134–37; Macbeth, 73, 111, 128–30; Richard III, 111, 124–27, 133, 136, 177
Shelley, Percy Bysshe, 152–53
Sin, 18, 111–19, 123, 133
Socrates: accused of impiety, 27–28, 30, 33–34, 39–40, 43, 47; interpreted by Hegel, 28–33, 41, 44, 46, 194n; irony of,

Socrates (*cont.*)
41, 43n; theological commitments of, 43–44
Soliloquy, 67–68, 89–93 passim; differentiated from self-address, 19n; divine, 111, 115–16; dramatic, 19, 111–33; identified with *daimōn* and *genius*, 67–68; psychological, 111, 119–33, 154, 156–68, 160–68 (*see also* Subjectivity)
Solitude, 6–7, 20, 153, 168, 186; in drama, 111–13, 115, 123, 133
Sophocles, 34
Spectator, 68–71
Stream of consciousness, 18–20, 22, 170
Stream-of-consciousness technique, 169–71, 180, 186; differentiated from internal monologue, 19–20, 170–71
Subject: "capsule-conception" of, 101–102; fictive, 168, 186–87
Subjectivity: in language, 16, 20–21, 92, 187; and monologue, 8, 15–16, 18, 67, 133, 168, 169, 192; self-determinative, 29, 46
Swerve, 17, 20–21, 38, 46, 59, 83, 112, 153, 154, 168, 190, 194
Synecdoche, 70, 72, 83, 138, 145, 181, 184, 189–90

Talmud, Babylonian, 48, 52n, 60–62
Tanchuma, 60, 62–64
Thales, 34
Theognis, 34
Theos, 29, 33, 35–37, 40–41, 44, 56, 189
Thibaudet, Albert, 187
Torah. *See* Bible, Hebrew
Transcendence, 16, 18, 83, 193; and being-in-the-world, 97–99, 101–102, 190; of

Dasein, 84, 95–103; in the eighteenth century, 82–83; in Heidegger's work, 95–103; in Husserl's work, 84, 86–89; and immanence, 53, 56, 86–89, 133; and intentionality, 97–100; as a step beyond, 100–101
Transzendenz, 95–103
Tropes, 140, 143, 152n; "divine speech" as, 107n, 194; master, 22–23, 189–90; Socrates' *daimonion* as, 28, 46. *See also* Chiasmus; Figuration; Introjection; Irony; Metaphor; Metonymy; Oxymoron; Personification; Prosopopoeia; Rhetorical devices; Synecdoche

Unconscious, 30, 146, 171, 193
Unit ideas, 22–23
Usener, Hermann, 36

Valéry, Paul, 187
Vygotsky, Lev, 91n, 191–92

Wakefield Master, 112n. Works: "The Creation," 115–16; "Mactatio Abel," 116–18
Williams, Raymond, 23
Witkowski, Georg, 25
Wordsworth, William, 134n, 136

Young, Edward, 8, 16, 39, 66–67, 135, 190; "Conjectures on Original Composition," 72–76, 78–81

Xenocrates, 34
Xenophon, 27–28, 30n, 31

Yes, 181–85, 187–88
YHWH, 42, 48–51, 61–64, 121, 190, 194

Library of Congress Cataloging in Publication Data
FRIEDEN, KEN, 1955–
    Genius and monologue.

    Bibliography: p.
    Includes index.
    1. English literature—History and criticism.
2. Monologue.   3. Soliloquy.   4. First person
narrative.   5. Stream of consciousness fiction.
I. Title.
PR408.M66F7   1985   820'.9   85–47700
ISBN 0–8014–1804–6